All the
COMMANDMENTS
OF GOD

Find Out the Secret to Inherit
All the Blessings of God

ESTHER V. SHEKHER

WestBow
P R E S S
A DIVISION OF THOMAS NELSON

WestBow Press books may be ordered through booksellers or by contacting:

WestBow Press
A Division of Thomas Nelson
1663 Liberty Drive
Bloomington, IN 47403
www.westbowpress.com
1-(866) 928-1240

Because of the dynamic nature of the Internet, any web addresses or links contained in this book may have changed since publication and may no longer be valid. The views expressed in this work are solely those of the author and do not necessarily reflect the views of the publisher, and the publisher hereby disclaims any responsibility for them.

Any people depicted in stock imagery provided by Thinkstock are models, and such images are being used for illustrative purposes only.
Certain stock imagery © Thinkstock.

ISBN: 978-1-4497-8523-9 (sc)
ISBN: 978-1-4497-9026-4 (e)

Library of Congress Control Number: 2013902909

Unless otherwise indicated, all Scripture quotations in this publication are from the New King James Version of the Bible © 1984 by Thomas Nelson, Inc., Publishers.

Scripture quotations noted KJV are from the Holy Bible, King James Version.

Scripture quotations noted NIV are from the Life In The Spirit Study Bible, New International Version © 1992, 2003 by Zondervan.

Our Contact Address:

Christ Rules
P.O Box: 994, Galt, CA - 95632, USA
Phone: Dr. Esther: 001- 626 - 450 - 5973
Michelle: 001- 480 - 251 - 1979
Email: christrulesnations@gmail.com
Website: www.christrulesnations.org

Printed in the United States of America
WestBow Press rev. date: 3/26/2013

Dedication

To My Beloved Savior and Lord,
Jesus Christ who is...
My Best Daddy,
My Best Mommy and
My Best Friend;
For Christ Rules My Heart.

Christ Must Rule Our Hearts.
Christ Must Rule Our Lives.
Christ Must Rule Our Families.
Christ Must Rule Our Cities.
Christ Must Rule Our Nations.
For Christ Rules Our Universe.

CONTENTS

PART I
Commandments of God

Jesus syas that ***unless your righteousness exceeds*** the righteousness of the Scribes and Pharisees, you will in *no case enter the Kingdom of Heaven.* (see Matt. 5:20)

Obedience to His Commandments listed in this Chapter will enable you to exceed the righteousness of the Pharisees to inherit Eternal Life.

PART II
God's Ways Higher Than Our Ways

PART III
Eternal Life Or Eternal Damnation? You Decide!

FOREWORD TO
ALL THE COMMANDMENTS OF GOD

By Rev. Dr. David E. Stewart

Missionary Teacher and Trainer for forty-three years
and Co-Founder of New Life Assembly of God Church,
Chennai with **Rev. Dr. D. Mohan, Senior Pastor**

Many of us who have served God in public places of ministry have been admonished from time to time that we should write a book. Sometimes the comment comes from an acquaintance who has enjoyed a particular story or recounting of a life experience. Such people encourage us to write a book of personal or family stories that they feel would be interesting, encouraging or inspiring. Other people have been encouraged or inspired by some exposition of Holy Scripture and thus feel they would like for us to write a book of sermons or some other form of written exposition. Even beloved family members have repeatedly stated with varying degrees of firmness that we should write a book for the sake of posterity, whatever that means to them. I must admit that I have often felt brief flashes of inspiration to put some of my experiences and ideas into book form. But then I come face to face with the realization that writing a book is not an easy task to set oneself to accomplish. Still, I deeply admire people who exhibit the self-discipline and dedication to the challenge that is required to write a book.

Dr. Esther V. Shekher is one such person. After a career of many years of service to mankind on more than one continent, Dr. Esther has accomplished another goal in her life by writing this special book that you now hold in your hands. This servant of God has a deep love for and abiding interest in the Word of God as revealed in the Holy Bible. This book is the result of hours, months and years of serious study of this holy book.

The Almighty God has given us this most special and holy of all books to serve as a guide through the maze of life. The Holy Bible also gives strength and inspiration to all who read and enters into its precepts with a determination to follow its teachings and instructions for daily living.

The Holy Bible is meant to be more than a rich source of history and knowledge, though it provides that in abundance. Through the history of mankind and the dealings of God with men down through the ages from the time of the creation of man our marvellous God shows us the way to live a fulfilling and richly happy life. This Holy Bible also shows us wonderful insights into the future including the unending ages of eternity set before us. Amazingly, it even shows us the way to eternal salvation and life through our Lord and Savior, Jesus Christ. Dr. Esther has developed a unique style and format to help honest seekers and believers to better understand "All the Commandments of God." While she has revealed to the reader some of her own thoughts and glimpses of her journey along the way of this Holy Book, it is mostly a restating of the great truths of the Holy Spirit of God revealed in the Holy Bible in easy to understand ways. The Index serves as an easy guide to find Biblical answers to many of the problems of life faced by people around the world.

This book will serve to remind those who take time to read it and meditate upon the Holy Scriptures contained in it that there is no higher goal than to seek and apply the wisdom of the Ancient of Days in our own lives.

While I commend Dr. Esther for her commitment and dedication to the writing of this book, I also deeply appreciate her deep desire for all seekers and believers to better understand and live by the commandments of our wonderful God. I sincerely hope that this book will create or awaken in every reader an insatiable hunger for the Word of God and the Righteousness revealed in this Holy Scripture given to us by our loving Father in heaven.

AUTHOR'S HEART

Introduction:

It is purely God's grace that He considered me worthy to write this book entitled "ALL THE COMMANDMENTS OF GOD." This was conceived into my spirit by the Lord God Almighty Himself and it is absolutely from the Throne-Room of God.

The Commandments are the desires of God's heart; His instructions for us to live a pleasing life before Him. God has promised that this book will bring reverential fear of God upon the face of the earth.

Purpose of the Book:

Jesus says, "If anyone hears My words and does not believe, I do not judge him; for I did not come to judge the world but to save the world. He who rejects Me and does not receive My words **-the Word that I have spoken will judge him in the last day.**" (see John 12:47-48) The Lord also states, My people are destroyed for lack of knowledge of God's Word. Ignorance of God's word is not an excuse for us to live in sin. (Hosea 4:6)

I have heard numerous messages on blessings of God. It is true that our God is a God of blessings, He cares for us, He gives us peace and prosperity but we should not see Him only as a Santa Claus who provides us with all that we need. The Scriptures clearly say that if we diligently obey the voice of the Lord our God, to observe carefully all His Commandments, then the blessings will come upon us and overtake us.(see Deut. 28:1-2, 9)

In desperation, I sought the Lord, inquiring, "What are the Commandments that we ought to obey to inherit Your blessings?" This question was burning in my heart, and praying much in the spirit for years, enabled me to get a revelation from the Lord. The Lord started revealing to me the Commandments hidden in the Word of God. *Whenever an instruction of the Lord is followed by rewards or consequences, and sometimes both, it is a Command. Some Commands are without any rewards but we still need to obey them because He says so.*

About the Book:

Part I and Part III of the book bring out **the Commandments of God** from the Gospels of Matthew and John. The rewards for obedience and consequences of disobedience are plainly explained in a simple table format.

Almost all the major topics in Christian faith are covered in this book. It points out how when we bring our lives in line with the Word of God, blessings will not only follow us but will overtake us.

Part II: God's Ways Higher Than Our Ways...

This is the Highlight of the Book.

'My thoughts are not your thoughts neither are your ways My Ways. As the Heavens are higher than the earth, so are My Ways higher than your ways' says the Lord God Almighty. (see Isa.55:8-9/NIV)

The Psalmist repeatedly stated, 'Teach me Your Precepts, Testimonies, Laws, Commandments, Statutes and Judgments (all mean the same) so that I may understand Your Ways.' (see Ps. 119:1; 18:30) Moses knew God's Ways, but the children of Israel only saw His deeds. We learn His Ways through the Word of God and from Christ's example. (Ps. 103:7)

We often mess up our lives by going in our own ways. God has revealed to me some of "His Ways" which I have brought out in this section, to help us understand the heart and mind of God so that we can live the abundant life that God intends for us to live.

This section of the book will be a blessing to you!

Conclusion:

This first book in the series is from the Book of Matthew and partly from John.

I believe that this book will tremendously help believers as well as non-believers to receive blessings from God. I have simplified this book enough for an average person to understand.

It is my prayer that every human being should have a copy of this book and be blessed!

Know that the Lord Your God, He is God, the faithful God

who keeps ***His covenant and mercy for a thousand generations***
with those who love Him and keep His Commandments.
(see Deut. 7:9)

PS: The Asterisk symbol (*) used in the book indicates Author's note.

Acknowledgments:

Special thanks to my loving family members for their encouragement and faithful support, and my dear friends Monica, Darla and George for their valuable insights, and countless hours of hard work in compiling this book.

I am so grateful to my beloved husband Vincent and my precious daughter Sarah for their selfless sacrifice and support. I am also indebted to all of those committed people who stood with me in prayer for the release of this book.

PART I

1. Adultery

1.1 Physical Adultery

In these last days, millions of people, including many in the Body of Christ, are involved in adultery. This Chapter on Adultery is placed at the beginning of this book by the leading of the Lord to benefit you to overcome the sin of adultery.

COMMANDMENT OF GOD FOR US TO OBEY	REWARD FOR OBEDIENCE/ CONSEQUENCE OF DISOBEDIENCE
You shall not commit adultery. (Matt.5:27/KJV)	The man who commits adultery with another man's wife, he who commits adultery with his neighbor's wife, the adulterer and the adulteress, shall surely be put to death. (Lev.20:10)
This is the 7th of the "Ten Commandments" written by our Lord God Almighty. In the Old Testament times, both the man and the woman caught in adultery were put to death. They were judged only when they committed physical adultery. (see Ex.20:14; Deut.22:22)	

1.2 Adultery Of The Mind

COMMANDMENT OF GOD FOR US TO OBEY	REWARD FOR OBEDIENCE/ CONSEQUENCE OF DISOBEDIENCE
Do not look at a woman lustfully. (see Matt.5:28/NIV)	For anyone who **looks** at a woman **lustfully** has already committed **adultery** with her in her heart. (Matt.5:28/NIV)

This is the **upgraded version** of the Commandment "You shall not commit adultery" by the Lord Jesus Christ. Our God is the Most Holy God and His standards are very high. In the eyes of God, even looking at a woman or a man lustfully is "adultery."

1.3 Spiritual Surgery

COMMANDMENT OF GOD FOR US TO OBEY	REWARD FOR OBEDIENCE/ CONSEQUENCE OF DISOBEDIENCE
1. Pluck out your eye and cast it from you if it causes you to sin. (see Matt.5:29) 2. Cut off your hand and throw it away if it causes you to sin. (see Matt.5:30/NIV)	1. It is better for you to lose one part of your body than for your whole body to go into Hell. (Matt.5:30/ NIV) 2. For adulterers will be cast into Hellfire. (see Rev. 21:8)

We should sincerely seek God's help to abstain from scenes of immorality in films, TV, internet, books, cell-phones, etc., in order to maintain purity before God.

1.4 Divorce & Remarriage

COMMANDMENT OF GOD FOR US TO OBEY	REWARD FOR OBEDIENCE/ CONSEQUENCE OF DISOBEDIENCE
Do not divorce your wife, except for sexual immorality, and marry another. (see Matt. 19:9)	For in God's eyes, *you are committing adultery.* (see Matt. 19:9)

A husband is not to divorce his wife. (see 1 Cor.7:11)

Consequences & Prevention of Adultery

Introduction: The sin of adultery is highly prevalent all over the world. In these modern days, we can commit any sin and come up with a lame excuse to justify our sin, why and under what circumstances we did it. The world may accept us but in the eyes of God "sin is sin."

The sin of adultery will lead you straight to Hell. So don't commit adultery just because people around you do it. Do not take God's grace in vain. Sudden destruction may come upon you. Be warned!

Consequences, If One Commits Adultery...
(see Prov.5, 6 & 7)

This is applicable to both genders.

1. He that commits adultery lacks judgment and **destroys his own soul**.

2. The lips of an adulteress drop as a honeycomb and her mouth is smoother than oil. But her end is bitter as gall.

3. If you go after an adulteress, you will follow her like an ox going to the slaughter.

4. Her house is the **way to Hell**, going down to the *chambers of death.*

5. Remove your way far from her, lest you give your honor to others.

6. Your years will be wasted to the cruel one, the devil.

7. Lest strangers feast on your wealth; and your labor enrich another man's house.

8. At the end of your life you will groan, when your flesh and body are consumed with diseases like AIDS, Sexually transmitted diseases, etc.

9. Your reproach will not be wiped away.

10. He who sleeps with another man's wife will not go unpunished. He will reap what he sows. (see Gal.6:7)

When King David Committed Adultery...

King David bore devastating consequences for committing adultery. Sexual abuse and murder never departed from his house. (see 2 Sam.12:10-12)

What are the consequences David had to face for the sin of adultery?

1. *Grief due to death of David's new born baby - death of first son:* As soon as the illegitimate son of David and Bathsheba was born, he died.

2. *Shame and pain of sexual abuse:* David's son, Amnon raped Tamar, his half sister and ruined her life.

3. *Murder & Grief of death in the family – death of second son:* Absalom, Tamar's brother killed Amnon two years after he molested Tamar.

4. *Agony of separation:* David grieved when his son, Absalom fled to another country and hid himself in fear for three years, away from his father.

5. *Pain due to son rising against the father:* Absalom rebelled and raised up an army against David to take away his kingdom from him.

6. *Disgrace due to son lying with father's wives and concubines:* Absalom lay with David's concubines.

7. *Pain of losing another son – death of third son:* Absalom was killed in the battle while fighting against his father's army.

8. *David, a bad role model to his children:* Since David had a weakness for women, the same weakness was also found in his sons because as a father he left a bad example to his children.

King David killed Uriah, the Hittite with the sword of the people of Ammon and had taken his wife, Bathsheba to be his wife. Since it was a grave sin in the eyes of God, the Lord sent Prophet Nathan to David.

When Prophet Nathan pointed out David's sin of adultery to him through an analogy, though David repented sincerely for his sin, yet the following judgment of God was pronounced to him by the Prophet.

The Prophet rebuked David saying, "Why have you despised the commandment of the Lord, to do evil in His sight. You have killed Uriah, the Hittite with the sword; you have taken his wife, Bathsheba, to be your wife, and have killed him with the sword of the people of Ammon." "Therefore,

1. The **sword** shall never depart from your house, because you have **despised Me,** and have taken the **wife of Uriah, the Hittite to be your wife**." For the last of the Ten Commandment says, Thou shalt not covet another man's wife. (see 2 Sam.12:10; Ex.20:17)

2. "Thus says the Lord: 'Behold, I will **raise up adversity** against you from your own house; (see 2 Sam.12:11)

3. I will take your wives before your eyes and give them to your neighbor and he shall lie with your wives in the sight of the sun. (see 2 Sam.12:11)

For you did it secretly but I will do this thing before all Israel before the sun.'" (see 2 Sam.12:12)

Fulfilment of the Lord's Judgment on David...

After having gone through a lot of trials and hardship to become the King of Israel, imagine the agony David had to go through again all his life because of this one sin of Adultery.

David lost three sons at their young age; two of them were killed by the sword. God allowed David's own son, Absalom to rise against him as his adversary just as it was prophesied. Thus all the judgments of God came to pass in David's life.

God forgave David when he truly repented of his sins yet he had to bear the above consequences of his sins of adultery and murder.

If God did not spare David, a man after His own heart and made him bear the consequences of his sin of adultery, where do you and I stand when it comes to the sin of adultery?

Another good attribute of David that comes out strongly is that though he knew very well that he was suffering because of the prophecy given to him by Nathan, yet he never murmured against God.

Three Stages Of Adultery You Must Overcome

First Stage - When You Initiate... If you are married and you interact with another man or woman to entice them into an illicit relationship with you, then you have entered into the first stage of adultery. Check your heart!

Second Stage - When Someone else Tempts you...What will you Do? After being married, if you are tempted by another man or woman, what will your response be? If you are not strong enough and you yield to the temptation, then you are in the second stage of adultery.

Third Stage - When Someone Chases after you Persistently...How will you React? You cannot overcome this stage with your own strength. You have to continually depend on the Holy Spirit everyday to protect yourself from committing adultery.

As long as you are willing to resist the temptation, *the Holy Spirit of God in you* will continuously counsel you and guide you in the right direction. He will not allow you to fall into the snare of the devil. Remember, adultery is the devil's snare. Therefore, submit to God, resist the devil and he will flee from you. (see Jam.4:7)

Godly Counsel For The Youth

If an Attractive Unbeliever Pursues You relentlessly, then what will you do?

We have a good illustration of such an incident in the Bible: the account of Potiphar's wife tempting Joseph daily, to lie with her. Because *Joseph feared God,* he resisted her and fled from that place. Although he was falsely accused and put in prison for two years, yet the Lord was with him and lifted him up as second to Pharaoh in all of Egypt. (see Gen.39-41)

"Do not be unequally yoked together with unbelievers. And what agreement has the temple of God with idols? For you are the temple of the living God." (see 2 Cor.6:14-15)

This truth of *God's Word,* if you obey it, will set you free. You can avoid facing unnecessary consequences in life.

How Do You Protect Yourself From Adultery?

Prevention: Following are some of the ways…

1. Guard All Your Senses, Especially Your Eyes

i. **Sight…**Eyes are the windows of our soul (mind).Temptations penetrate through our eyes and corrupt our thoughts. When we entertain lustful or vain thoughts, we may eventually become slaves to the enemy and end up fulfilling Satan's will for our lives rather than God's will. Scripture says, 'Do not let her captivate you with her eyelids.' (see Prov.6:25) If you turn and give a second glance at a man or a woman, then watch out!

ii. **Smell…**Don't be lured by the smell of sweet perfume.

iii. **Touch…**Don't be tempted by the **tender touch** of the opposite sex.

iv. **Sound…**Shun listening to **heart-melting words.**

v. **Speech…**Avoid flirting and keep your distance from the person you are attracted to.

2. Constantly Renew Your Mind With The Word Of God

"An idle mind is the devil's workshop." Scripture says that we must not be conformed to this world; but be transformed by the renewing of our minds with the Word of God. (see Rom.12:2)

Whatever things are true, honest, just, pure, lovely and whatever things are of good report; if anything is excellent or praiseworthy, think on such things instead of the vain and lustful thoughts. (see Phil.4:8)

We ought to meditate on God's Word and continue to dwell on it day and night; **for God's Word is true, honest, just, pure and lovely.**(see Ps.119)

You must gird the loins of your mind with the belt of Truth i.e., the Word of God. When your thoughts go wild and cannot be controlled, the only way out is to put a tight belt around your mind with the Word of God.

You can also listen to the Word of God, Bible teachings and songs to renew your mind. When you do so, you will no longer have the desire to sin. This victory over sin is glorious.

3. Flee From The Place Of Temptation

i.   Flee from the place where there is temptation; if you give in to temptation, it is like playing with fire.

ii. Stay far from the path of evil; avoid it, do not set foot on the path, turn from it and pass away.

iii. Occasionally, the Lord might ask you to stay in the same place and overcome the temptation for specific reasons. This is generally applicable to mature Christians, who are over-comers. For example, Joseph, a bond servant fled from the person who tempted him but did not flee from the place. (see Prov.4:14-15;6:27-28;Gen.39:9-10)

4. Resist The Devil

Exposing the Devil's Tricks…Everything the devil tempts you with, he makes it look attractive, beautiful, and irresistible so that you fall prey to his trap. As you yield, the devil sends one arrow after another and builds a stronghold in your mind, making you his easy target. For example, David and Bathsheba. (see 2 Cor.10:4-5; 2 Sam.11-12)

It can all start innocently in the flesh and as you give in, the devil takes over the situation. The devil uses your characteristics or any other entry point to divert you from your *calling* and ruin your life. For example, weakness for women, rage, bitterness, fear, self-pity, depression, pride or even a kind, forgiving and patient spirit can be used by Satan as an open entry to entangle you in his trap. You can give place to the devil even by talking about the temptation. (see Eph. 4:27; Heb.13:4/NIV)

The devil does not give up easily. He studies you for a long time before he tempts you. He is **subtle, cunning and very patient.** He knows your weaknesses and is always waiting for the right opportunity to attack you.

Be vigilant, because your adversary the devil walks about like a roaring lion, seeking whom he may devour. Therefore, you must resist the devil and also **bind the spirit of lust,** spirit of fornication and spirit of adultery in the mighty Name of Jesus Christ. Be not deceived. God is not mocked. In the end, nobody can escape His wrath. (see Gal .6:7; 1 Pet.5:8-9)

Ways to overcome Satan are listed in *Chapter 10.* "Fear Not Satan, The Wicked One."

5. Heed The Guidance Of The Holy Spirit

Scripture says, "No temptation has overtaken you except what is common to man; but God is faithful, He will not let you be tempted beyond what you can bear; *God will, with the temptation, also make a way to escape*, that you may be able to bear it." (see 1 Cor.10:13)

First of all, you should have a constant relationship with the Holy Spirit of God by whom you are sealed when you invite Jesus into your heart. The Holy Spirit in you will guide you and help you resist the temptation, as long as you are willing to cooperate with Him.

But if you handle the situation in your own way, God may allow you to get hurt. Therefore, be sensitive to the Holy Spirit's promptings everyday and obey Him. (see Eph.1:14)

Listen & Follow…

6. Fear The Judgment of God

Jesus states, "If anyone hears My words and does not believe, I do not judge him; for I did not come to judge the world but to save the world.

He who rejects Me, and does not receive My words - the Word that I have spoken will judge him in the last day." (see John 12:47-48)

"Till Heaven and earth pass away, one jot or one tittle will by no means pass from the Law (Word of God) till all is fulfilled." (Matt. 5:18)

The Scripture very clearly says that the **adulterers,** fornicators, idolaters, homosexuals and those who abuse themselves, including those who commit masturbation, will **not inherit the Kingdom of God** but end up in Hell Fire. (see 1 Cor.6:9-10; Rev 21:8; Gal.5:19-21).

Marriage should be honored by all, and the marriage bed kept pure, for God will judge the adulterer and all the sexually immoral. (see Heb.13:4/NIV)

Therefore, be not deceived. God is not mocked. In the end nobody can escape His wrath. (see Gal.6:7)

7. Reverential Fear For "The Word of God"

The Lord says, **I will look upon those who tremble at My Word.** If you truly love and fear God, then you will follow all His Commandments given in His precious Word. (see Is.66:2)

Let's look at what the Word of God says concerning our body and adultery...

i.   The body is not for fornication (i.e., pre-marital sexual relationship) but for the Lord.

ii. He who is joined to a harlot or any other woman besides his own wife, is one with her in body; for it is said, 'The two will become one flesh.'

iii. Every sin that a man does is outside the body but he that commits fornication, sins against his own body. Therefore flee sexual immorality.

iv. Do you not *know that your body is the temple of the Holy Spirit* and you are not your own? For you are bought with a price, the precious Blood of Jesus Christ. Hence, the Lord expects you to keep your body holy and acceptable unto Him. (see 1 Cor.6:13-20; Rom.12:1)

8. Spiritual Adultery

Friendship with the world is spiritual adultery, i.e., unfaithfulness to Jesus Christ, our Bridegroom.

Friendship with the world is enmity with God; for it involves embracing the world's attitudes, values and sinful ways. (see James 4:4) For example, if you have friends who do things that you know are morally wrong, then you should not do what they do simply because they are your friends and you want to please them. If you feel obligated to do so, then this implies that they are not truly your friends. True friends will not care whether you are "cool" or not. They will accept you just as you are!

Unfaithfulness... Once you surrender 100% of your spirit, mind and body to the Lord, then if you give precedence to some worldly matter above the Lord in your mind, it is spiritual adultery before God. Jesus, your bridegroom wants to keep you, His bride, all for Himself; for He is a *jealous* God and a *consuming fire.* Jesus will not accept your friendship with the world. He will judge you for this sin if you don't repent and forsake it, especially if you are called to be the *"Bride of Christ."* Therefore, protect yourself from spiritual adultery.

9. Golden Nuggets

i. If you are single, it is better to marry than to burn with passion. (see 1Cor.7:9)

ii. If it is simply lust, it may quickly turn into hatred. E.g. Amnon and Tamar (see 2 Sam.13:12-19)

iii. True love waits - it will not hasten you into having pre-marital sexual relationships. But if you feel obligated to give in, then that person is not the one God has chosen for you.

iv. Don't keep "cutesies" close by at your workplace, especially when you are attracted to them. This can be an unnecessary temptation as it is said "opposites attract."

v. It is commonly said, "Grass is always greener on the other side but you still have to mow it." Learn to appreciate your spouse.

vi. You can put up pretence before men that you are faithful to your spouse but in your mind, you might have lusted after a man or a woman. In God's eyes this is adultery though you might have had no physical contact with him/her.

vii. Adultery is the devil's snare. It is a snake-pit. So take your hands off of it quickly. Otherwise the snake will bite you hard.

10. God, A Witness Of Your Marriage Covenant

God instituted marriage and He has been witness between you and the wife of your covenant. In flesh and spirit you are God's. Because He is seeking Godly offspring, the Lord has made you one.

When you commit adultery, you deal treacherously against your covenant spouse. If you then flood the Lord's altar with tears, He will still not accept your offerings with pleasure and the Lord will cut off the man who does this.

So guard yourself in your spirit, and let none deal treacherously against the wife of his youth. (see Mal. 2:12-15; Gen. 2:24)

2. Beatitudes Of Righteousness

2.1 Dependence On God

COMMANDMENT OF GOD FOR US TO OBEY	REWARDS FOR OBEDIENCE
Be poor in spirit. (see Matt.5:3)	1. For you are *blessed* and 2. Yours is the Kingdom of *Heaven.* (see Matt. 5:3)

To be poor in spirit is to depend on God for everything rather than on your own abilities. Depending on God is telling God, "I can't but only you can." Depend on the Lord in whatever you do, and your plans will succeed. (Prov.16:3/NCV).

2.2 Repentance

COMMANDMENT OF GOD FOR US TO OBEY	REWARDS FOR OBEDIENCE
Mourn. (see Matt.5:4)	1. For you are blessed and 2. You shall be comforted with righteousness, peace and joy in the Holy Spirit. (see Matt.5:4; Rom. 14:17)

Reasons to Mourn: 1. To grieve over your own weaknesses in relation to God's standard of righteousness.
2. To lament over lost souls.

1.3 Mercy

Be merciful. (see Matt. 5:7)	1. For you are blessed and 2. You will obtain mercy. (see Matt.5:7)

God expects us to be full of compassion and love towards those who are suffering.

2.4 Humility

COMMANDMENT OF GOD FOR US TO OBEY	REWARDS FOR OBEDIENCE
Be humble (meek). (see Matt.5:5)	1. For you are blessed. 2. And you will inherit the earth. (see Matt.5:5) 3. He who humbles himself will be exalted. (Lk. 18:14/NIV)
To be humble is to be submissive before God. It is like telling God, "I can't do it on my own. I need you, Lord."	

2.5 Purity

COMMANDMENT OF GOD FOR US TO OBEY	REWARDS FOR OBEDIENCE
Be pure in heart. (see Matt.5:8)	1. For you are blessed and 2. You shall *see God.* (see Matt.5:8)

Desire For Purity... First of all, desire to be pure in heart. As God reveals your sins, repent immediately and seek His help to set things right before Him.

Prayer: Make me so pure that I will be able to see You, Lord.

1. If you seek Him early, you will find Him. (see Prov.8:17)
2. If you draw near to God, He will draw near to you. (see James 4:8)
3. If you seek Him with all your heart and with all your soul, you will find Him. (see Deut.4:29)

God Cannot Lie... God is not a liar to put such a verse in His Word, if it is not possible for us to see Him.(see Matt.5:8)

God Is Not a Respecter of Persons... If Moses, a man like us, could see the Lord, why can't we?

For our God is not a respecter of persons. God doesn't care whether you are rich or poor. He cares because you are His child. (see Rom. 2:11/KJV)

2.6 Peace

COMMANDMENT OF GOD FOR US TO OBEY	REWARDS FOR OBEDIENCE
Be peacemakers. (see Matt.5:9)	1. For you are blessed and 2. You will be called sons of God. (see Matt.5:9)
1. Be at peace with God through the cross. (see Rom.5:1) 2. Be at peace with one another. (see Rom.12:18)	

2.7 Persecution

COMMANDMENT OF GOD FOR US TO OBEY	REWARDS FOR OBEDIENCE
Rejoice and be glad when people insult you, persecute you, and falsely say all kinds of evil against you because of Me. (see Matt.5:11-12/NIV)	1. For you are blessed and 2. Great is your reward in **Heaven.** (see Matt.5:11-12/NIV)
If you endure, you will also reign with Him. (see 2 Tim.2:12)	

2.8 Sufferings

Suffer persecution for righteousness' sake. (see Matt.5:10)	1. For you are blessed and 2. Yours is the Kingdom of **Heaven.** (see Matt.5:10)

1. When you want to follow God's standard of truth, justice, and purity and refuse to compromise with the present worldly standard, you will suffer persecution by those of the world. But in the end, it will be worth the suffering as you will be rewarded greatly in Heaven.

2. Those who are Christ's will crucify the sinful nature of the flesh with its passions and desires. (see Gal. 5:24)

2.9 Righteousness

COMMANDMENT OF GOD	REWARDS FOR OBEDIENCE
Hunger and thirst for righteousness. (see Matt. 5:6)	1. For you are blessed and 2. You will be filled with all the physical and spiritual blessings in Christ Jesus. (see Matt.5:6)
1. We must hunger and thirst after Christ's righteousness. When we abide in Christ, He clothes us with His righteousness. (see 1 Cor.1:30) 2. A righteous man's path is a *Royal path*.	

What is Righteousness?

Righteousness is "right-standing" and "right-doing" before God.

"Right standing" is having the right relationship with God through the free gift of Salvation.

"Right doing" is working out your own Salvation with fear and trembling before God, by obeying His Commandments.

Righteousness By Abiding In Christ...

If any man *be in Christ*, he is a *new creature*. God has made Jesus to be sin for us, who knew no sin; that *we might be made the Righteousness of God in Him*. (2 Cor.5:17, 21)

We must hunger and thirst for...
1. The Presence of God. (see Deut. 4:29)
2. The Word of God (see Ps.119)
3. Intimacy with Jesus (see Phil.3:8-10)
4. Fellowship of the Holy Spirit (see Jn.7:37-39)
5. Righteousness of God (see Matt. 5:6)
6. Kingdom of God (see Matt. 6:33)
7. Return of Christ (see 2 Tim.4:8)

We can abide in Christ by desiring all that is indicated above; for **Christ is our**

Righteousness, wisdom, sanctification and redemption. God sees the finished work of Christ and accepts us as His saints.

Our self righteousness is like filthy rags before God. We don't need to strive to be righteous. If we seek God's help, He will help us to achieve that status. (see 1Cor.1:30; Is.64:6; Phil.2:12)

3. Believers, The Chosen Of God

Spiritual Blessings For Believers In Christ Jesus (Eph.1:3-14)

1. Christ Jesus has **chosen us** in Him even before the *foundations of the world* that we should be holy and without blame before Him.

2. In love He predestined us to be *adopted as **His sons*** through Jesus Christ, in accordance with His pleasure and will - to the praise of His glorious grace.

3. He has accepted us in the beloved.

4. We have *redemption* through His precious blood.

5. We have the **forgiveness** of sins according to the riches of His grace.

6. He has abounded towards us in all wisdom and prudence.

7. He has made known to us the **mystery of His will**; according to *His good pleasure* which he has purposed in Himself.

8. In the fullness of times Christ will **gather** together in one all things in Him, both which are in heaven and which are on earth.

9. In Christ we also have obtained an **inheritance**, being pre-destinated according to the purpose of Him.

10. We, who were the first to believe in Christ, should be for the praise of His glory.

11. We are privileged to **trust** in Jesus Christ.

12. We also were included in Christ when we heard the **Word of Truth.**

13. It is His abundant grace that enabled us to receive the gospel of **Salvation.**

14. Having believed, you were sealed with that **Holy Spirit** of promise; who is a deposit guaranteeing our inheritance.

15. The Holy Spirit will help us to endure until the redemption of those who are *God's possession.*

Do you know how much God values *you* that He has thought about *you* even before the foundations of the world and predestinated you to Himself? He has a *specific will* for you. *Wait on Him to find out the "Mystery of God's Will" for Your Life.*

3.1 Repentance Through Godly Sorrow

Begin your journey with the Lord Jesus, as a Believer, through repentance.

COMMANDMENT OF GOD FOR US TO OBEY	REWARD FOR OBEDIENCE/ CONSEQUENCE OF DISOBEDIENCE
1. Repent.(see Matt. 3:2; 4:17) 2. Repent.(see Lk.13:3,5)	1. For the Kingdom of Heaven is near. (see Matt. 3:2; 4:17) 2. Or else you will all perish. (see Luke 13:3,5)

1. Jesus began His ministry with the message of repentance. He assured people of their inheritance in Heaven when they truly repent of their sins.
2. *Godly sorrow* from the heart brings repentance that leads to *salvation* and leaves no regret.
3. *Worldly sorrow* which is merely a lip service before God brings death to the soul. (see 2 Cor.7:10/NIV)

What Is Sin?

Sin is breaking the Law of God. All unrighteousness is sin. Whatsoever is not of *faith* is sin. He who commits sin is of the devil. (see 1 Jn.3:4,8; 5:17; Rom.14:23)

What Is Repentance?

To repent means to make a firm, inward decision to change and turn 180 degrees from our sinful ways, back to God.

How Do You Return To God?

Three 'R's - Remember, Repent and Redo.
Remember from where you have fallen.
Repent of your sins and weaknesses.
Redo the right things that you first did, if you have backslidden from God. (see Rev. 2:5)

* *When I was young, I used to write down all the sins I had committed and repented for them one by one and also set things right with people. This helped me not to commit those sins again.- Author*

Consequences...If you Refuse to Repent

1. **Judgment of God:** If you are stubborn and refuse to repent, you are storing up indignation and wrath against yourself for the Day of Judgment. 'I will come unto you quickly and will remove your place, the lamp stand, from My kingdom' says the most Holy God. (see Rev. 2:5; Rom. 2:5, 8)

2. **Your Soul will Die and You will Not Prosper in Life:** The soul that sins and not truly repents will surely die; for the wages of sin is *death*. (see Ezek.18:20)
   He that covers his sins shall not prosper. (see Prov.28:13; Rom. 6:23; 2 Cor.7:10-11/KJV)

3. **The Holy Spirit will Depart from You:** The Holy Spirit in you, the very gentle spirit, will not strive forever but slowly withdraw from you leaving your soul to die. When the world comes in, the Holy Spirit walks out. (see Eph.4:30)

4. **God will Hide His face from You:** Your iniquities will separate you from your God; your sins will hide His face from you. (see Is.59:2)

5. **God will Reject You if You are Luke warm:** 'I know your works. You either be hot or cold. If you are lukewarm, I will spit you out of my mouth.' says the Lord. (see Rev.3:15-16) You are called to walk either closely with the Lord (hot) or to walk in the ways of the world (cold) but do not be in-between (lukewarm); unfortunately, where majority of the Christians are today.

6. **You Crucify The Lord Jesus All Over Again:** *If you keep on sinning after being saved,* disregarding the conviction of the Holy Spirit and taking God's grace in vain, then you are crucifying the Lord on the cross all over again and putting Him to an open shame. (see Heb: 6:4-6)

7. **God will Not Answer when You Call upon Him:** If you continue to ignore God's reproof, He will laugh when calamity befalls you and will not answer your prayers. (see Prov.1:24-28)

Rewards...If you Truly Repent

1. **<u>God will Grant You Eternal Life:</u>** When you genuinely repent and be born again, God will forgive you and grant you *eternal life*.(see Jn.3:3, Mark 1:15)

2. **<u>You will Find Mercy of God:</u>** Whosoever confesses and forsakes his sins will have the mercy of God. For our God is a God of second chances. (see Prov.28:13/KJV)

3. **<u>All of Heaven will Rejoice over You:</u>** There will be more rejoicing in Heaven over one sinner who repents than over ninety-nine righteous persons who do not need to repent. (see Luke 15:7)

4. **<u>God will Return to You:</u>** 'Return unto Me in repentance and I will return to you,' says the Lord Almighty. (see Mal. 3:7)

5. **<u>God will Forgive Your Sins and Heal Your Land:</u>** 'If My people humble themselves and turn from their wicked ways, then will I hear from heaven and will forgive their sins and will heal their land' says the Lord God. (see 2 Chr.7:14)

6. **<u>You will be Blessed by Go</u>d:** Blessed are those who mourn over their weaknesses, for they will be comforted. (see Matt. 5:4)

7. **<u>You will be a New Creation in Christ:</u>** If any man be in Christ, he is a new creation; old things are passed away; All things have become new. (see 2 Cor.5:17)

3.2 The Word of God

(a) Ignorance of God's Word

COMMANDMENT OF GOD FOR US TO OBEY	REWARDS FOR OBEDIENCE
1. Do not live by bread alone, but by every word that proceeds from the mouth of God. (see Matt. 4:4)	1. We are **born again through the Word of God** which lives and abides forever. (see 1 Pet.1:23) 2. As new born babies, desire the pure milk of the Word that you may **grow** thereby. (see 1 Pet.2:2)

1. Our spirit which exists forever lives by the Word of God.
2. The meditated Word of God is the right kind of food for our spirit to grow deeper in the Lord.

COMMANDMENT OF GOD	SUPPORTING SCRIPTURES
2. Do not tempt the Lord your God. (see Matt. 4:7)	Satan said to Jesus, "If you are the Son of God, throw yourself down. For **it is written**: *'He will give His angels charge concerning you.'*" Then Jesus said to Satan, "**It is written again,** 'You shall not tempt the Lord your God.'" (see Ps. 91:11-12; Matt. 4:5-7)

1. Jesus quoted this to Satan in the wilderness, when Satan tried to divert Jesus from the path of perfect obedience to His Father's will, by using the word of God. Remember, Satan knows God's Word!

2. Satan tempted Jesus three times by saying, ***"If you are the Son of God..."*** and tried to ensnare Him in the areas of ***pleasure, pride, and power.*** These are the three most powerful areas of life through which the devil tries to tempt us even today, as he did with Jesus. (see 1 Jn.2:15-17)

Lessons To Learn From The Temptations Of Jesus...

1. Do Not Tempt The Lord:

Though God promises His protection, we should not tempt Him unnecessarily by getting into trouble because of our pride or ignorance of God's ways and still expect God to deliver us. He may not deliver us. (see Matt. 4:7)

2. Know the Scriptures well:

Since Jesus knew the Scriptures well and His Father God's ways, He did not fall for the devil's snare and did not jump from the mountain top.

Ignorance of God's Word is not an excuse you can give to God for the wrong choices you make in life. For the Lord says, *'My people **perish** for lack of knowledge of God's Word.'* (see Hos.4:6)

3. Compare Precept with Precept :

The Bible says that we should compare "precept upon precept, line upon line" of God's Word, as Jesus did. Therefore, we should not take one verse out of context, misinterpret it and use it for our selfish purposes. (see Is. 28:10).

4. Quote "The Word" to the Devil:

The devil, by using the Word of God, enticed Jesus to cast Himself down from the mountain top. But Jesus quoted another Scripture and did not fall prey to the snare of the devil. We must follow our Master's example to overcome the devil. (see Matt. 4:5-7)

3.2(b) Be Ye Doers Of God's Word & Not Hearers Only

In the parable of the sower, Jesus explains how *salvation and fruitfulness* of a person depends on how one responds to God's Word.

The Lord says, "Hear ye the parable of the sower."

COMMANDMENT OF GOD	CONSEQUENCES OF DISOBEDIENCE
Hardened Hearts: 1(a) Do not let your heart be hardened like the wayside where the seeds cannot grow. (see Matt.13:4,19) (b) Hear the Word of the Kingdom and understand it. (see Matt.13:19)	a. For the birds will come and devour the seed. (see Matt. 13:4) b. Or else the evil one will come and snatch away the Word that is sown in his heart. (see Matt.13:19/NIV)

1. The seed is the Word of God. The bird is symbolic of the devil, the wicked one. The wayside represents the heart of a person who does not understand the Word when he hears it.
2. **Don't Let The Devil Snatch away "The Word"**...If anyone hears the Word of God and does not understand it, then the devil comes and snatches away the Word that is sown in his heart. This is he who received seed by the wayside. (see Matt. 13:19)

COMMANDMENT OF GOD	CONSEQUENCE OF DISOBEDIENCE
Shallow Believers: 2. Do not let your heart be shallow like the **rocky place** where it does not have much soil for the seeds to grow. (see Matt.13:5-6/NIV)	The seeds will spring up quickly because the soil is shallow. But when the sun comes up, the plants will be scorched, and they will wither away because they have no root. (see Matt.13:5-6/NIV)

1. The rocky place represents the heart of a person.
2. Here, the people immediately receive the Word with joy. But **when persecution arises because of the Word, they quickly fall away** from Christ. For they don't understand Christ's love and His sacrifice for them on the Cross. (see Matt.13:20-21)

COMMANDMENT OF GOD	CONSEQUENCE OF DISOBEDIENCE
Unfruitful Believers: 3. Do not let your heart be unfruitful like the **thorny ground** which yields no fruit. (see Matt. 13:7, 22)	The seeds that fall among thorns will be choked by the thorns. (see Matt. 13:7)

1. The thorny ground represents the heart of a person.
2. This represents people of God who hear the Word; but when the cares of this world and the **deceitfulness of riches enter in, they choke the Word and** they become unfruitful for the Kingdom of God. (see Matt. 13:22)

COMMANDMENT OF GOD	REWARDS FOR OBEDIENCE
Fruitful Believers: 4. Let your heart be fruitful like the good soil which produces crop. (see Matt.13:8, 23/NIV)	For the seeds that fall on the good ground will yield a crop; some a hundredfold, some sixty, some thirty. (see Matt. 13:8)

1. The good soil represents the heart of a person.

2. **"30, 60, 100 Fold Fruit" Bearing Believers...**This represents people who hear, understand and obey the Word. They will produce 30, 60 or 100 fold fruit for the kingdom of God, **depending on the price** they are willing to pay for Christ's sake. ***What kind of a Believer are you?***

3.2(c) Do You Know What "BIBLE" Stands For?

Basic

Instructions

Before

Leaving

Earth

The BIBLE is the Holy Word of God and a love letter from God to mankind. It is the most read book in the world.

The Bible is the "Basic Instruction Manual" by which we ought to live on this earth. It enables us to live the kind of abundant life, full of joy and peace which God intends for us.

Proof... The Bible is archaeologically, scientifically, historically, medically, mathematically and geographically 100% proven, word for word from Genesis to Revelation.

Price Paid... Many servants of God have literally shed their own blood to translate the Bible from the original language into the languages of present day.

Must Be Desired More Than Gold... The law of the LORD is perfect, ***converting the soul***.

The statutes of the LORD are right, ***rejoicing the heart***:

The commandment of the LORD is pure, ***enlightening the eyes***.

By them is thy servant ***warned:*** and ***in keeping of them*** there is ***great reward***.

Therefore more to be desired are they than gold, yea, than much fine gold. (See Ps.19:7-11)

All Scripture is given by inspiration of God, and is profitable for doctrine, for reproof, for correction, for instruction in righteousness. (2 Tim.3:16/KJV)

His Name is Called The Word of God... The Word of God is Jesus Himself. (Rev.19:13)

Blessings From "The Word"

1. **To know the Lord Jesus...** We need to study the Word of God, to know Jesus, His nature and to understand what kind of God we serve. For in Him we live, and move, and have our being. (see Acts 17:28) Jesus' *Name* is called "The Word of God." (see Rev. 19:13)

2. **To Renew your Soul...** The Word of God is perfect. The Word revives the soul. (see Ps.19:7)

3. **Your Children...** If you forget My Word, I will forget your children, says the Lord. (see Hos.6:4)

4. **Wisdom & Joy...** The Word enlightens the eyes and makes wise the simple. The Word brings joy to the heart. (see Ps. 19:7- 8)

5. **Protection from Sin & the Devil ...** The Word protects you from sin and from the devil. For the psalmist says "I have hidden your Word in my heart that I might not sin against you." (Ps.119:11/NIV) As for the deeds of men, by the Word of your lips I have kept myself from the ways of the destroyer, the devil. (see Ps. 17:4)

6. **To know God's Ways...** The Psalmist, knowing the importance of God's Word, repeatedly cried out to God, 'Teach me Thy Law, Thy Precepts, Thy Commandments, Thy Statutes, Thy Testimonies, Thy Judgments and Thy Word' so that I may *know Your ways.'* (see Ps.119)

7. **Prosperity...** 'Blessed is the man who delights in the Law of the Lord and meditates His word day and night. And whatsoever he doeth will *prosper.* (see Ps 1: 1-3)

Hence "The Word" must be desired more than gold, yea, than much fine gold. (see Ps. 19:10)

3.3 The Fruit Bearing Life

COMMANDMENT OF GOD FOR US TO OBEY	REWARD FOR OBEDIENCE
1. Be like the good tree that bears good fruit. 2. Be not like the bad tree that bears bad fruit. (see Matt.12:33)	For a tree is known by its fruit. (see Matt.12:33)

1. After being born again, we should strive to become "Christ-like." For the Lord expects us to grow from glory to glory; it is an ongoing process. 2. We should not be stagnant in our spiritual growth, or else we will backslide. (see 2 Cor.3:18)	

COMMANDMENT OF GOD FOR US TO OBEY	REWARD FOR OBEDIENCE
3. *Go and bear fruit - fruit that will last.* (see John 15:16)	1. Then the Father will *give you whatever you ask* in My Name. (see John 15:16) 2. My *Father is glorified* when you bear much fruit; so you will be *My disciples*. (see John 15:8)

"I am the true vine, and My Father is the gardener. He **cuts off** every branch in Me that bears no fruit, while every branch that does bear fruit **He prunes** so that it will be even more fruitful." (see John 15:1-2/NIV)

How Can You Bear Good Fruits?

1. Jesus says "I am the Vine; you are the branches. If a man remains in Me and I in him, he will bear much fruit; **apart from Me you can do nothing.**"

    Always stay connected with Jesus Christ. (see Jn.15:5/NIV)

2. *Fruit of the Holy Spirit...*As God's child, if you allow the Holy Spirit to direct and influence you, then your life will bring forth the *"fruit of the Spirit"* which is love, joy, peace, long suffering, gentleness, goodness, meekness, faith and self-control.

    We can bear good fruits by living a lifestyle that reflects the image of Christ and by winning souls for His Kingdom. (see Col.1:10)

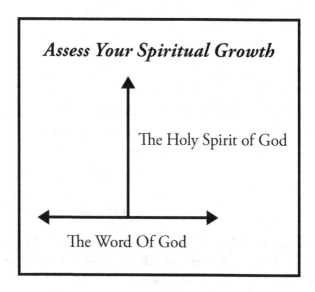

The Word of God is the foundation of your spiritual growth and it helps you to grow stronger in the Lord.

Prayer increases the anointing of the Holy Spirit upon you. The Presence of the Holy Spirit transforms you into the image of God and the gifts of the Holy Spirit help you to go deeper in the things of the Lord.

Seven Levels In God's Kingdom

Do you want to receive rewards in Heaven?

A believer can reach the following *"Seven Levels"* by paying the required price and by bearing fruits for His kingdom. We will be rewarded accordingly in Heaven :

1. Be Born Again

Steps to follow - as simple as A, B, C...

Admit that you are a sinner before God, and truly repent for your sins.

Ask God to forgive you; and He is faithful and just to forgive. Accept His forgiveness by faith; for it is a *free gift*. (see Prov.28:13; Rom.3:23; Eph.2:8).

Believe in your heart that Christ died for your sins and rose up from the dead;

Confess with your mouth Jesus Christ as your Savior and Lord; and then you shall be *saved* and be *born again*. (see Rom. 10:9)

Pray... Invite Jesus into your heart and ask Him to wash your heart with His precious Blood and fill you with the *peace* that the world cannot give you. (see Rev.3:20; Jn.14:27)

Reward... You will be rewarded with *"Eternal Life"* for being born again. (see Jn.3:3, 16)

2. Be a Disciple of Jesus Christ

A disciple of Christ is someone who walks in His footsteps, has Christ as his role model and obeys every command of his Master.

Being a disciple is a costly affair; for Jesus says, 'Anyone who does not carry his cross and follow Me, cannot be My disciple; whosoever does not forsake all that he has, cannot be My disciple.' (see Luke 14:27, 33)

Reward... You will be rewarded with hundredfold blessings on earth along with *Eternal Life*. (see Matt.19:29)

For more details, please refer to Chapter 7 on "Disciples: Co-Laborers With Christ."

3. Be a Priest Unto Christ

Rev. 1:5-6 says, Christ loved us, and washed us from our sins in His own Blood, and *has made us kings and priests unto God.*

Priest's job … A priest's main job is to intercede for the people. The priest has to stand in the gap between the perishing souls and the hellfire; or else the Lord will make him accountable for the lost souls. (see Ezek. 22:30; Jer.2:34-35)

Reward…"The Lord is his inheritance" on earth and he will also be rewarded accordingly in Heaven. (see Deut. 10:9; 18:1-2)

4. Be a King Unto God

Christ has *made us kings* and priests unto God. (see Rev. 1:5-6)

When we sacrifice all of our desires for the Lord, we will "Rule with Him."

Reward…Jesus says, "To him that overcomes, I will grant to sit with Me in My throne." (see Rev 3:21)

5. Be a Judge In His Kingdom

Jesus stated 'In the resurrection, when the Son of Man sits on His glorious throne, you who have followed Me will also sit on twelve thrones, judging the twelve tribes of Israel.'

Reward…If you forsake all and follow Christ, then you will receive a *"Judge's Reward."* (see Matt. 19:28; Rev.20:4)

6. Be the Bride of Christ

The bride of Christ should be fully clothed in the "righteousness of saints" and be delivered from all impurity.

Let us be glad and rejoice, and give honor to Him; for the marriage of the Lamb is come, and His bride, the Church has made herself ready.

The *Most Honorable Reward* one can receive is to be the "Bride of Christ." (see Rev. 19:7-9; Hos.2:19-20; 2 Cor.11:2)

7. Be a Martyr For Christ

1. John said, "I saw thrones on which were seated those who had been given authority to judge.

And I saw the souls of those who had been *beheaded* because of their testimony for Jesus and for the Word of God. They had not worshipped the beast i.e., the anti-Christ or his image and had not received his mark on their foreheads or their hands."

Reward…The martyrs came to life and ***reigned with Christ a thousand years***. (see Rev. 20:4)

2. John also stated "I saw under the altar the souls of martyrs, crying in a loud voice, 'How long, Sovereign Lord, Holy and True, until you judge the inhabitants of the earth and avenge our blood?'"

Reward…Then each of them was given a *white robe;* and they were told to *wait* a little longer, until the number of their fellow servants and brothers, who would be killed as they were, was completed. (see Rev. 6:9-11)

3. Some believers are called to be *"living martyrs"* on earth. A living martyr must daily die to "self" ('I', ego, pride, own ways, and self-reliance). He must crucify his desires, goals, ambitions on the cross every moment of the day and totally depend on God.

Only by strictly following the guidance of the Holy Spirit, one can be a living martyr. (see Rom. 12:1)

3.4(a) Be Ye Salt Of The World

COMMANDMENT OF GOD FOR US TO OBEY	CONSEQUENCE OF DISOBEDIENCE
1. Be ye salt of the earth. (see Matt.5:13/KJV)	*If salt loses its saltiness,* how can it be made salty again? It is no longer good for anything, except to be thrown out and be trampled by men. (see Matt.5:13/NIV) Similarly, if we become lukewarm in our spiritual walk and quench the conviction of the Holy Spirit, we will be *cast out* by God and be reproached by men. Therefore, we must be godly examples in this world and must resist the moral decay and corruption. (see Rev.3:15-16)

We get certain insights from the characteristics of salt...

1. As salt is white, we should be pure before God in our thoughts, words, and actions.
2. As salt quickly dissolves in the water, we should be ready to serve Christ in ministry.
3. As salt is a preservative, our lives should be as preservatives, protecting this wicked world from the wrath of God.

3.4(b) Be Ye Light Of The World

COMMANDMENTS OF GOD FOR US TO OBEY	REWARDS FOR OBEDIENCE
1. Be ye the light of the world. (see Matt.5:14/KJV)	For "*I am the light* of the world; Whoever follows Me *will never walk in darkness,* but will have the Light of Life," says the Lord. (see Jn.8:12/NIV)
2. Do not light a lamp and put it under a basket, but on a lamp-stand. (see Matt.5:15)	For it gives light to all who are in the house. (see Matt. 5:15) **You might be** *the only Jesus people around you see* **and observe.**
3. Shine your light before men. (see Matt. 5:16)	For people may see your good works and glorify your Father in Heaven. (see Matt.5:16) You might be the only *"Bible"* those around you read.

1. Our lifestyle must radiate the light, Jesus Christ, to the world.
2. You were once darkness, but now you are light in the Lord.
3. Live as children of light, for the fruit of the light consists in all goodness, righteousness and truth.
4. Have nothing to do with the unfruitful deeds of darkness. (see Eph. 5:8-11/NIV)

3.5 How Far Will You Go To Reconcile?

(When Your Brother Sins Against You)

COMMANDMENT OF GOD FOR US TO OBEY	REWARD FOR OBEDIENCE/ CONSEQUENCE OF DISOBEDIENCE
Settle the matter privately: 1. If your brother sins against you, go and tell him his fault; **between you and him alone.** (see Matt. 18:15)	1. For if he hears you, you have won your brother over. 2. If a man is overtaken in any trespass, you who are spiritual **restore** such a man in a spirit of gentleness. (see Matt. 18:15; Gal. 6:1)

1. If a brother/sister sins against you, settle the matter privately with him/her.
2. Do not expose the sin in public and humiliate him/her; for you will never know how much you hurt that person. It should not become a matter of gossip.

COMMANDMENT OF GOD	REWARD FOR OBEDIENCE
Don't give up, Try again: 2. Take with you one or two more, if your brother will not hear you. (see Matt. 18:16)	For by the testimony of two or three witnesses, every matter may be established. (see Matt. 18:16/NIV)

1. Do not be quick to judge others based on assumptions.
2. Remember, until a person is proven guilty, he/she is innocent of the crime. Therefore, the mediator must listen to both sides of the story before passing judgment.

COMMANDMENTS OF GOD FOR US TO OBEY	REWARD FOR OBEDIENCE/ CONSEQUENCE OF DISOBEDIENCE
Go one step further, involve the Church: 3. Tell it to the church, if your brother refuses to hear the two or three witnesses. (see Matt. 18:17) *Final Resort:* 4. Consider him as a heathen and a sinner, if he neglects to hear the church. (see Matt. 18:17)	1. When your brother hardens his heart in such a way that he will not heed to many attempts of correction, then the church, as a final resort, should expel him. Sins within the church concerning sexual immorality must be dealt with as in 1 Cor.5:1-5. 2. If your brother repents and turns around from his sin, then he may be forgiven and restored to fellowship again. (see 2 Cor.2:6-8)

These Commandments show us that God gives much importance to reconciliation among brothers.

1. Our God is a God of second chances. He wants us to go to any extent to restore the strained relationship to maintain unity among believers.

2. For *Christ is our Head* and we are the different members of His Body. (see Eph.5:30)

3.6 Greatness In God's Kingdom

COMMANDMENT OF GOD	REWARD FOR OBEDIENCE
1. Be a minister unto others. 2. Be a servant to others. (see Matt. 20:26-27; 23:11/KJV)	1. Whosoever will be **great** among you, let him be your minister. 2. Whosoever will be **chief** among you, let him be your servant.

1. Even as the Son of Man, Lord Jesus, came not to be ministered unto, but to minister; and *to give His life a ransom for many.* (see Matt. 20:25-28/ KJV)
2. *In this world,* those who have power and authority are considered great.
3. *In the Kingdom of God, greatness is measured not by our authority* over others but by our service to others.

3.7 Unity Is Strength

United We Stand, Divided We Fall...

Christ's heart must be bleeding to see us divided and diverted from our God-given destiny. We are blinded by our superstitions, rituals, traditions, doctrines and various denominations, thereby causing great damage to the Body of Christ.

The only thing that matters is that ***we are all bought by the priceless Blood of our Lord Jesus***. Remember, Christ is our Head and we are the different members of His Body, regardless of who we are. So let us be united in Christ. (see Eph. 5:30)

COMMANDMENTS OF GOD FOR US TO OBEY	REWARD FOR OBEDIENCE/ CONSEQUENCE OF DISOBEDIENCE
Called to Live in Harmony: 1. Do not be divided in your kingdom. (see Matt. 12:25) 2. Do not be divided in your city. (see Matt. 12:25) 3. Do not be divided in your house. (see Matt. 12:25	1. For every kingdom divided against itself is brought to desolation. 2. Every city or house that is divided against itself will not stand. (see Matt. 12:25

Who Divides Us?

From the beginning of creation, Satan has been using the same strategy "***divide and conquer***" to destroy the human race.

Satan is always at work. Remember, Satan never takes a vacation. We must not be ignorant of Satan's schemes. (see 2 Cor.2:11)

COMMANDMENT OF GOD FOR US TO OBEY	REWARD FOR OBEDIENCE
4. All of you, live in harmony with one another. (see 1 Pet.3:8/NIV) 5. Be perfect, be of one mind and live in peace. (see 2 Cor.13:11/KJV)	So that you may inherit a *blessing* and the God of love and *peace* will be with you. (see 1 Pet.3:9; 2 Cor.13:11)

How can we live in harmony?

Be sympathetic, compassionate and humble and love as brothers.
Do not repay evil with evil or insult with insult but with blessing; because to this you were called so that you may inherit a *blessing*. (see 1 Pet.3:8-9/NIV)

COMMANDMENT OF GOD FOR US TO OBEY	REWARD FOR OBEDIENCE
Power in United Prayer: 6. Agree with another person in prayer. (see Matt. 18:19)	If two of you on earth agree about anything you ask for, **it *will be done for you*** by My Father in Heaven. (Matt. 18:19/NIV) **Jesus in your midst…**For where two or three are gathered together *in My Name*, I am there in the midst of them. (Matt. 18:20)

Tremendous **power of God** is released when we pray in unity. God is not even asking for three to unite but a bare minimum of two of us to agree on earth, to answer our prayers from Heaven.

4. Christ's Righteousness

Jesus states that unless your righteousness exceeds the righteousness of the Scribes and Pharisees, you will **by no means enter the Kingdom of Heaven.** (see Matt. 5:20)

How do we Surpass The Righteousness of the Pharisees?

When we obey Christ's upgraded version of the Old Testament Commands, we exceed the righteousness of the Scribes and Pharisees to inherit Eternal Life. (see Matt. 5:20).

For example, the OT command, "Thou shall not commit adultery" i.e., physical adultery, the Pharisees would have obeyed without much difficulty.

But Christ upgraded the above commandment for us, as "Anyone who looks at a woman lustfully has already committed adultery with her in his heart" i.e., committing adultery in the mind.

Similarly, Jesus has upgraded several OT commandments regarding various aspects of life, for us to obey which are listed in this chapter.

COMMANDMENT OF GOD FOR US TO OBEY	REWARD FOR OBEDIENCE
Let your righteousness exceed the righteousness of the Scribes and Pharisees. (see Matt. 5:20)	Only then you will enter into the Kingdom of Heaven. (see Matt.5:20)

1. Most of the Pharisees and the Scribes diligently followed all the rules in the Law but still did not make it to Heaven because their hearts were not right before God. (see Matt. 23:5; 33)

2. You can keep most of the rules in the Law of God, as the Pharisees did. You can pray, fast, praise God, read God's Word and attend worship services and still not enter into heaven; all these can be just *outward acts,* depending on the motives behind them.

3. Are you doing all these things to please yourself, to impress others or to please the Almighty God?

4.1 Obey His Commands & Be Great In Heaven

"If you love Me, you will keep My Commandments" **says our Lord Jesus.**

Our obedience is directly proportionate to our love for the Lord. **(see John 14:21-23)**

COMMANDMENT OF GOD FOR US TO OBEY	CONSEQUENCE OF DISOBEDIENCE
Obey and Teach: 1. Do not break even the least of God's Commandments and teach men so. (see Matt.5:19) 2. Let not many of you become teachers. (see James 3:1/NIV)	1. Or else, you will be called *least* in the Kingdom of Heaven. (see Matt.5:19) 2. Not many of you should be *Teachers* because you will receive a stricter judgment. (see James 3:1/NIV)

God has bound Himself with such a law whereby a disciple cannot prepare another disciple/an intercessor/a laborer above his own spiritual standard. For a disciple is not above his master. (Luke 6:40) So strengthen yourself first in the Lord and then strengthen others. (see Luke 22:32)

COMMANDMENT OF GOD	REWARD FOR OBEDIENCE
3. Obey His Commandments and teach others so. (see Matt.5:19)	1. For you will be called *great* in the Kingdom of Heaven. (see Matt.5:19) 2. Keep My Commandments so that My joy might remain in you, and that *your joy might be full*. (see Jn.15:10-11/KJV)

1. We must obey God's Commandment. For it is the Way, the Truth, and the Life. (see Jn.6:63; 17:17; Ps.119:37)

2. Apostle Paul said "I beat my body and bring it into subjection so that after I have preached to others, I myself will not be disqualified for the prize." (see 1 Cor.9:27)

3. Only by the power of the Holy Spirit, we can obey Him and live a victorious life.

Obey & Receive More Blessings

1. **Christ manifests Himself to you...**Jesus says "Whoever has My Commands and obeys them, he is the one who loves Me.

    He who loves Me will be...
    Loved by My Father and
    I too will love him and
    Show Myself to him and
    We will come to him and
    Make our home with him." (see Jn.14:21-23/NIV)

2. **Jesus becomes your friend...**"You are My friends, if you do whatever I command you." says our Lord Jesus. (see Jn.15:14)

3. **Work of your hands will be blessed...**The Lord will open His good treasure, the Heavens, to bless all the work of your hands. (see Deut. 28:12)

4. **Prosperity...**You shall lend to many nations but you shall not borrow. You shall be above only and not be beneath, if you heed the Commandments of the Lord your God. (see Deut. 28:12-13)

5. **Security...**Blessed shall you be when you come in, and blessed shall you be when you go out. (see Deut. 28:6)

6. **Your children will be blessed...** Blessed shall be the fruit of your body. (see Deut. 28:4)

7. **Your enemies will be defeated...**The Lord will cause your enemies who rise against you one way to flee before you seven ways. (see Deut. 28:7)

4.2   Adultery

The topic on adultery, being important, is given as a separate chapter in the beginning of the book.

4.3 Anger Equivalent To Murder

COMMANDMENT OF GOD FOR US TO OBEY	CONSEQUENCE OF DISOBEDIENCE
Physical Murder: 1. You shall not murder. (OT) (Matt.5:21)	Whoever murders will be in ***danger of the judgment.*** (Matt. 5:21)
This is the 6th of the Ten Commandments in the OT which the Pharisees would have easily obeyed. (see Ex.20:13)	

COMMANDMENT OF GOD	CONSEQUENCE OF DISOBEDIENCE
Heart Murder: 2. Do not be angry with your brother without a cause. (see Matt.5:22)	Whoever is angry without a cause will be in ***danger of the judgment.***
1. This is the upgraded version of the above Commandment by Christ. 2. Anger without a cause is like breaking the 6th commandment in the eyes of God. (see Matt. 5:22) 3. In order to exceed the righteousness of the Pharisees, Jesus commands us to overcome anger since it may lead to murder.	

COMMANDMENT OF GOD	CONSEQUENCE OF DISOBEDIENCE
Tongue Murder: 3. Do not say to your brother, "Raca!" in your anger. (see Matt.5:22)	For you will be in danger of the council. (see Matt. 5:22)

"Raca" is a scornful word, which means "Thou empty fellow" and it comes due to one's pride, anger and malice.

COMMANDMENT OF GOD FOR US TO OBEY	CONSEQUENCE OF DISOBEDIENCE
Tongue Murder: 4. Do not say to another "You fool!" (see Matt.5:22)	For you will be in danger of **Hell Fire**. (see Matt. 5:22)

1. "You fool" is a spiteful word, and comes from hatred. It is looking down upon someone, not only as mean and unworthy but also as a wicked person who does not deserve to be loved.
2. Ask God to help you control your tongue.

COMMANDMENT OF GOD	REWARD FOR OBEDIENCE
Be Reconciled: 5. First be reconciled to your brother who has something against you. (see Matt.5:23)	To be worthy to offer your gift unto God. (see Matt.5:24)

Make every effort to live in peace with all men and to be holy; without holiness no one will see the Lord. (Heb.12:14/NIV)

COMMANDMENT OF GOD	CONSEQUENCE OF DISOBEDIENCE
Be a Peacemaker: 6. Settle matters quickly with your adversary who is taking you to court. (see Matt.5:25/NIV)	For the judge may find fault in you and hand you over to the officer and you be thrown into prison. (see Matt.5:25)

Agreeing with the wicked is wrong before God; but settling the matter with your adversary is right in the eyes of God.

4.4 Divorce Due To Hardness Of Hearts

COMMANDMENT OF GOD	SUPPORTING SCRIPTURES
God Hates Divorce: 1. Let not man separate what God has joined together. (see Matt. 19:6)	Moses permitted divorce because of the hardness of people's hearts but from the beginning it was not so. (see Matt. 19:8)
1. "God hates divorce." (Mal.2:16) 2. Only by pride comes contention. Hence it is better to lose an argument and win your spouse rather than living in strife which may end up in divorce. So protect your marriage at any cost. (see Prov. 13:10/KJV)	

Exception for Divorce: 2. Do not divorce your wife for any reason except sexual immorality. (see Matt.5:32)	1. For if you do so, you will cause her to commit adultery. 2. And anyone who marries her who is divorced commits adultery. (see Matt.5:32) 3. Adulterers will not inherit the Kingdom of Heaven. (see Gal.5:19-21)
Jesus made an exception for divorce only in the case of sexual immorality.	

Divorce & Remarriage: 3. Do not divorce your wife, except for sexual immorality, and marry another. (see Matt. 19:9)	For in God's eyes, *you are* committing adultery. (see Matt. 19:9)

1. A husband is not to divorce his wife. (see 1 Cor.7:11)

2. A man shall leave his father and mother and be united to his wife, and the two will become one flesh. (see Eph.5:31)

3. ***If you have married an unbeliever*** before your salvation, then you should not initiate divorce if your spouse wants to stay with you. But if the unbelieving spouse wants divorce then you are not bound. (see 1 Cor.7:12-16)

4.5 Do Not Break Your Oaths

COMMANDMENT OF GOD FOR US TO OBEY	CONSEQUENCE OF DISOBEDIENCE/ SUPPORTING SCRIPTURES
1. Do not break your oath, but keep the oaths you have made to the Lord. (see Matt.5:33/NIV)	Pay what you have vowed. It is better not to vow than to make a vow and not pay.
2. When you make a vow to God, do not delay in fulfilling it; for God has no pleasure in fools. (see Eccl. 5:4)	Do not let your mouth cause you to sin. Do not say before the angel of God that the vow you made was an error. God will be angry at your excuse and destroy the work of your hands. Therefore, stand in awe of God. (see Eccl. 5:4-6)

COMMANDMENT OF GOD	SUPPORTING SCRIPTURES
2. Do not swear at all; neither by Heaven nor by the earth; neither by Jerusalem nor by your head. (see Matt.5:34-36)	For Heaven is God's throne; The earth is His footstool; Jerusalem is the city of the great King; and you should not swear even by your head because you cannot make one hair black or white. (see Matt.5:34-36)

The 3rd of the Ten Commandments instructs us not to take the Name of the Lord, our God, in vain. (see Ex.20:7)

4.6 Do Not Fight For Your Rights

COMMANDMENT OF GOD FOR US TO OBEY	SUPPORTING SCRIPTURES
Do not strike back: 1. Do not resist an evil person; Turn your other cheek also when you are slapped on one. (see Matt.5:39)	If it is possible, as far as it depends on you, live at peace with everyone. (Rom. 12:18/NIV)
This is Jesus' upgraded version of the OT command "An eye for an eye" and "A tooth for a tooth."	

COMMANDMENT OF GOD	SUPPORTING SCRIPTURES
Give up your Rights: 2. When you are sued for a tunic, give away your cloak also. (see Matt.5:40) 3. When someone compels you to go one mile, go with him two miles. (see Matt.5:41) 4. Give to the one who asks you. 5. Do not turn away from the one who wants to borrow from you. (see Matt.5:42)	As we have opportunity, let us do good to all people, especially to those who belong to the family of Christ. (see Gal.6:10)

When you are approached for help, make it a habit to help.

Do not fight for your rights but be at peace with all. It is alright to lose the argument or your rights if you can win the person for Christ.

But see to it that no one takes advantage of you and takes your kindness for weakness.

4.7 Do Good To Those Who Hate You

COMMANDMENT OF GOD FOR US TO OBEY	REWARD FOR OBEDIENCE/ SUPPORTING SCRIPTURES
1. **Love** your enemies, **bless** those who **curse** you, **do good** to those who **hate** you, **pray** for those who **spitefully use you**, and **persecute you**. (Matt.5:44)	1. Love your enemies so that you may be the ***children of your Father*** in Heaven. 2. Jesus said, 'Even the tax collectors love those that love them and salute their brothers.' (see Matt.5:45-47)
2. Do to others what you would have them do to you. (see Matt.7:12/NIV)	For this is the Law and the Prophets. (see Matt.7:12)

1. This is the Lord's upgraded version of the OT command, "You shall love your neighbor and hate your enemy."
2. When we behave like the tax collectors, then there is no reward for us in Heaven. (see Matt.5:45-47)
3. You can love your enemies only by the love of God that is poured into your hearts by the Holy Spirit. (see Rom. 5:5)
4. If someone says, "I love God," and hates his brother, he is a liar; for he who does not love his brother whom he has seen, how can he love God whom he has not seen. (1 Jn.4:20)

COMMANDMENT OF GOD	CONSEQUENCE OF DISOBEDIENCE
Jesus, The Prince of Peace: 3. Put your sword back in its place. (Matt. 26:52/NIV)	For all who take the sword will perish by the sword. (see Matt. 26:52)

Jesus Did Good To Those Who Hated Him…When the soldiers came to arrest Christ; Peter immediately reached for the sword and cut off the soldier's ear, desiring to protect the Lord. Jesus was compassionate enough to fix the soldier's ear, not worrying about His forthcoming crucifixion. We ought to follow the Lord's example and solve all our problems amicably, without violence.

4.8 Forgive Seventy Times Seven

COMMANDMENT OF GOD FOR US TO OBEY	REWARD FOR OBEDIENCE/ CONSEQUENCE OF DISOBEDIENCE
1. Forgive your debtors. (see Matt. 6:12) 2. Forgive men when they sin against you. (see Matt.6:14/ NIV) 3. Forgive your brother who sins against you seven times in a day and **seven times in a day returns to you,** saying, "I repent." (see Luke 17:4) 4. Forgive your brother's sins not seven times, but up to seventy times seven i.e., 490 times. (see Matt. 18:22)	Forgive men when they sin against you, only then your Heavenly Father will forgive you. If you do not forgive men their trespasses, ***neither will your Father forgive*** your trespasses. (see Matt.6:14-15)
5. Forgive a man who has grieved you; comfort him and reaffirm your love to him. (see 2 Cor.2:5-8)	So that he will not be overwhelmed by excessive sorrow as the punishment inflicted on him by the majority is sufficient for him. (see 2 Cor.2:6-8)

1. Forgiveness is the best gift we can give to one another.
2. **Satan, The Offender...** We ought to forgive such a man in order that Satan might not take advantage over us; for we are not ignorant of Satan's schemes. (see 2 Cor.2:10-11)
3. Bind the spirit of unforgiveness and bitterness.

Is God's Forgiveness Conditional?

The forgiveness of God, though freely given to us when we repent, yet is conditional, according to a person's willingness to forgive others.

In other words, if we are unkind and unforgiving towards another person, it will block the flow of God's forgiveness and blessings towards us. E.g. Esau. (see Heb.12:15-17)

Therefore, bear with each other and forgive whatever grievances you may have against one another, as the Lord has forgiven you. (Col. 3:13/NIV)

Unforgiving People Face God's Judgment

COMMANDMENT OF GOD FOR US TO OBEY	CONSEQUENCE OF DISOBEDIENCE
Parable of The Unforgiving Servant: Forgive your brother's trespasses, from your heart. (see Matt. 18:35)	If you do not forgive, your Heavenly Father will call you a wicked servant and will deliver you to the ***tormentors.***(see Matt. 18:32-35)

God forgives and forgets our worst sins...

When God has freely forgiven all our sins and iniquities, can we not forgive others who have harmed us in small matters?

In the parable of the Unforgiving Servant, Jesus spoke about a certain king who forgave his servant that owed him ten thousand talents. When the king found out that the same servant did not in turn forgive his debtor, who owed him only a hundred pence, he became furious and cast that wicked servant into the prison and gave him up to the tormentors.

Our heavenly Father will do the same to us if we do not forgive our fellow brethren. (see Matt. 18:23-35)

4.9 Prayers Of The Righteous Avail Much

Prayer is merely talking to Jesus, our daddy and best friend who loves us so much.

You must have balanced proportions of Prayer, the Word and the anointing of the Holy Spirit in order to keep your spirit alive.

i. "Prayer" can be compared to the Air we breathe...

Scripture says that you should pray without ceasing just as you breathe continuously. When you stop breathing, you die, so also when you stop praying, your spirit dies. (see 1 Thess.5:17)

If you are *too lazy to pray* and you always depend on others to pray for us, then you are like a person who is connected to *"the ventilator"* and is breathing artificially instead of breathing on his own.

ii. The "Word of God" can be compared to the Food we consume...

If there is no intake of food for a few days, one may become weak, mal-nourished and can eventually go into coma;

Similarly, without the Word of God, your spirit inside becomes skeleton-like, weak and useless for the Kingdom of God. (see Matt. 4:4)

iii. The "Holy Spirit" can be compared to the Water we drink...

Just as you get dehydrated without water; your spirit also can become dry and powerless, without the anointing of the Holy Spirit. (see Jn.7:37-38)

4.9(a) How Should We Pray?

COMMANDMENT OF GOD FOR US TO OBEY	REWARD FOR OBEDIENCE
Pray, Not To Be Seen By Men: 1. When you pray, do not be like the hypocrites, who love to be seen by men. (see Matt.6:5)	They have their reward on earth in full and therefore they receive **no rewards in Heaven.** (see Matt. 6:5)

The Pharisees, who were hypocrites, loved to pray in public just to be seen and honored by men. But Jesus, our Master stated, "I do not receive honor from men." (see Jn.5:41)

Pray In Secret:	*Reward for Obedience:*
2. When you pray, go into your room, shut your door, pray to your Father. (see Matt.6:6)	For your Father who sees in secret will reward you openly. (see Matt.6:6)

Use God's Word in Prayer…When you use God's Word in your prayers, you will receive answers to your prayers quickly; for the Lord says, My Word shall not return to Me void, but it shall accomplish what I please. (see Is. 55:11) When you pray for 30 minutes, you need to read the Word for at least 15 minute; in the ratio of 2:1.

3. Do not use vain repetitions as the heathen do. Do not be like the heathen. (see Matt.6:7-8)	For your Father knows what you need before you ask Him. (Matt.6:8/NIV)

No Vain Repetitions…

1. The heathen think that they will be heard because of their many words. (see Matt. 6:7)

2. Jesus often prayed very short prayers. For example, He said **"Peace, be still"** and the raging storms calmed down. (see Mark 4:39)

3. If you pray enough in secret, all you have to do is to say a few words in public to bring forth miracles.

Ask, Seek & Knock

COMMANDMENT OF GOD FOR US TO OBEY	REWARD FOR OBEDIENCE
4. Ask. (see Matt.7:7)	And it will be given to you. For everyone who asks, receives. (see Matt.7:8)

"Asking" implies simply making God aware of your needs and believing that God hears your prayers.

COMMANDMENT OF GOD FOR US TO OBEY	REWARD FOR OBEDIENCE
5. Seek and you will find. (see Matt.7:7)	For he who seeks, finds. (see Matt.7:7)

1. *"Seeking"* implies intense pleading along with obedience to the will of God.
2. **Seek ye first the kingdom of God** and His righteousness. (see Matt. 6:33)

COMMANDMENT OF GOD FOR US TO OBEY	REWARD FOR OBEDIENCE
6. Knock and it will be opened to you. (see Matt.7:7)	To him who knocks, the door will be opened. (see Matt. 7:7)

1. *"Knocking"* implies banging on the door of Heaven and persisting in prayer until He responds.

2. If you truly want to receive an answer from God, you must be ready to sacrifice or pay any price for it, even if it requires changing your attitude and lifestyle.

3. **Persevere in Prayer...** Jesus encourages perseverance in prayer. He expects us to keep on asking, seeking and knocking or sometimes banging on Heaven's door until it opens. Make breakthrough prayers until you receive answers.

4.9(b) Ways To Pray Efficiently

1. **Find a Covenant Partner** with whom you can agree in prayer.

    "If two of you agree on earth about anything you ask for, it will be done for you by My Heavenly Father" says the Lord. (see Matt. 18:19)

    * From my personal experience, I can guarantee, it works! When I prayed along with my covenant prayer partner, God answered all our prayers. - Author

2. **Prayer Saves You From Unseen Dangers...**Everyday, you can **wake up at least half an hour early** and spend that extra time alone with God. This time with God will protect you from a lot of troubles that the devil has planned against you for the day.

3. **Pray in the Spirit...**Scripture says, 'The Spirit of God helps us in our weaknesses. For we do not know what we ought to pray for, but the Spirit Himself intercedes for us with groaning which cannot be uttered.' If you have the gift, speak in tongues as much as possible, as apostle Paul did.

    When you speak in tongues, you speak *mysteries* with the Almighty God. The Holy Spirit will intercede for you and will bring your life in line with His will. (see Rom. 8:26-27; 1 Cor.14:2)

    * By His grace, God has enabled me to speak much in tongues in the past ten years which opened my spiritual ears to hear the voice of the Holy Spirit everyday. It has helped me to understand the Word of God better and it has also deeply impacted my spiritual life. - Author

4. **Join A Prayer Group** where you can grow in prayer, with other believers.

    Do not forsake the assembling of the church, for it is difficult to grow spiritually by yourself. (see Heb. 10:25)

4.9(c) What Should We Pray For?

COMMANDMENTS OF GOD FOR US TO OBEY	REWARDS FOR OBEDIENCE
1. Ask. (see Matt.7:7) 2. Know what to ask for in prayer. (see Matt. 20:22)	1. And it will be given to you. (see Matt.7:7) **2. Ask for the Holy Spirit:** If you, being evil, know how to give good gifts to your children, how much more will your Father in Heaven give good gift i.e., the Holy Spirit, to those who ask Him. (see Matt.7:11; Luke 11:13)

What to pray for...

1. Pray for the infilling of the Holy Spirit everyday to help you overcome sin, Satan, and the world. Pray for the outpouring of the Holy Spirit; the former and the latter rains to be poured upon your nation. (see Zech.10:1; Matt.7:11; Luke 11:13)

2. Ask God for *wisdom,* if you lack it. (see James 1:5)

3. Pray for the *mantle of prayer* and the *Spirit of Intercession* to fall upon you. Pray for the burden of Christ for lost souls to fill your heart. (see Rom 8:26)

4. Pray that God should send forth the **right kind of laborers** to work in His harvest field. (see Matt. 9:38)

5. Pray for "Revival" in your country. (see Dan. 9:3-24)

6. Pray that the Lord may show you great and mighty things which you do not know. (see Jer.33:3)

7. Pray for the peace of Jerusalem; for they that love her will prosper. (see Ps. 122:6)

4.9(d) Model Prayer of Christ

COMMANDMENTS OF GOD FOR US TO OBEY	SUPPORTING SCRIPTURES
1. Pray ye after this manner -"The Lord's Prayer." 2. Pray to your Father in Heaven 'Hallowed be Your Name.' 3. Pray for His Kingdom to come. 4. Pray for His will to be done on earth as it is in Heaven. 5. Pray that He should give you daily bread. 6. Pray for forgiveness of your debts as you forgive your debtors. 7. Pray not to be led into temptation but ask to be delivered from the evil one. (see Matt.6:9-15)	Now it came to pass, as Jesus was praying in a certain place, when He ceased, *that* one of His disciples said to Him, "Lord, teach us to pray." Then Jesus taught them the Lord's Prayer to His disciples. (see Luke 11:1)

1. **Hallowed Be Your Name**: Our God is a God of Holiness who detests sin; though He is our Father, He will not tolerate evil and will always discipline His children. (see Matt.6:9)

2. **Let Thy Kingdom come:** We must pray for Christ's second coming and for the establishment of God's Eternal Kingdom. (see Rev.21:1; Matt.6:10)

3. **Thy Will be done:** Sincerely desire for God's will to be fulfilled in your lives. Find out what God's will is through His revealed Word (the Bible) and through the Holy Spirit's leading in your hearts. (see Rom.8:4-14; Matt.6:10)

4. If we pray according to the Lord's prayer, our petitions will be answered quickly. (see Luke 11:5-9)

4.9(e) "My House Shall Be Called A House Of Prayer"

COMMANDMENTS OF GOD FOR US TO OBEY	CONSEQUENCE OF DISOBEDIENCE
1. Call My house, "A house of prayer." (see Matt. 21:13) 2. Do not make My Father's house, a house of merchandise! (see Jn.2:16)	1. "My house shall be called a house of prayer for all nations but you have made it a den of thieves." (see Mark 11:17) 2. If any man defiles the temple of God, God will destroy him; for the temple of God is holy. (see 1 Cor.3:17)

1. In these last days, there will be many who lack the fear of God in the churches. They will have an outward form of godliness. But Christ expects His house to be a place of unceasing prayer.
2. A *believer's spirit* is also God's house of prayer. So keep it pure and consecrated. If any man defiles the temple of God, God will destroy him; for the temple of God is holy and you are that temple. (see 1 Cor.3:17)

3. Do not make My house a den of thieves. (see Matt. 21:13)	Jesus went into the temple of God, and drove out all those **who bought and sold in the temple,** and overturned the tables of the *money-changers,* and the seats of those who sold doves. (see Matt. 21:12)

1. Jesus very well understood that everything depended on prayer for He knew the true value of prayer.
2. We must not be worldly minded and profane the house of God, by making it means for **social gathering, monetary gain and entertainment etc.,** preying on the fear of God that people have. (see 1 Tim. 6:5)

Imitate Christ in Prayer... The Lord Jesus is our role model in prayer. He is a great prayer-warrior. Jesus has a permanent priesthood and He is still interceding for us. (see Heb. 7:25; Rom. 8:34)

Jesus' whole life on earth was taken up by prayer. Jesus always lived in His Father's Presence. He occasionally came away from praying to do His Father's will and went back to prayer as soon as the mission was completed. He always chose to be in the house of God. *Prayer was His very life.* So should prayer be to us believers.

4.10 (a) No Rewards For Fasting Like Hypocrites

COMMANDMENT OF GOD FOR US TO OBEY	CONSEQUENCE OF DISOBEDIENCE
Motive for Fasting: 1. Do not fast like the hypocrites, with a sad countenance. (see Matt. 6:16)	For the hypocrites disfigure their faces to show men they are fasting; and they have received their reward in full. (see Matt. 6:16/NIV)
2. But when you fast, put oil on your head, wash your face, do not show men that you are fasting, but only to your Father who is unseen. (see Matt.6:17-18/NIV)	*Reward for Obedience:* For your Father who sees in secret, will reward you openly. (see Matt.6:18)

1. When you fast to be seen by men, you receive your rewards in full from people on earth and you will not be given any rewards in Heaven.
2. When you fast, make sure you spend time in prayer and the Word for at least 3 to 6 hours. Do not take up a 40 day fast unless the Lord clearly instructs you to do so.

You should fast for the following reasons:

1. To serve God. E.g. Anna (see Luke 2:37)
2. To experience God's intimate Presence.
3. To place Christ's will, desires and His interests above your own.
4. To intercede for the lost souls with Christ's burden and agony.
5. To repent over the sins of the church, nation and world. (see Neh.9:1-2)
6. To humble yourselves before God and to experience more of His grace.
7. To repent over personal sins and failures. (Ezra 8:21)
8. To receive answers to your specific prayer requests. (see Is:58:6-9)
9. To overcome sin, Satan and the world.

4.10(b) Cast Out Demons By Prayer & Fasting

COMMANDMENTS OF GOD	SUPPORTING SCRIPTURES
Healing of a demoniac boy: 1. Do not be a faithless and perverse generation. *Jesus' Command to His Disciples:* 2. 'Bring the boy to Me.'	**Jesus Condemns Unbelief...**Jesus rebuked the disciples harshly for their lack of faith, saying, How long shall I put up with you? And then Jesus delivered the boy from the demon. The disciples asked the Lord why they could not cast the demon out. Jesus said to them, ***Because of your unbelief;*** However, these kinds of demons *cannot be cast out but by prayer and fasting.*(see Matt. 17:14-22
Jesus said this to His disciples, when a certain man approached the Lord for the deliverance of his son from demonic attacks. (see Matt. 17:17)	

Points to Ponder:

1. **Faith Required To Cast Out Demons...**We should neither doubt *God's power* nor the *authority* given to us by the Lord to cast out demons. (see Luke 10:19)

2. **Prayer & Fasting...**Some kind of demons can be cast out only by prayer and fasting. Prayer with fasting will release the anointing of the Holy Spirit to empower you to drive out the demons.

4.11(a) Is Money Your Idol?

COMMANDMENTS OF GOD	CONSEQUENCE OF DISOBEDIENCE
Do Charitable Deeds: 1. Take heed that you do not do your charitable deeds before men, to be seen by them. 2. Do not sound a trumpet before you as the hypocrites do when you do a charitable deed. (Matt.6:1-2)	Otherwise you have no reward from your Father in Heaven. (Matt.6:1)
3. When you give to the needy, do not let your left hand know what your right hand is doing. (Matt.6:3/NIV)	For your Father who sees in secret will Himself reward you openly. (see Matt.6:4)

1. We can never out-give God. He who is kind to the poor lends to the Lord, and He will reward him for what he has done. (Prov.19:17/NIV)
2. When we give alms to be seen by men, we receive our rewards and glory from people on this earth and therefore, no rewards in Heaven.

Give unto God: 4. Give. (Luke 6:38)	1. And it will be given to you. (Luke 6:38) 2. When you give to God, it will be given back to you; Good measure, Pressed down, Shaken together and Running over, will be poured into your lap. (see Luke 6:38/NIV) 3. For with the same measure that you use, it will be measured back to you. (Luke 6:38)

1. He who sows sparingly will also reap sparingly, and he who sows bountifully will also reap bountifully. (2 Cor.9:6)

2. **God Gave His Best**, His only begotten Son, Jesus Christ, to die in our place. *How Can We Repay Him?*

COMMANDMENT OF GOD FOR US TO OBEY	CONSEQUENCE OF DISOBEDIENCE
Lust for Money: 5. Do not store up for yourselves treasures on earth. (see Matt. 6:19/NIV)	If you store up on earth, moth and rust will destroy and thieves will steal. (see Matt.6:19)
6. Store up for yourselves treasures in Heaven. (see Matt.6 :20/NIV)	1. Store up treasures in heaven, where moth and rust do not destroy and thieves do not steal. 2. For where your treasure is, there your heart will be also. (see Matt. 6:20-21/NIV)

1. Only what we do for Jesus Christ on earth will bring us rewards in Heaven.
2. It is wise to use our possessions and money to promote God's interest i.e., for the *Salvation of lost souls,* to receive rewards in Heaven; for he who wins souls is wise. (see Prov.11:30)

Godliness with contentment is great gain...

i.   The rich in this present world are ***commanded not to be arrogant,*** nor to put their hope in wealth, which is so uncertain, but to put their hope in the Living God, who richly gives us all things to enjoy.

ii. They are commanded to do good, ***be rich in good works***, be generous and be willing to share. (see 1 Tim. 6:17-18)

iii. For we brought nothing into the world when we were born, and we can take nothing out of it when we die. So do not live only for the earthly life. (see 1 Tim.6:6-7/NIV)

iv. We should not value our fellowmen based on their riches on earth.

COMMANDMENT OF GOD FOR US TO OBEY	REWARD FOR OBEDIENCE/ CONSEQUENCE OF DISOBEDIENCE
Whom do you Serve? 7. Do not serve two masters; God and money. (see Matt.6:24/NIV)	1. For either you will hate the one (God) and love the other (money), or else you will be loyal to the one and despise the other. 2. For no one can serve two masters. (see Matt.6:24)

Who is Your Master, God or Money?

1. Give God what is due unto Him - His *glory*, at least one tenth of your *time* and *money*. God wants to have first place in your heart.
2. To serve money is to place such a high value on it that we put our trust and faith in it, look to it for our ultimate security and joy, and desire it more than we desire God's kingdom and His righteousness.

4.11(b) Serve God Through Your Tithes

Scripture says, Give to Caesar what is Caesar's (Government); and to God, what is God's. (see Matt. 22:21/NIV; Deut.26:13;14:28-29)

*Blessings...*You should be faithful in paying your tithes that belong to God; then He will open for you the windows of Heaven and pour out such blessing that there will not be room enough to receive it.

*Curse...*We are **cursed with a curse if we rob God in tithes** and offerings. (see Mal. 3:8-12)

*Your attitude counts...*Bring your tithes and offerings to Him with a cheerful heart; for God is pleased with a cheerful giver. For example, God rejected Cain's offering but accepted Abel's. (see 2 Cor.9:7; Gen.4:4-5)

4.11(c) Pay Your Taxes Promptly, As Jesus Did

COMMANDMENTS OF GOD FOR US TO OBEY	SUPPORTING SCRIPTURES
Jesus Paid His Taxes: 1. Pay your taxes. (see Matt. 17:24-27) 2. Give to the Government what belongs to the government. 3. Give to God what is God's. (see Matt. 22:21/NIV) *Jesus' Command to Peter:* 4. Go to the lake and throw out your line. Take the four-drachma coin out of the first fish's mouth and pay our tax. (see Matt. 17:27/NIV)	In order to pay taxes to the government, Jesus even performed a miracle, by bringing a coin out of a fish's mouth. (see Matt. 17:24-27)
As believers, Jesus expects us to be honest and faithful people. From Jesus' example, we learn that we should abide by the laws of the government. We should not evade paying taxes or give false accounts to the authorities. (see Rom. 13:6-7)	

4.11(d) Balance Your Physical Life With Spiritual Life

We are made up of *spirit, soul and body*. Once the spirit leaves our body, the physical body has no value at all. It goes back to the dust as the Lord said, 'Dust you are, and to dust you will return.' (see Gen. 3:19; 1 Thess.5:23)

Psalm 90:10 says that the average life of a human being is 70 or may be 80 years at the most. But our spirit will live not for 100, 1000, 10,000 years or millions, billions or even trillions of years but for *Eternity*. Think about it!

So learn to balance your physical life with your spiritual life.

4.12 Eyes & Ears - Windows Of Your Soul

COMMANDMENT OF GOD FOR US TO OBEY	REWARDS FOR OBEDIENCE
Guard Your Eyes: 1. Let your eyes be good. (see Matt.6:22)	1. So that your whole body will be full of light. (see Matt.6:22) 2. For the lamp of the body is the eye. (see Matt.6:22)
2. Do not let your eyes be bad (corrupt). (see Matt.6:23)	1. So that your whole body will not be full of darkness. (see Matt.6:23) 2. If your eye is bad, then the light within you is darkness, how great is that darkness! (Matt.6:23/NIV)
3. See with your eyes and perceive (the spiritual things). 4. Hear with your ears (what the Spirit of God says). 5. Understand with your heart (the mysteries of the Kingdom of Heaven). (Matt. 13:11-16)	1. Blessed are your eyes for they see and your ear for they hear, says the Lord to His disciples. (see Matt. 13:16) 2. The people's hearts are hardened, their ears are dull of hearing and their eyes are closed to the ways of God, lest they should understand with their heart and turn from their wicked ways; so that I should heal them, says the Lord. (Matt.13:13-15)
Listening Ears: 6. He who has ears to hear, let him hear! (Matt. 11:15)	"Hear this, you foolish and senseless people, who have eyes but do not see, who have ears but do not hear: ***should you not fear Me?***" declares the Lord. (Jer.5:21,22/NIV)

1. You can keep your eyes clean before God by abstaining from the scenes of immorality displayed in films, TV, internet, books, cell-phones, etc.

2. Pray that God would open your spiritual eyes to see Heavenly visions. (see Jer. 33:3)

3. Pray until your spiritual ears are opened to hear the Spirit of God; for the Lord says, ***"My sheep will hear My voice."*** (see Jn.10:27)

4.13 Be Not Anxious But Rest In Him

COMMANDMENT OF GOD FOR US TO OBEY	SUPPORTING SCRIPTURES
Be not Anxious about Food & Water: 1. Do not worry about your life, what you will eat or what you will drink. (Matt.6:25)	1. Is not life more important than food? (Matt.6:25/NIV) 2. Your Heavenly Father feeds even the birds of the air. Are you not of more value than the birds of the air? (see Matt.6:26) 3. Which of you by worrying can add one cubit to his stature? (Matt. 6:27)
Be Not Anxious About Clothing: 2. Do not worry about your body; what you will wear. (Matt.6:25/NIV)	1. Is not the body more important than clothes? (see Matt.6:25/NIV) 2. Even King Solomon in all his glory was not dressed like one of the lilies of the field which God so clothed. 3. For the *gentiles* seek after all these things. 4. And **your Heavenly Father knows** that you need them. (see Matt.6:28-29, 32) 5. If God so clothes the grass of the field, which today is, and tomorrow is thrown into the oven, will He not much more clothe you. O you of little faith? (Matt. 6:30)

1. Jesus did not mean to say that it is wrong to make provision for your future needs. But He does forbid anxiety which shows your lack of faith in His fatherly love and care.

2. For Scripture says, If anyone does not provide for his own, and especially for those of his household, he has denied the faith and is worse than an unbeliever. (1 Tim.5:8)

COMMANDMENT OF GOD FOR US TO OBEY	REWARDS FOR OBEDIENCE
3. Do not worry about tomorrow. (Matt.6:34/NIV)	1. For tomorrow will worry about itself. Each day has enough trouble of its own. (see Matt.6:34/NIV)
	2. But seek first the Kingdom of God and His righteousness; and all the things that you need, will be added to you. (see Matt. 6:33)

1. God who did not spare His own Son, but gave Him up for us all - how will He not also, along with Him, graciously give us all things? (see Rom.8:32)
2. How comforting it is to hear from our Creator who cares so much for us, not to worry about anything!

COMMANDMENTS OF GOD FOR US TO OBEY	REWARDS FOR OBEDIENCE
Come, Jesus Invites You:	1. And I will give you rest.
1. Come to Me, all you who are weary and burdened.	2. For I am gentle and humble in heart, and you will find rest for your souls.
2. Take My yoke upon you and learn from Me. (Matt. 11:28-29/NIV)	3. For My yoke is easy and My burden is light. (Matt. 11:28-30/NIV)

Our Way... Many times we mess up our lives by going in our own way. If we are wise in our own eyes, God will not respect us. (see Prov.3:5)

His Way... When we walk in Jesus' ways, and heed the guidance of the Holy Spirit, He will free us from our heavy burdens and give us rest, peace and joy in our lives. (see Rom.14:17)

4.14 Seek Ye First His Kingdom (All Things Will Be Added To You)

COMMANDMENT OF GOD	REWARD FOR OBEDIENCE
Make God Your Priority: 1. Seek ye first the Kingdom of God, and His righteousness; (Matt.6:33/KJV)	Then all the things that you need will be added to you. (see Matt.6:33)

We are commanded to seek two things -

1. The Kingdom of God 2. Christ's Righteousness

1. What is the Kingdom of God?

The Kingdom of God is the *"Rule and Power of God"* in our lives which we must earnestly seek. The Kingdom of God is not a matter of eating and drinking, but of *righteousness, peace and joy* in the Holy Spirit. (see Rom. 14:17/NIV)

We must accept Christ not only as our Savior but also as our *"Lord"* and totally surrender to Him to bring His rule and power in our lives. We should pray for the Kingdom of God to come in the mighty power of the Holy Spirit to set people free from their sin and bondage. (see Matt. 6:10)

2. How do we become righteous?

The *"Gift of Righteousness"* shall reign in your life by Jesus Christ. Therefore, righteousness is a gift that we receive when we abide in Christ. (see Rom.5:17)

You are in Christ Jesus, whom God has made unto us *Righteousness, Holiness, Wisdom and Redemption.* (see 1 Cor.1:30)

COMMANDMENT OF GOD	REWARD FOR OBEDIENCE
Pursue with Holy Violence: 2. Be forceful in laying hold of the Kingdom of Heaven. (see Matt. 11:12/NIV)	For the Kingdom of Heaven has been forcefully advancing, and forceful men lay hold of it. (Matt. 11:12/NIV)
The violence that Jesus mentions here is "holy violence" that is one needs to have determination, and earnest desire for His power and purity to possess the kingdom of God in the midst of opposition.	

4.15 Judge Not That You Be Not Judged

COMMANDMENT OF GOD FOR US TO OBEY	CONSEQUENCES OF DISOBEDIENCE
As you judge, you will be Judged: 1. Do not judge. (see Matt.7:1/NIV)	1. Or you too will be judged. (see Matt.7:1/NIV) 2. For with what judgment you judge, you will be judged. 3. With the same measure you use, it will be measured back to you. (Matt.7:1-2)

Jesus condemns the habit of judging others while ignoring one's own faults.

COMMANDMENTS OF GOD FOR US TO OBEY	REWARD FOR OBEDIENCE
Behold the Beam In Your Eye: 2. Do not look at the speck in your brother's eye but consider the plank in your own eye. (see Matt.7:3) 3. "You hypocrite! First remove the plank from your own eye. (see Matt.7:5)	Then you will see clearly to remove the speck out of your brother's eye. (Matt.7:5)

You must first surrender yourself to God's righteous standard, before attempting to examine and influence the conduct of other Christians. (see Matt. 7:1-5)

Do Not Give Godly Counsel To The Hardened Scorners: 4. Do not give dogs what is sacred (Matt.7:6/NIV) 5. Do not cast your pearls before swine. (Matt.7:6)	Lest they trample them under their feet, and turn and tear you in pieces. (see Matt.7:6)

1. Do not give godly counsel to the hardened scorners because they will not heed your counsel but rather mock you and find fault in you.

2. Do not rebuke a mocker or he will hate you; rebuke a wise man and he will love you. (Prov.9:8/NIV)

4.16 Narrow Gate To Heaven
(Few Shall Find It)

COMMANDMENT OF GOD FOR US TO OBEY	REWARDS FOR OBEDIENCE/ CONSEQUENCES OF DISOBEDIENCE
1. Enter through the narrow gate. (see Matt.7:13/NIV)	For wide is the gate, and broad is the way that leads to destruction. And there are many who go in by the wide gate. Because narrow is the gate and difficult is the way which leads to *Life* and there are ***few who find it***. (see Matt.7:13-14)
Make sure you are one of the few who enter through the narrow gate.	

To Go Through The Narrow Gate -

*Repent...*Be humble and truly repent for your sins before God.

Have reverential fear of God and walk in His righteousness.

*Obey Him...*Sincerely strive to obey His commandments.

*Die to Self...*Deny yourself and follow Jesus Christ.

Guard your Salvation with fear and trembling and *endure till the end* in true faith, purity and love.

It is a difficult path and not many choose this way**.**

4.17 Test Of False Prophets

COMMANDMENT OF GOD FOR US TO OBEY	CONSEQUENCE OF DISOBEDIENCE/ SUPPORTING SCRIPTURES
Beware of false prophets. (Matt.7:15)	The false prophets come to you in disguise, in sheep's clothing, but inwardly they are ravenous wolves. (see Matt.7:15-16) **You will know the false prophets by their fruits...** Do people pick grapes from thorn-bushes, or figs from thistles? Likewise, every good tree bears good fruit, but a bad tree bears bad fruit. Every tree that does not bear good fruit is cut down and thrown into the fire. Thus, by their fruit you will recognize them. (see Matt.7:17-20; 12:33/NIV)

How Do You Identify The False Prophets?

1. The doctrine of a false prophet will be self-centred rather than God-centred. (Matt. 7:21-23)

2. Their teachings will not be based on sound doctrine of God's Word and they will compromise with the truth of God.

3. They will offer salvation through the "broad road of unrighteousness."

4. They will be men-pleasers rather than God-pleasers.

5. They will be concerned about their own glory rather than God's glory and honor.

6. They accept human teachings and traditions even when those teachings contradict the Word of God.

7. The fruits of false teachers will be unholy behaviour manifested in the lives of their followers. (1 Jn.4:5-6)

4.18(a) Fulfil God's Will For Your Life

COMMANDMENT OF GOD FOR US TO OBEY	CONSEQUENCES OF DISOBEDIENCE
1. Do not say to Me, 'Lord, Lord' but do the will of My Father in Heaven – Jesus. (see Matt.7:21)	1. So that you enter the Kingdom of Heaven. (see Matt.7:21)
	2. You can **prophesy** accurately in Jesus' Name.
	You can **cast out demons** in His Name.
	You can **do many wonders** in His Name.
	And you can say to *Jesus, 'Lord, Lord.'*
	But after having done the above four things, if you have still not done the will of the Father, you will not enter in to Heaven,
	For Jesus will say to you, *"I never knew you;* depart from Me, you who practice lawlessness!" (see Matt.7:22-23)

Servants of God but not in God's Will…When God equips His servants with gifts of prophecy, casting out demons and working miracles, if they *get carried away with fame, money and power* the gifts bring them and not fulfil the specific will of God for their lives for which God had equipped them, then God calls such people as "workers of iniquity."

Unrighteous Preachers…God does not approve of any unrighteous preacher of the gospel. But, out of His mercy, He still works miracles for those who receive the Word of God preached by those preachers.

No Burden For Lost Souls…When preachers do not have true burden for perishing souls but seek to expand their own ministry and fame making God's work a business to gain wealth, then they are not in the will of God. Jesus calls them "workers of iniquity."

Sometimes the working of *miracles can be of Satan.*

COMMANDMENT OF GOD FOR US TO OBEY	REWARDS FOR OBEDIENCE/ CONSEQUENCES OF DISOBEDIENCE
2. Do the will of My Father in Heaven. (see Matt. 7:21)	1. To enter the Kingdom of Heaven. (see Matt. 7:21) 2. *The servant who knows his master's will* and does not get ready, or does not do what his master wants, will be beaten with many blows. 3. *But the one who does not know* and does things deserving punishment, will be beaten with few blows. 4. From everyone who has been given much, much will be demanded. (see Luke 12:47-48/NIV)

1. *First, you find out God's specific will* for your life by waiting on Him. Then, fulfil God's will for each and every day of your life, as Jesus did. For example, if God sends you to proclaim the gospel in the orphanages, youth camps, villages, small churches etc., then obey Him rejoicingly. God will honor you. Do not wait for big opportunities to come your way.

2. *If God asks you to do* something, then step out in faith and do it, even if the whole world comes against you. If God be for you, who can be against you? (see Rom.8:31)

Are You Fulfilling God's Will For Your Life?

Is your whole life centred on money? Is lust for money diverting you from doing the will of God for your life? Pause & think…

Scripture says *"Godliness with contentment is great gain."* Let us be content if we have food and clothing. People who want to get rich fall into temptation and a trap and into many foolish and harmful desires that plunge men into ruin and destruction. For the love of money is the root of all kinds of evil.

But you, man of God, flee from all this, and pursue *righteousness, godliness, faith, love, endurance and gentleness.* Fight the good fight of faith. Take hold of the *Eternal Life* to which you were called by the Lord Jesus Christ. (see 1 Tim.6:6-12/NIV)

God's "Perfect Will" as Revealed in His Word…

1. **None should perish…**It is the will of your Father that none of the souls should perish but that all should come to repentance and be saved. (see 2 Pet. 3:9; Matt. 18:14; 1 Tim.2:4)

2. **Believe in His Son, Jesus…**God's will is that everyone who *believes in the Son* shall have *Eternal Life.* (see Jn.6:40/NIV)

3. **Be filled with the Holy Spirit…**It is the will of the Father that we be not drunk with wine but be filled with His Spirit. (see Eph. 5:18)

4. **Keep your vessel sanctified…**It is the will of God that everyone of you should know how to possess his vessel in sanctification and honor. (see 1Thess. 4:3-7)

5. **Be joyful always.** (see 1 Thess.5:16)

6. **Pray** without ceasing. Pray that God's will be done on earth. (see Matt. 6:10)

7. In everything **give thanks**; for this is the will of God for you in Christ Jesus. (see 1 Thess.5:16-18)

4.18(b) Obedience To Your Father God's Will

COMMANDMENT OF GOD FOR US TO OBEY	REWARD FOR OBEDIENCE
Parable of Two Sons: 3. Do the will of My Father who is in Heaven - Jesus. (see Matt. 12:50, 21:28-31)	Then you will be My brother, sister and mother - Jesus. (see Matt. 12:50, 21:28-31)

Parable of Two Sons...

1. A certain man had two sons; and he came to the first, and said, "Son, go work today in my vineyard." He replied, "I will not" but afterwards he repented and went.

    And the father came to the second, and said likewise. He replied, "I go, sir" and went not. (see Matt.21:28-30/KJV)

    "Which of the two did the will of his father?" asked Jesus to the chief priests and the elders. They said to Him, "The first."

    Then Jesus said to them "Assuredly, the tax collectors and harlots enter the Kingdom of God before you. (see Matt.21:31)

2. As Jesus always fulfilled the will of His Father for His life, we should also strive to do His will at all times. (see John 5:30)

3. It Is Not The Words But Your Obedience That Matters...

The first son, though he said in the beginning "I will not" later on, pleased his father by obeying him.

You cannot please God with your words but only by your obedience.

4.19 Build Your House On Christ, The Rock

COMMANDMENT OF GOD FOR US TO OBEY	REWARD FOR OBEDIENCE/ CONSEQUENCE OF DISOBEDIENCE
Doers - The Wise Builders: 1. Hear the sayings of Mine and do them - Jesus. (see Matt.7:24)	1. For I will liken him to a wise man who built his house on the rock. 2. And the rain descended, the floods came and the winds blew and beat on that house and it did not fall, for it was founded on the rock. (Matt. 7:24-25) 3. Similarly, if we build our lives on the foundation of Christ, The Rock, then when storms of life blow in our path, we will not be moved but stand firm.
Disobedient Men - The Foolish Builders: 2. Do not disobey when you hear the sayings of Mine - Jesus. (see Matt. 7:26)	For he will be like a foolish man who built his house on the sand; and the rain descended, the floods came, and the winds blew and beat on that house; and it fell. And great was its fall. (see Matt. 7:26-27)

1. ***How Can We Be Doers of God's Word?***
   We can be doers of God's Word by walking in total submission to God; by relying on the power of the Holy Spirit and by desiring to please the Lord at any cost.

2. The Lord let the Israelites die in the desert after wandering for forty years because of their disobedience and rebellion. Ask God to fill you with the *"Spirit of obedience."* (see Rom. 8:13)

4.20 Be Perfect As Your Father In Heaven Is Perfect

COMMANDMENT OF GOD	REWARD FOR OBEDIENCE
Be perfect, just as your Father in Heaven is perfect. (see Matt.5:48)	By obeying all the above upgraded Commandments of Christ, we can exceed the righteousness of the Scribes and Pharisees and thereby become worthy to enter into the Kingdom of Heaven. (see Matt.5:20)

When you obey all the above upgraded Commandments of Jesus Christ, you become perfect in the eyes of God.

5. Children - Heritage Of The Lord

"**Children**…Obey your parents in the Lord; for this is right.
Honor your father and your mother; that you may enjoy long life on the earth."
This is the first Commandment of God with a promise, given unto children. (see Eph.6:1-3; Ex. 20:12/NIV)

Parents…God expects parents to instruct their children in the ways of the Lord when they are young. If you forget God's Word, He will forget your children. (see Deut.6:1-9; Hos.4:6)

The Tree and the Shoot alike…*As much as you, parents, compromise* with *God's standard of righteousness,* to the same extent God will allow your children to compromise with the world. If the Tree is green, the Shoot also will be green.

COMMANDMENTS OF GOD FOR US TO OBEY	CONSEQUENCES OF DISOBEDIENCE/ SUPPORTING SCRIPTURES
For Salvation: 1. Be ye converted and become as little children. (see Matt. 18:3/ KJV)	1. Or else, you will by no means ***enter*** the Kingdom of ***Heaven.*** (see Matt.18:3/KJV) 2. Jesus said, 'Let the little children come to Me, for of such is the Kingdom of God.' (Matt.19:14) 3. "Assuredly, I say to you, whoever does not receive the Kingdom of God as a little child will by no means enter it." (Lk.18:17)

The gift of salvation is through simple faith in Jesus Christ. We receive this free gift, when we have at least one of the following qualities inherent in a little child: innocence, humility, dependence, teachable and trustful nature.

The Truth i.e., Jesus, will come your way; only humility will accept it, or else the Truth will pass you by.

COMMANDMENT OF GOD FOR US TO OBEY	REWARDS FOR OBEDIENCE
Child like Humility: 2. Humble yourself as a little child. (see Matt. 18:4)	1. For you will be the **greatest** in the Kingdom of Heaven. (see Matt. 18:4) 2. The humble will be **exalted** and the proud will be abased by God. (see Matt. 23:12)

We must come to the Lord as a little child with the spirit of humility. For God resists the proud but gives **grace** to the humble. (1 Peter 5:5)

COMMANDMENT OF GOD FOR US TO OBEY	REWARDS FOR OBEDIENCE
Receive with love: 3. Receive a little child in My Name - Jesus. (see Matt. 18:5)	"Whoever receives a little child in My Name, receives Me." (see Matt. 18:5)

1. Ps.127:3 says that children are a heritage of the Lord; and the *fruit of the womb (a child) is His reward.*
2. The Lord delights in the praise and worship of little children. (Ps. 8:2)

COMMANDMENT OF GOD FOR US TO OBEY	SUPPORTING SCRIPTURES
Despise not the little ones: 4. Take heed that you do not despise one of the little ones. (see Matt. 18:10)	1. For their angels always see the face of My Father in heaven.(see Matt. 18:10) 2. For the Son of Man (Jesus) **has come to save** that which was lost. (see Matt. 18:10-11)

We should not despise any believer based on their social status or degrees following their names. They are so precious before God, for He has bought them with the Blood of Jesus Christ, His only begotten Son.

COMMANDMENT OF GOD FOR US TO OBEY	CONSEQUENCES OF DISOBEDIENCE
Hinder Not the Little Ones: 5. Do not cause one of the little ones who believe in Me, to sin. (see Matt. 18:6)	1. Or else, it would be better that a millstone were hung around your neck and you were drowned in the depth of the sea. **2. *Woe*** to that man by whom the offence comes to the little one. 3. It is better for you to lose one of your eyes or hands or feet and enter into Heaven; rather than having two eyes or two hands or two feet, and be cast into the everlasting fire.(see Matt. 18:6-9)

1. Here, the little one represents a child or a child like believer.
2. **Preachers, being the Shepherds** and role models for many, should be very careful in their walk before God.
3. They should set a good example for others to follow. If not, great will be their punishment.
4. *Let not many of you become teachers,* because you know that we who teach will be judged more strictly. (see James 3:1)
5. God will judge you harshly, if you are an offence to a growing believer by your lifestyle and attitude.

Love the Little Children:	For the Kingdom of ***Heaven***
1. 'Let the little children come to Me - Jesus; and do not hinder them.' (see Matt. 19:14/NIV)	belongs to such as the little children. (see Matt. 19:14/NIV)

1. Jesus spent His precious time with little children. He loved to embrace them and bless them

2. Parents should ***spend time*** with their children, listen to their problems and try to solve them. Do not be caught up with your busy schedule but keep aside some time for your children.

3. ***Develop a relationship with your kids.*** Go to their level, interact with them and try to understand their feelings.

6. Crucifixion & Resurrection Of Christ

6.1. The Cross

COMMANDMENTS OF GOD FOR US TO OBEY	CONSEQUENCES OF DISOBEDIENCE
1. Do not crucify the Son of God, Jesus Christ, as the gentiles did. (see Matt. 20:19) 2. Do not fall away and crucify the Son of God all over again. (see Heb: 6:4-6)	1. Behold, He is coming with clouds, and every eye will see Him, even they who pierced Him. And all the tribes of the earth will mourn because of Him. (see Jn.19:37; Rev.1:7) 2. How can you crucify the Lord all over again? It is impossible for those... who have once been enlightened, who have tasted the heavenly gift, who have shared in the Holy Spirit, who have tasted the goodness of the Word of God and the powers of the coming age, if they fall away, to be brought back to repentance, because *to their loss they are crucifying the Son of God all over again and subjecting Him to public disgrace.* (see Heb: 6:4-6/NIV)

Unfailing Love of Christ... No one on this earth would ever love you as Jesus loves you; not even your own parents will love you as much as He does. Jesus says, I will never forsake you even if your mother forsakes you. (see Is.49:15; Heb.13:5)

If you truly understand Jesus' love and the price He has paid on the Cross to redeem you, you will never want to grieve His loving heart by continuing in sin.

When *you keep on sinning* after being saved, disregarding the conviction of the Holy Spirit and taking God's grace in vain, then, *to your loss you are crucifying Jesus Christ* all over again and putting Him to an open shame.(see Heb: 6:4-6)

Jesus Died On The Cross For You
What Have You Done For Him?

Sufferings of Jesus: Jesus Christ has borne the following sufferings on the Cross, for our sake :

1. Jesus Christ was **despised** by men; so that we can be loved.
2. He was **rejected** by all; so that we can be accepted.
3. He **carried** our sorrows; so that we can be joyful.
4. He **bore** our grief and iniquities.
5. He was **lonely;** so He understands our loneliness.
6. He was **dishonored.** (see Is. 53:3)
7. Jesus was **wounded** for our transgressions.
8. He was **bruised** for our iniquities.
9. He was **chastised** for our peace.
10. He was **whipped;** so that we can be healed. (see Is.53:5)
11. Jesus was **oppressed;** so that we can be freed from bondage.
12. He was **afflicted;** yet He opened not His mouth.
13. He was **slaughtered** like a lamb. (see Is. 53:7)
14. Jesus was **judged** instead of us and **punished** for our sins.
15. He was **cut off** from the land of the living.
16. He was **stricken** for our transgressions.
17. He was **buried** with the wicked.
18. He **did not defend** Himself.
19. He was **not dishonest** in His words. (see Is. 53:8-9)
20. He was **smitten** and **bruised** by God.
21. He was made a **sin offering** for our sake.
22. He **travailed** in His soul.
23. He was **numbered with the transgressors.**
24. He **shed His precious blood** for us. (see Acts 20:28)
25. He **poured out His soul unto death.**

Christ died and rose again to set us free from sin, Satan and the world. He was made a **curse** for us, to redeem us from the curse of the law; for it is written, Cursed is everyone that hangs on a tree. (see Gal.3:13)

Reward for Jesus: Since our Lord Jesus died in our place, He shall see His seed, (the perishing **souls) saved** and rejoice over it. (see Is. 53:10)

Agony Of Christ - 7 Stages

Stage 1 - Abandoned by His Own Disciples

1. Jesus was **betrayed with a kiss** by Judas Iscariot. It must have been more agonizing for Jesus to be let down by His own friend and disciple, who was with Him for 3 ½ years. (see Matt.26:49)

2. When the soldiers came to arrest Jesus, *all His disciples forsook Him and fled.* Not even one of His disciples stood by the Lord. (see Matt. 26:56)

3. Peter, one of Jesus' closest disciples not only **denied** Him thrice but also **cursed** and swore that he did not know who Jesus was. (see Matt. 26:69-74)

Stage 2 - Accused by His own Jewish Leaders out of Envy

1. Jesus was found guilty of death for claiming to be the Son of God. He was **accused by false witnesses** arranged by the Jewish leaders**.**

2. He was **blindfolded**.

3. They **mocked** Him repeatedly.

4. They **spat on His face**.

5. They **struck** Him in the face with their fists.

6. Some **slapped** Him.

7. They **preferred a notable prisoner** and a murderer called Barabbas to be released instead of Jesus. (see Matt.26:57-67; 27:20-22)

Stage 3 - Trial before the Roman Governor, Pontius Pilate

The next morning, Jesus, **battered and exhausted**, was brought before Pilate for trial.

The Roman Governor did not find any fault in Him; washing his hands before the multitude, he said, I am innocent of the blood of this just person. See you to it. But His own Jewish race wanted Him to be crucified. Pilate, compromising what he knew to be true and right, wanting to please the Jewish leaders, scourged Jesus and handed Him over to be crucified. (see Matt.27:1-2, 11, 24)

Stage 4 – Jesus Scourged

Scourging was a **gruesome torture**. The scourge was made of several leather thongs attached to a short wooden handle with *bits of iron or bones tied to the thongs.* During the flogging, the flesh was cut to such an extent that *veins and arteries* and even **internal organs were exposed**.

Jesus was **stripped** and **flogged** 39 times and *His back* was like a ploughed land and He could number all *His bones.*

Stage 5 – Tortured at the hands of the Romans (Gentiles)

1. Jesus was handed over to the Roman soldiers to be crucified.

2. The soldiers placed a **crown of thorns** upon *His head* so that we can have a crown of righteousness in Heaven.

3. They made **mockery** of Him.

4. The Roman **soldiers spat** upon Christ.

5. They took a reed, **struck Him** across *the face* and *the head,* **driving the thorns deeper** into *His scalp* and led Him away to be crucified. (see Matt. 27:27-31)

Stage 6 - Crucifixion of Jesus by the Romans

1. Jesus had to *carry the heavy beam of His own cross* on His already **bruised and bleeding** *shoulders.*

2. The soldiers crucified Jesus on that awful cross. Heavy, square wrought-iron nails were **pierced** through His *hands* (or wrists) and His *feet.*

3. The weight of His whole body was held by those three nails. **His breathing** must have been **extremely painful** because He had to lift His body against those nails to breathe.

4. Jesus hung on the cross, **blood-streaked**, covered with **wounds** and exposed to the view of the people as a **pathetic display**. He experienced **hours of pain** in His entire body, **fatigue** in His *arms,* great waves of **cramps** in the *muscles* and *skin torn* from His back.

5. He was poured out like water and His *tongue* stuck to His palate, all His *bones were out of joint* and He could count all His *bones.* And His *heart* had turned to wax and **melted away**. His **strength was dried up** like a potsherd. He was aware of the **abuse** and **ridicule** of those who passed by the cross.

6. He felt an intense thirst and the soldiers gave Him vinegar to drink mingled with gall. Jesus had to taste the sour drink to take away the bitterness from our lives. (see Matt. 26-27; Is. 53; Ps. 22)

Stage 7 – Climax of Jesus' Sufferings

Jesus' **sorrow, grief and pain were at their worst** when **He was forsaken by His own Father**. He cried out in deep agony, "My God, My God, why have You forsaken Me?" There was no one to help Him.

When Jesus took upon Himself the sin of mankind, the Holy One, who cannot tolerate sin, *hid His face* from His own son, Jesus, and **deserted** Him in His darkest hour.

Redemption of Mankind...Jesus uttered His final words with a loud cry, **"It is Finished."** (Jn.19:30). This *signifies the completion of the Redemption work*. The penalty for our sin had been paid in full, and the plan of Salvation established. Only then, He offered His Spirit into the hands of His Father.

*He who knew no sin, God made Him **to be sin for us**; that we might be made the righteousness of God in Him.*

Jesus died **forsaken** that we might never be forsaken.

Christ gave Himself as **"a ransom for many"** and thus we are redeemed by His sufferings. (see Matt. 20:28, 2 Cor.5:21, 1 Tim. 2:6, 1 Peter 1:19)

In obedience to His Father's will, Jesus became a **curse** to make the way of salvation for us.

Remember, Jesus endured all this agony for you.

6.2 Believe In God's Power To Resurrect You

COMMANDMENT OF GOD	SUPPORTING SCRIPTURES
1. Do not be in error; know the Scriptures and the power of God to resurrect. (see Matt. 22:23-29/NIV)	At the resurrection people will neither marry nor be given in marriage. But they will be like the angels of God in Heaven. (see Matt. 22:30/NIV)

1. This was Jesus' reply to the Sadducees who questioned Him concerning life after death.
2. Our God is proud to call Himself "the God of Abraham, Isaac and Jacob" for He is not the God of the dead but of the living. (see Matt. 22:30-32)

COMMANDMENT OF GOD	SUPPORTING SCRIPTURES
Jesus' Command to the women at the tomb: 3. ***Be not afraid***; go and tell my brothers to go to Galilee; and there they will see Me. (see Matt. 28:10)	As Jesus had declared while He was alive "After three days I will rise again," He arose.(see Matt. 27:63) An angel of God descended from heaven, rolled back the stone and said to the women at the tomb, 'Jesus is not here; ***for He is risen from the dead, as He said.'***(see Matt. 28:6)

The risen Lord Jesus gave this command to the women at the tomb, who were loyal to the Lord, to announce His resurrection to His disciples.

Life After Death...

We have the *assurance of being resurrected* after death because Christ rose up from the dead on the third day. We can be confident that there is life after death, for Jesus said, ***I go to prepare a mansion*** for you in Heaven and I will come again to receive you unto Myself. (see Jn.14:2-3)

At the second coming of Christ, His faithful children will have no reason to fear if they have remained loyal to Him in the midst of a world that rejects His love and salvation. (see 1 Jn.2:28)

Importance of Jesus' Resurrection to the Believers:

1. The resurrection of Christ proves to the world that *Jesus is the Son of God*. (see Rom. 1:4)

2. It emphasizes His *redemptive power*. (see 1 Cor.15:17)

3. It confirms the *truth of Scripture*. (see Luke 24:44-47)

4. It guarantees believers of their future *heavenly inheritance* and of their resurrection after death. (see Jn.14:3)

5. It enables us to enjoy the ***presence of Christ*** and His power over sin in our everyday lives. (see Eph.1:18-20)

6.3 Supernatural Events

Proof of His Lordship: The occurrence of supernatural events at Christ's death and resurrection proves to the world that Jesus Christ is risen from the dead and is truly the Son of God.

At Christ's Death:

1. The **veil** of the temple was torn into two from **top to bottom**. This signifies that a way into the most holy place is now open for all believers so that we can boldly enter into His Presence where only the high priests could go.

2. The **earth quaked** and the **rocks split**. (see Matt.27:51)

3. The **sun stopped** *shining* and **darkness** covered the whole land for three hours. (see Luke 23:44-45)

At Christ's Resurrection:

1. At the resurrection of Jesus, there was **another great earthquake**.

2. The **angel** of the Lord descended from heaven, and came and **rolled back the stone** from the tomb of Jesus and sat upon it. The Roman soldiers who were guarding the tomb of Jesus stood in awe.

3. The *angel declared* to the women at the tomb that *Jesus had risen* from the dead and commanded them to go quickly and announce His resurrection to all His disciples.

4. The *linen clothes* and the napkin were *folded* neatly and kept separately.

5. **Two angels** in white were seen by the disciples, sitting, one at the head and the other at the feet where the body of Jesus had been. (see Matt. 28:2-7)

6. The **tomb was empty**. Christ is risen; alive forevermore. He has *conquered death and grave*. (1 Cor.15:55-56)

7. After Jesus' resurrection, the **graves were opened** and bodies of many **saints** who had died were **raised to life** and appeared to many people in the city. This event is symbolic of our glorious resurrection at Christ's return. (see Matt. 27:53; 1Thess.4:14; 1 Cor.15:50-58).

8. **Jesus appeared** personally to all His disciples and to more than **five hundred people at once**, before ascending to heaven. (see 1 Cor.15:6)

9. **Two men in white** apparel said to the crowd that Jesus would come back in the same way as He had ascended into heaven.

10. Watching all this, the **Roman centurion** and the soldiers fearing greatly, declared **"Truly, Jesus was the Son of God."** (see Acts 1:9-11; Jn.20; Matt. 26: 27- 28)

6.3 Events Related To The Crucifixion Of Christ

6.3 (a) Jesus, Our No. 1 Priority

COMMANDMENT OF GOD	SUPPORTING SCRIPTURES
Jesus' Command to His Disciples: 'Let her alone; do not trouble the woman who poured a very expensive perfume on my head for my burial.' (see Mark 14:3-9; Matt. 26:10-12/NIV)	1. Jesus said, 'She has done a good work for Me. 2. For you have the poor with you always, but Me you do not have always. 3. For in pouring this fragrant oil on my body, she did it to prepare Me for burial. 4. Assuredly, I say to you, wherever this gospel is preached in the whole world, what she has done will also be told as a memorial to her.' (see Matt. 26:10-13)

Jesus stated this to the disciples who rebuked the woman for wasting her money on the Lord.

Lessons We Learn...

1. **Place Jesus above Charity:** Jesus must be our "No.1 Priority" and preaching the gospel must take precedence over every other charitable work; for salvation is the greatest miracle one can receive. (see Matt. 26:11)

2. **Majestic Lord:** Always remember how majestic Jesus is. We must have reverential fear for the Lord and should never comment disrespectfully about the Lord as the disciples did. (see Matt. 26:8)

3. **Profound Love For Jesus:** Jesus honored the woman because she exhibited profound love and devotion to Jesus. This should be the *characteristic of every disciple.*

4. Christianity is not a ritualistic religion but a personal devotion to the Lord Jesus. The Lord enjoys our devoted love for Him more than our ministry. (see Luke 7:38)

6.3(b) Salvation, Not To Be Taken For Granted

COMMANDMENT OF GOD FOR US TO OBEY	CONSEQUENCES OF DISOBEDIENCE
Betrayal of Judas Iscariot: Do not betray the Son of man, Jesus Christ, at any cost as Judas did. (see Matt. 26:15-16, 24, 47-50)	1. **Woe to that man** who betrays the Son of Man (Jesus). 2. It would be better for that man if he had not been born. (see Matt. 26:24/NIV)

Points to Ponder:

1. **Jesus' love for Judas…**The Lord had so much love for Judas that He tried to prevent Judas as much as possible from betraying Him.

2. **Salvation lost…**Judas had hardened his heart so much that he ignored the Lord's repeated warnings. He went in his own way, heeding the voice of the devil. He lost his salvation by betraying Jesus.

3. **A Disciple Deceived?** Having paid the price to become a disciple of Christ and having been with Christ for three and a half years, it is sad that Judas allowed himself to be deceived by the devil.

4. **Do not take your salvation for granted…**Only those who endure till the end will be saved. (see Matt. 10:22)

6.3(c) "My Body Broken For You"

COMMANDMENTS OF GOD FOR US TO OBEY	REWARD FOR OBEDIENCE
The Lord's Supper: 1. Take and eat the bread; this is My Body. 2. Drink from the cup, all of you; for this is My Blood. (see Matt. 26:26- 28/NIV) 3. Do this in remembrance of Me. (1 Cor.11:24)	Jesus took bread and when He had given thanks, He broke it and said, Take, eat; this is My Body which is broken for you. Jesus took the cup, gave thanks, and offered it to them saying, "This is My Blood of the new covenant which is ***shed for many for the remission of sins.***" (see Matt. 26:28; 1 Cor.11:24-25)

COMMANDMENTS OF GOD FOR US TO OBEY	CONSEQUENCES OF DISOBEDIENCE
Unworthy Participation: 4. Do not eat the bread and drink the cup of the Lord in an unworthy manner. (see 1 Cor.11:27) 5. Let a man examine himself before partaking in the Lord's Supper.(see 1 Cor.11:28)	1. If you partake unworthily, you will be **guilty** of sinning against the Body and Blood of the Lord. 2. For he who eats and drinks unworthily, eats and drinks **judgment** to himself, not discerning the Lord's Body. 3. For this reason many are **weak and sick** and a number of you have **fallen asleep**. 4. You will be **judged and chastened** by the Lord. (see 1 Cor.11:27-32)

Significance of The Lord's Supper...

1. **He Died For You...**We participate in the Lord's supper in remembrance of Christ's death for our sake.

2. **Give Thanks...**It is our thanksgiving to God for Christ's sacrifice on the cross.

3. **Have Fellowship...**It is a fellowship with Christ as well as with other believers.

4. **Have Reverential Fear of God...**We must partake in the Lord's supper with reverential fear of God and in true faith.

6.3 (d) Jesus' Blood Shed For You

Blessings Through The Blood of Jesus...

1. **Forgiveness...**The Blood of Jesus Christ cleanses us from all sin and justifies us. (see 1 Jn.1:7; Rom. 3:24-25)

2. **Reconciliation With God...**The Blood of Christ reconciles us with God. (see Col. 1:20)

3. **Eternal Life ...**The Blood of Christ gives us Eternal Life. (see Jn.6:54)

4. **His Blood Purges Your Conscience...**Since Jesus offered Himself without spot to God, His precious Blood purges your conscience from dead works to serve the living God. (see Heb. 9:14)

5. **Entry Into The Most Holy Place...**The Blood of Jesus gives us boldness to enter into the Most Holy Place. (see Heb. 9:12; 10:19)

6. **The Church of God has been purchased** by the Blood of Christ. (see Acts 20:28)

7. **Victory Over the Devil...**The Blood of Christ helps us to overcome the devil. (see Rev. 12:11)

6.3 (e) Overconfidence In The Flesh

COMMANDMENTS OF GOD FOR US TO OBEY	CONSEQUENCES OF DISOBEDIENCE/ SUPPORTING SCRIPTURES
1. Do not deny Me before men - Jesus. (see Matt. 10:33) *Peter's Denial of Christ:* 2. Do not disown Me - Jesus. (Matt. 26:34)	1. For Jesus says, "I will also deny you before My Father in Heaven." (see Matt.10:33) 2. Jesus said to Peter, 'Before the cock crows, you will deny Me thrice.' Peter declared to the Lord, 'Even if all fall away on account of you, I never will. Though I should die with you, yet I will not deny you.' (see Matt. 26:33-35, 69-74)

Jesus said this to His disciples. On the night of Christ's arrest, anticipating persecution, all His disciples including Peter, deserted Him and fled. We should not put our confidence in the flesh like Peter did. Do not deny Jesus at any cost.

6.3 (f) Die To Self

Wretchedness of Peter Revealed

Peter was overconfident when he boldly confessed that he would even die for Jesus because of his love for him. But within a short while, he denied Christ thrice and even cursed that he did not know Him.

Jesus, wanting to show Peter his frail nature, foretold about his denial of the Lord. When Peter was convicted of his own wretchedness, he wept bitterly and repented of his weakness.

Peter's Calling Restored…Though Peter had denied the Lord thrice, Jesus came back to Peter after His resurrection and restored his calling, by saying to him thrice, 'Feed My lambs and sheep.' Thus the Lord delivered Peter of his guilt and condemnation.

Later on, after the Lord molded Peter's character by filling him with the anointing of the Holy Spirit, he became so humble that when he was to be crucified for his faith in Jesus, he said that he was not worthy to be crucified in the same manner as his *Master*. So he was **crucified upside down** on the cross.

Isaiah's Uncleanness Revealed

In another instance, when Isaiah was in the Presence of God, his wretched nature was revealed to him. In the light of God's holiness, Isaiah saw his filthiness and cried out, '**Woe is me**! I am ruined; because I am a man of unclean lips and I dwell in the midst of a people of unclean lips; for mine eyes have seen the King, the Lord of Hosts.' (see Is. 6:5)

The Lord's Chosen Emptied of "Self"

Scripture says, "Many are called but only a few are chosen." You can be one among the few that are chosen if you wholeheartedly surrender your life to God. Once you accept His calling, He patiently prepares your vessel. It may take 1 or 10 or even up to 20 years…as you yield to the ways of the Holy Spirit. (see Matt. 20:16)

When the Lord empties the "self and ego" from you, **then you will not touch God's glory** when God uses you greatly.

The Lord may take you through the following **four tests** before using you in His service.

1. *Character test*

2. *Faith Test*

3. *Word (Scripture) Test*

4. *Obedience Test*

Which grade are you in with regards to the above 4 tests?

Still at School level, Graduate level or Ph.D. level…

6.3(g) Pray That You Enter Not Into Temptation

COMMANDMENTS OF GOD FOR US TO OBEY	CONSEQUENCES OF DISOBEDIENCE
1. Watch and pray at least for one hour. (see Matt. 26:40-41) *Jesus' Command to His Disciples at Gethsemane:* 2. Sit here while I go and pray. (Matt. 26:36) 3. Stay here and watch with Me. (Matt. 26:38) 4. Sleep on now and take your rest; for the hour is at hand. (Matt. 26:45) 5. Rise, let us be going. (Matt. 26:46)	1. For the Son of Man is betrayed into the hands of sinners. 2. **Watch and pray** that you enter not into temptation. 3. The spirit indeed is willing but the flesh is weak. (Matt. 26:41, 45)

Be Alert In Prayer

The Lord, anticipating His crucifixion, strengthened Himself in prayer. Therefore, he was able to fulfil His Father's will and died on the Cross for our redemption. Having known the importance of prayer, the Lord asked His disciples to watch and pray for at least an hour so that they too could overcome temptation.

The disciples, including Peter, *did not heed the Lord's repeated pleas to pray* but fell asleep. That is why, when Peter was faced with the temptation, he could not overcome it and *denied the Lord thrice.* The other disciples also feared for their lives and fled, leaving Jesus alone.

Failure in Christian life is absolutely certain when you do not spend enough time in prayer. Be alert in prayer so that when trials come your way, you are equipped with His power to have victory over the enemy.

You Can Follow These Steps To Pray Efficiently...

i.   *Confess and repent* of your sins until you feel the peace of God in your heart.

ii.   *Praise and worship* God by singing to Him until you feel His Presence.

iii. *Give thanks* to the Lord for all His blessings.

iv.   *Wait on the Lord quietly until you are filled with His Holy Spirit;* focus your mind on the Lord; yearn for His Presence.

v.   *Allow Him to speak* and you listen to the voice of the Holy Spirit.

vi.   *Read and meditate the Word* of God; let the Lord speak to you through His Word.

vii. *Pray and intercede* not only for your needs but also for the Salvation of perishing souls; pray as much as you can, in the Spirit which will enable you to hear the Lord speak.

7. Disciples: Co-Labourers With Christ

7.1 Calling Of The Disciples For Ministry

COMMANDMENT OF GOD FOR US TO OBEY	REWARDS FOR OBEDIENCE
"Follow Me" (see Matt.4:19, 9:9)	1. "And I will make you **fishers of men**" i.e., bringing lost souls to salvation in Christ. (see Matt. 4:19) 2. You who have followed Me will also **sit on thrones,** judging the twelve tribes of Israel.(see Matt. 19:28)

1. This was Jesus' command to four of His disciples, Peter, Andrew, James and John and later on to Matthew, to follow Him.
2. They immediately obeyed the Lord, left their professions and families and went with Him. Jesus did not keep them idle but gave them a *new job of fishing for men* and a purpose driven life.
   Do you hear the gentle voice of your Master calling you to serve Him?

* In the year 1992, the Lord asked me, (the Author) "I died on the cross for you, what have you done for Me? Will you serve me until you have your last breath? Will you follow Me to do My ministry?"

I immediately responded "Yes, Lord." That was the beginning of my calling.
- Author

Count The Cost

A disciple of Jesus is someone who walks in His footsteps, keeping the Lord as his role model and obeys every command of His Master. Being a disciple of Jesus is a costly affair.

Are You Prepared To Be His Disciple?

First count the cost whether you can follow Jesus all the way or not. Once you put your hand to the plough, there is no turning back. You should be ready to deny your desires, goals, give up your rights and worldly pleasures. God's interests must rule your life and you should be willing to say, "Break me, shape me and use me, Lord, according to Your will."

You must overcome all that is in the world, the lust of the flesh and the lust of the eyes and the pride of life, which is not of the Father, but is of the world. (see 1Jn 2:16). *A Disciple must overcome the 3 'P's – Pleasure, Power and Pride.*

If any servant of God is careful in following the three principles given below, he/she will be mightily used by God. The 3 "G's" are

*"Never touch **Gold**"* meaning, Do not serve God for money.

*"Never touch God's **Glory**"* meaning, Do not take credit for what God is doing through you. Make sure you give Him all the glory.

*"Never touch a **Girl/Guy**"* with the wrong motive.

What about you and me?

When Jesus called His disciples for ministry, they had not witnessed any of His miracles nor had Jesus died for them. Neither had they known the depth of His love nor had they seen His power; yet they left everything and followed Him. It must have been Jesus' *Majestic and Powerful voice* that drew them to Him. (see Psalm 29)

Today, we know the price Jesus has paid on the Cross to deliver us from Eternal damnation. Having experienced the free gift of Salvation, many of us are so hardened in our hearts that we are reluctant to leave our comfort zone to serve the Lord, when millions of souls around us are perishing. Shame on us!

7.2 The Cost Of Discipleship

COMMANDMENT OF GOD FOR US TO OBEY	REWARD FOR OBEDIENCE/ SUPPORTING SCRIPTURES
High Calling of God: 1. "Follow Me; and let the dead bury their own dead." (see Matt. 8:21, 22)	Jesus stated "No one who puts his hand to the plough and looks back is fit for service in the Kingdom of God." (Luke 9:62/NIV)

1. "Let the dead bury their dead"- This implies **let the spiritually dead people bury the physically dead ones.**

2. The disciple who wanted to follow Christ probably wanted to stay with his elderly father until his death. After receiving the call for ministry from the Lord, we should not turn back to the worldly life.

3. Do not expect the path of discipleship to be always smooth. (see Matt. 8:20)

COMMANDMENT OF GOD FOR US TO OBEY	CONSEQUENCE OF DISOBEDIENCE
Be Worthy of Christ: 2. Do not love your father or mother more than Me. (see Matt. 10:37)	For then you are **not worthy of Me.** (see Matt. 10:37)

1. God must be your priority, even above your parents. But it is your responsibility to make sure their needs are met.

2. The higher the price you pay in denying yourself, greater will be the anointing of the Holy Spirit you receive. For example, Jesus was filled with the Holy Spirit without measure because of the price He paid on this earth. (see John 3:34)

COMMANDMENT OF GOD FOR US TO OBEY	CONSEQUENCE OF DISOBEDIENCE
3. Do not love your son or daughter more than Me. (see Matt. 10:37)	For then you are **not worthy of Me.**(see Matt. 10:37)

1. God must be your priority, even above your children. 2. Commit your children into the mighty hands of the Lord and the Lord will make your seed *great.* (see Job 5:25)	

COMMANDMENT OF GOD	CONSEQUENCE OF DISOBEDIENCE
4. Deny yourself, take up your cross and follow Me - Jesus. (see Matt. 10:38, 16:24)	And he who does not take his cross and follow after Me is **not worthy of Me - Jesus.** (Matt. 10:38)

Strive to deny yourself of vain thoughts, filthy words and deeds which are pleasing unto you and not unto God.

* At every stage of my spiritual training, the Lord would ask me "Are you ready to walk in the path of your Redeemer? For it is a path of suffering." And every time I said "Yes, Lord!" – Author

COMMANDMENT OF GOD FOR US TO OBEY	REWARD FOR OBEDIENCE/ CONSEQUENCE OF DISOBEDIENCE
Your Life Not For Yourself: 5. Do not find your life. (meaning, do not live your life for yourself.) (see Matt. 10:39)	1. For "he who finds his life will lose it. 2. He who loses his life for My sake will find it." (see Matt. 10:39) 3. For what good will it be for a man if he gains the whole world, yet loses his own soul? (see Matt.16:26/NIV)

Live for Jesus! It's worth it ! For Jesus is "The Way, The Truth and The Life." When we have Jesus, we have "True life." (see Jn.14:6)

COMMANDMENT OF GOD FOR US TO OBEY	REWARD FOR OBEDIENCE
Sacrifice & Find Life: 6. Lose your life for My sake (i.e., sacrificing your life for Christ's sake.) - Jesus. (see Matt. 10:39)	For then you will find life. (see Matt. 10:39)

Sacrifice your life for Christ...

1. Isaiah 43:4 says "I will give men (i.e., lost souls) in exchange for you, and people in exchange for your life." - A *promise given to the author in 1995.*
2. Sometimes you may need to change your environment, your comfort zone for the Lord's sake. God is always looking for "**yielding vessels**" who would pay the price.
3. The number of souls you win is directly proportional to the measure of sacrifice you make for Christ's sake. Pay the price on your knees in prayer and in obedience to His Word.
4. Jesus and I - We are Majority.

COMMANDMENT OF GOD	REWARDS FOR OBEDIENCE
Receive 100 Fold Blessings: 7. 'Forsake houses or brethren or sisters or father or mother or wife or children, or lands for My Name's sake.'(see Matt.19:29/ KJV)	For you shall receive a hundredfold blessing - houses and lands, brothers and sisters, fathers and mothers, and children on this earth with persecutions and also **Eternal Life.** (see Mark 10:30)

1. When we forsake our all for the Lord's sake, He promises us hundredfold blessing on earth, which may not be literal.
2. When we are in His perfect will for our lives, God will bring **spiritual relationships** in our path such as, brothers, sisters or parents in the Lord, who will bring us much blessings and joy.

COMMANDMENT OF GOD	REWARD FOR OBEDIENCE
Honor & Bless the Servants of God: 8. Receive a disciple of Christ (i.e., a servant of God (Matt. 10:40)	For he who receives you, receives Me and My Father who sent Me. (see Matt. 10:40)
9. Receive a prophet because he is a prophet. (see Matt. 10:41/NIV)	For you will receive *a prophet's reward.* (see Matt. 10:41)
10. Receive a righteous man because he is a righteous man. (see Matt. 10:41/NIV)	For you will receive a righteous man's reward. (see Matt. 10:41)
11. Give a cup of cold water to one of the little ones because he is My disciple. (see Matt. 10:42/NIV)	For you will certainly not lose your reward. (see Matt. 10:42)

1. When you receive God's servants and prophets who are righteous, then your **reward will be the same as that of the prophet** or righteous person you help. (see Matt. 10:40)
2. Do not muzzle the ox while it treads out the grain. And the worker is worthy of his wages. (see 1 Tim. 5:18/NIV)
3. Make sure you give glory only to God but bless the servants of God who have been a blessing to you.
4. Honor a true prophet of God who operates under the anointing of the Holy Spirit. *If you support a false prophet* or a man of God who is living a compromised life, then you are causing more damage to the Kingdom of God and also partaking in their evil deeds.
5. The leaders judge for a bribe, the priests teach for a price, and *the prophets tell fortunes for money*, yet they lean upon the Lord and say, "Is not the Lord among us?" The Lord says, Because of you the city will become a heap of rubble. (see Micah 3:11-12)
6. Ask God to give you wisdom and the gift of discerning of spirits to identify a true servant of God.
7. **Show Gratitude...**Make it a habit to bless the servants of God who brought fruitfulness in your life by investing their prayers, time and counsel.

Deny Yourself & Follow Christ

Living Martyrs

Those who are Christ's will crucify the flesh with its passions and desires.
If we live in the Spirit, let us also walk in the Spirit. For as many as are led by the Spirit of God, these are Sons of God. (see Gal.5:24-25; Rom.8:14)

Living martyr…Every believer is called to live as a "living martyr" on earth but only a few yield to the Spirit's guidance. **A** living martyr must daily die to "self" and crucify his desires, goals, ambitions on the cross every moment of the day and totally depend on God.

Rees Howells, one of the greatest intercessors that ever lived was called to live as a living martyr by our Lord.

* The Lord made me read the autobiography of Rees Howells to train me as a living martyr.

Everyday, the Lord schedules my day when I am in prayer between 3 am and 6 am. Some days, the Lord says, "Rest in Me and learn from Me," other days, "Go to Church and pray in the Spirit."

At times, He says, "work on the Book." The Lord promised me, "Every time you obey, there is a blessing awaiting you." - Author

It is extremely hard to change all your plans for the day as the Lord instructs you. But if you obey just as He counsels you, He makes life lot easier for you. He will help you avoid the snares of the devil for the day.

It is wonderful to be led by the Holy Spirit of God because He is Omniscient i.e., He is the all-knowing God. So we can safely entrust our lives and future in His hands.

Holy Spirit…Only by strictly following the guidance of the Holy Spirit, one can be a living martyr. (Rom. 12:1)

Those who are called to be living martyrs must not only obey the commandments given in the Word of God; but also obey the counsel given by the Holy Spirit for their specific situations on a daily basis; just as the *"Cloud"* symbolic of the Holy Spirit, led the Israelites through their journey in the wilderness. Whenever the cloud stopped, they had to stop their journey. Whenever the cloud lifted above the tabernacle, the Israelites would set out. (see Ex. 40:36-38; Num. 9:15-23)

7.3 The Mission Of The Disciples

COMMANDMENT OF GOD	SUPPORTING SCRIPTURES
To whom should you Preach? 1. Do not go among the gentiles or enter any town of the Samaritans. Go rather to the lost sheep of Israel. (Matt. 10:5-6/NIV)	For Jesus says, There will be more rejoicing in Heaven over one sinner who repents than over ninety-nine righteous persons who do not need to repent. (see Luke 15:7)

1. This was a specific command given to the twelve disciples to first go to the lost souls of Israel.
2. Since our God is a covenant-making and *covenant-keeping God,* He sent Jesus Christ first for the Jews to receive salvation remembering His covenant with Abraham, thereby honoring his faith and obedience to God. (see Gen. 12:2-3; Deut. 7:9)
3. *Today, we are commanded to reach out to the lost souls instead of preaching to the already saved believers over and over again.*

COMMANDMENTS OF GOD FOR US TO OBEY	REWARD FOR OBEDIENCE/ CONSEQUENCE OF DISOBEDIENCE
What should you Preach? 2(a) Go, preach this message: "The Kingdom of Heaven is near." (see Matt. 10:7/NIV) (b)Go ye into all the world, and preach the gospel to every creature. (see Mark 16:15/KJV)	Whoever believes and is baptized will be saved, but whoever does not believe will be condemned. (see Mark 16:16)

1. Preach the Word of God which is the Truth. (see Jn.17:17)
2. For the lips of a priest should keep knowledge and people should seek the Law from his mouth; for he is the messenger of the Lord of Hosts. (see Mal.2:7)
3. Teach the way of God in *truth* as Jesus did. (see Matt. 22:16). We understand God's ways through the Word of God. (see Ps. 119)

COMMANDMENT OF GOD FOR US TO OBEY	REWARD FOR OBEDIENCE/ SUPPORTING SCRIPTURES
Do Signs and Wonders: 3. "Heal the sick, cleanse the lepers, raise the dead, cast out devils." (see Matt. 10:8/KJV)	For Jesus said, "These signs will follow those who believe; in My Name, they will cast out demons; they **will lay hands on the sick, and the sick will recover** etc." (see Mark 16:17-18)

As we heed the calling of the Lord and obey Him, He will empower us with His anointing. He will also equip us with the gifts of the Holy Spirit to do miracles as the early apostles did. (see 1 Cor.12:7-11; Acts 2-3)

COMMANDMENT OF GOD	REWARD FOR OBEDIENCE
What to Take For Journey? 4. Do not take along any gold, or silver, or copper (money) in your belts. (see Matt. 10:9/NIV) 5 Take no bag for the journey, or extra tunic, or sandals, or a staff. (see Matt. 10:10)	For a worker is worthy of his keep. (Matt. 10:10/NIV)

1. If God calls, He provides. (see Phil. 4:19)
2. **None of Jesus' disciples murmured** about lacking anything because their focus was on things above. They had absolute trust in God who had called them. Hence, they achieved greater things for God. Trust God at all times to meet your financial needs.

For example, Peter said to the crippled man who begged for alms at the temple gate, '**Silver and gold I have none**, but what I have I give you. In the name of Jesus Christ of Nazareth, rise up and walk.' Instantly the man jumped to his feet and began to walk.

Peter did not have silver or gold with him but he had the *power of the Holy Spirit* to accomplish God's will. (see Acts 3:2-8)

COMMANDMENTS OF GOD FOR US TO OBEY	REWARD FOR OBEDIENCE/ CONSEQUENCE OF DISOBEDIENCE
Where Should You Stay? 5. Enquire first who is worthy when you enter into a city for ministry and stay there till you go out. (see Matt. 10:11) 6. And whatever house ye enter, first say, peace be to this house and in that same house remain, eating and drinking as they give. 7. ***Go not from house to house.*** (see Lk.10:5,7/KJV)	1. For the laborer is worthy of hire. 2. Whosoever will not receive you, when ye go out of that city, shake off the very dust from your feet for a testimony against them. (see Lk.9:5/KJV)

1. When God sends you to some place for ministry, He will take care of your accommodation, but wherever God makes the provision, you should be willing to stay without murmuring.
2. For example, Prophet Elijah was not sent to the palace but to a poor widow's house during the famine. (see 1 Kings 17:8-9) We should learn from God's ways.

COMMANDMENTS OF GOD FOR US TO OBEY	REWARD FOR OBEDIENCE/ CONSEQUENCE OF DISOBEDIENCE
What to say as you enter a home? 8. When you go into a household, greet it. (see Matt. 10:12/KJV)	1. If the house is worthy of your salutation, then let your peace come upon it; but ***if it is not worthy***, then let your peace return to you. (see Matt.10:13) 2. ***If the Son of peace be there,*** your peace shall rest upon it. If not, it shall turn to you again. (see Lk.10:6/KJV)

1. If you welcome a true servant of God into your house, God's peace and blessings will enter your home.
2. When you accept the gospel of the Prince of Peace, the peace that the world cannot give will fill your heart.

COMMANDMENT OF GOD FOR US TO OBEY	SUPPORTING SCRIPTURES
Expect Not Anything In Return: 9. Freely you give. (see Matt.10:8)	For freely you have received. (see Matt.10:8)

1. Jesus has given us Salvation, His Word and the anointing of the Holy Spirit for free.
2. When your intention is not to make money through the ministry, then God will make sure your needs are met. (see Phil. 4:19)
3. A true laborer will have deep burden for perishing souls and will tirelessly work for God's Kingdom. He will not work for money, his own fame or to expand his own ministry. He will not make God's work a business. (see 1 Tim.6:5)
4. "The Lord is my Shepherd; I shall not want. Surely goodness and mercy shall follow me all the days of my life." (see Ps. 23:1,6)

COMMANDMENT OF GOD FOR US TO OBEY	SUPPORTING SCRIPTURES
Be Innocent but Wise: 10. Be wise as serpents and harmless as doves. (see Matt. 10:16)	For you are sent as sheep in the midst of wolves. (see Matt. 10:16)

Knowledge is powerful... Believers should not be ignorant of God's ways, the devil's ways as well as the ways of the world. Update your knowledge from time to time.

7.4 Sufferings Of A Disciple

COMMANDMENTS OF GOD FOR US TO OBEY	CONSEQUENCES OF DISOBEDIENCE
Betrayal by Men: 1(a) Beware of men. (see Matt. 10:17/KJV) (b) Be on your guard. (Matt. 10:17/NIV)	1. "For they will deliver you up to councils and 2. They will scourge you in their synagogues. 3. You will be brought before governors and kings for My sake."(see Matt. 10:17-18)

1. *If Jesus was called "Beelzebub"* how much more will they call you and persecute you. Do not be discouraged but look forward to your reward in Heaven. (see Matt.10:23-25)
2. *For Christ's sake –*
    1. Your own brother will deliver you to death.
    2. A father will betray his own child.
    3. Children will rise up against their parents and cause them to be put to death.
    4. You will be hated by all men for Christ's name sake.
    5. Sufferings and persecution are part of life when you truly want to serve God. (see Matt. 10:21-22)

COMMANDMENT OF GOD FOR US TO OBEY	REWARD FOR OBEDIENCE
Be Not Anxious What to Reply: 2. Do not worry about what to say or how to say when they arrest you. (see Matt. 10:19/NIV)	1. For it will be given to you, in that hour, by the Holy Spirit, who is inside of you, what you should speak. (see Matt. 10:19-20) 2. For I will give you words and wisdom that none of your adversaries will be able to resist or contradict. (see Lk.21:15/NIV)

The Spirit of God will give you boldness and wisdom to speak forth for Christ. For example, on the day of Pentecost, Peter, an illiterate fisherman, preached the gospel under the anointing of the Holy Spirit and three thousand souls were saved in one day. (see Acts. 2:14-41

COMMANDMENT OF GOD FOR US TO OBEY	REWARD FOR OBEDIENCE
Finish Your Race Well: 3. Endure till the end. (see Matt.10:22)	So that you will be **saved.** (see Matt.10:22)

1. We should be faithful to God until the very end of our lives, for our Salvation to be complete.
2. Many started out well but lost their Salvation along the way. E.g., Judas Iscariot, King Saul, Lot's wife, Ananias and Sapphira, etc. (see Matt. 27:3-5; 1 Sam. 28:16-18; Gen. 19:26; Acts 5:3-10)
3. **Endured till the end...**Apostle Paul said, I have fought the good fight, I have finished my race, and I have kept the faith. Now there is in store for me the **crown of righteousness**, which the Lord, the righteous judge will award to me on that day; and not only to me, but also to all who long for His appearing. (see 2 Tim.4:7-8/NIV)

COMMANDMENTS OF GOD FOR US TO OBEY	SUPPORTING SCRIPTURES
What to do When Persecuted: 4. Flee to another place when you are persecuted in one. (see Matt. 10:23/NIV) 5. Do not be above your Master, Jesus Christ. (see Matt. 10:25)	1. Truly I tell you, you will not finish going through the towns of Israel before the Son of Man comes. (see Matt.10:23/NIV) 2. It is enough for the disciple that he be as his master; and the servant as his lord. (see Matt.10:25/KJV)

1. God expects you to **use your wisdom,** whenever possible, to escape from the place of persecution.
   For example, **Jesus fled** from Judea into the outskirts of Galilee when John, the Baptist was cast into prison. (Matt. 4:12-16)
2. We should not be **"over-righteous,** over-compassionate and over-wise" than Jesus Christ, our Master. (see Eccl. 7:16)

Nothing Can Separate You From The Love of Christ...

Apostle Paul said,

Hard work...I have worked much harder.

Prison...I have been in prison more frequently.

Flogged more severely, *five times* I received from the Jews *thirty nine lashes each time.*

Exposed to death *again and again.*

Beaten... Three times I was beaten with rods.

Stoned... Once I was stoned.

Shipwrecked thrice.

In the Open Sea... I spent a night and a day in the open sea.

On the Run...I have been constantly on the move.

Dangers...I have been in danger from **rivers,**

in danger from **bandits,**

in danger from my **own countrymen,**

in danger from **gentiles,**

in danger in the **city,**

in danger in the **country,**

in danger **at sea**; and

in danger from **false brothers**.

No Sleep...I have labored and toiled and often gone without sleep.

No Food and Water...I have known hunger and thirst and have often gone without food.

No clothes...I have been cold and naked besides everything else.

Burdened for Churches... I face daily the pressure of my concern for all the churches.' (see 2 Cor.11:23-33).

Yet Apostle Paul could say, "Neither death nor life, neither angels nor demons, neither the present nor the future, nor any powers and principalities, neither height nor death nor anything else in all creation, will be able to separate us from the love of God in Christ Jesus, our Lord." (Rom. 8:38)

The revelation of Christ's love enabled apostle Paul to endure the above afflictions. Ask God to reveal to you the depth of His love, as He did to apostle Paul. *Will you endure sufferings as apostle Paul did and still serve the Lord?*

7.5 The Worth Of A Disciple

COMMANDMENTS OF GOD	REWARD FOR OBEDIENCE
Hear From the Lord and Preach: 1(a) Speak in the daylight what I tell you in the dark. (b) Proclaim from the roofs what is whispered in your ear. (see Matt. 10:27/NIV)	"My sheep will hear My voice," says the Lord. (Jn.10:27)

When Will You Not Hear the Lord's voice?

1. The Holy Spirit longs to commune with you but if your spiritual ears are plugged with the worldly cares, you will not hear Him even if He shouts loudly in your ears.
2. Never go too far away from the Holy Spirit where He cannot give you a message to preach to the congregation.
3. You might be damaging God's Kingdom without your knowledge by giving messages in the flesh.
4. If you desire to hear the Lord speaking to you, wait on Him in prayer in the early morning hours, especially between **3 am and 6 am,** when your mind is at rest. Don't quit until you hear Him.

* By God's grace, I have been hearing His audible voice in the early morning hours since 1992 until today - Author

COMMANDMENTS OF GOD	SUPPORTING SCRIPTURES
Do not fear Men: 2(a) Do not be afraid when you are persecuted. (see Matt.10:23,26/NIV) (b) Endure hardship as a good soldier of Christ Jesus. (see 2 Tim. 2:3/KJV)	For there is nothing covered that will not be revealed, and hidden that will not be known. (Matt. 10:26)

When you begin your ministry, Satan will try to scare you by bringing obstacles in your way to discourage you and make you give up your calling before you could establish God's ministry. But you must remain faithful to the Lord in fulfilling His will for your life. (see 1 Thess.3:2-4)

1. Do not fear, for the Holy Spirit will counsel you to avoid the dangers but if you have to go through the trial; He will help you to endure it. *If God is for us, who can be against us?* (see Rom. 8:31)

2. The truth will eventually come out. The Lord may lift you up and honor you in the same place where you were persecuted. For example, Daniel, Shadrach, Meshach and Abed-Nego, Joseph and David. (see Dan. 6:24-28; 3:28-30)

COMMANDMENT OF GOD FOR US TO OBEY	REWARD FOR OBEDIENCE/ SUPPORTING SCRIPTURES
3. **Don't be afraid.** (see Matt. 10:31/NIV)	1. For you are of more value than many sparrows which are sold just for a penny and not one of them falls to the ground apart from your Father's will. 2. The very hairs of your head are all numbered by your Father in Heaven. (Matt. 10:29-30)

1. You are of great worth to God. God is more concerned about you, your personal needs, trials and sorrows than you can comprehend.
2. God loves you so much that He sent His only Son, Jesus Christ, to die on the cross for you. He will carry you through your difficult times. (see Jn.3:16)

COMMANDMENT OF GOD FOR US TO OBEY	REWARD FOR OBEDIENCE / CONSEQUENCE OF DISOBEDIENCE
4. Do not deny Me before men - Jesus. (see Matt. 10:33)	Whoever shall deny Me before men, I will also deny him before My Father in Heaven - Jesus. (see Matt. 10:33)
5. Confess Me before men - Jesus. (see Matt. 10:32)	Whoever shall confess Me before men, I will also confess him before My Father in Heaven - Jesus. (see Matt. 10:32)

COMMANDMENT OF GOD FOR US TO OBEY	REWARD FOR OBEDIENCE/ SUPPORTING SCRIPTURES
Fear Not Death: 6. Do not fear those who kill the body but cannot kill the soul; but rather fear God. (see Matt. 10:28)	1. For He is able to destroy both soul and body in Hell. (see Matt. 10:28) 2. *I, even I, am He who comforts you.* 3. *Who are you that you should be afraid of a man who will die,* and of the son of a man who is made like grass? 4. And you forget the Lord your Maker. You have feared continually everyday because of the fury of the oppressor, when he has prepared to destroy. 5. And *where is the fury of the oppressor?* declares the Lord of Hosts. (see Is. 51:12-13)

1. There is one life to live on earth and then there is judgment. Our lives do not end in death but continue forever; either in Heaven or in Hell. (see Heb. 9:27)
2. Nowadays, people who live in compromise have come up with a **convenient theory that there is no "Hell."**
3. But Jesus used the term "Hell" for the place of Eternal damnation, where there is unquenchable fire, reserved for the ungodly. (see Mark 9:43,48)
4. We must obey God rather than men. (see Acts. 5:29)
5. If you die with Him, you will also live with Him. (see 2 Tim.2:11)

8. Faith

Our Father God is seated on the throne as the King of kings. We, being His dear children should know how to go into His throne room and take anything we need from His hands, by faith.

We don't need to beg Him; *for an Obedient child knows his rights.* If we cry and plead in prayer, God will also cry with us; His face will move but His hands will not move to do miracles.

Only by faith, we can receive miracles from God. Our Lord will never test us beyond our level of faith. Even faith, as small as a mustard seed, can bring forth great miracles for us. We must not only express our faith in the Lord's ability to do a miracle but also act upon it.

Without faith, it is impossible to please God. (Heb. 11:6)

8.1 Faith Can Move Mountains

COMMANDMENT OF GOD FOR US TO OBEY	REWARDS FOR OBEDIENCE
Have faith and do not doubt. (see Matt. 21:21-22)	1. So that you will receive all things you ask in prayer. (see Matt. 21:21-22) 2. Jesus said to His disciples, "In faith, if you say to a mountain, 'Be removed and be cast into the sea; and it will be done. 3. *All things,* whatever you ask in prayer, *believing,* you will receive." (see Matt. 21:21-22)

What is Faith?

Faith is being sure of what we hope for and certain of what we do not see. (Heb. 11:1/NIV)

* To me, faith is "child-like belief" in the Name of the Lord and in His love and power. – Author

8.2 Persistent Faith Brings Deliverance

COMMANDMENTS OF GOD FOR US TO OBEY	REWARD FOR OBEDIENCE
Have great faith as the Canaanite woman had. (see Matt. 15:28)	"Woman, your request is granted; *for you have great faith"* (see Matt. 15:28/NIV)
	And her daughter was made whole from that very from a demon. This was the test of faith for her. (see Matt. 15:28)

Reasons why the Canaanite woman received deliverance for her daughter...

1. She, being a gentile, called Jesus, "Lord" and worshipped Him.
2. She cried out for His mercy.
3. She persevered in her faith in the Lord. Though the Lord did not seem to answer her, still she did not give up.
4. The Canaanite woman was one of the two gentiles who were appreciated by the Lord for their great faith.

How Do You Receive Faith?

Remember, God has dealt to every man the measure of faith. (see Rom.12:3/ KJV)

1. **Through the Word of God:** *Faith comes by hearing the Word of God.* Meditating the "Miracles of God" will increase your faith. (see Rom. 10:17).
   * *When the Lord was taking me through many trials to increase my faith, I cried out to the Lord in frustration, "How do I get this faith, Lord?" I heard His audible voice saying to me, "**Meditate My Miracles.**" - Author*

2. **Through the Holy Spirit:** The Holy Spirit of God imparts different measure of faith to each and every one of us. (see Rom. 12:3) The "*gift of faith"* is the highest level of faith. It is one of the nine gifts of the Holy Spirit. (see 1 Cor.12:9)

3. **Through Prayer:** You can pray and ask the Lord to increase your faith as the apostles did. (see Lk. 17:5)

Seven Blessings Through Faith In Jesus

1. *Salvation through Faith...* If you confess with your mouth "Jesus is Lord" and **believe** in your heart that God raised Him from the dead, you will be **saved.** Whoever believes and is baptized will be saved. (Rom. 10:9; Mark 16:16)

2. *Eternal Life through Faith...* He who *believes* in Christ is not condemned but has *"Everlasting Life."* And he who does not believe the Son is condemned already and will not see Life. (see John 3:18, 36)

3. *Holy Spirit through Faith...* Jesus says, 'If anyone is thirsty, let him come to Me and drink. Whoever *believes* in Me, rivers of **living waters** will flow out of him. (see John 7:37-38)

4. *Answers to Prayers through Faith...* All things, whatsoever ye shall **ask** in prayer, *believing,* ye shall receive.' (see Matt. 21:21-22/KJV)

   Believe that God is able to answer your prayers. Nothing will be difficult for you to receive from God,

   i.   if you ask in prayer,

   ii. according to God's will and

   iii. without wavering in faith.

5. *Greater Works through Faith...* "Verily, verily, I say unto you, he that *believes* in Me, will do what I do also; and he will do even **greater things than what I did**" says the Lord Jesus. (Jn.14:12/KJV)

   The "greater works" will include greater number of souls saved and greater scope of ministry.

6. *Healing through Faith...* When the woman with the issue of blood touched Jesus' garment in faith, Jesus said to her, "Daughter, **thy faith has made thee whole.** Go in peace." And she was healed immediately. (see Mark 5:25-34)

7. *Perfect Peace through Faith...* God will keep in perfect peace him whose mind is steadfast, because he **trusts** in Him. Trust in the Lord forever. (see Is. 26:3-4)

   Remember, Israelites were judged for their sin of unbelief.

9. Fear of God - Beginning Of All Wisdom

Who shall not Fear You and glorify Your Name? For You only are Holy; all nations will come and worship before You. (Rev. 15:3)

To fear the Lord is to hate evil. Obedience to God is directly proportionate to the fear of God you have. (Prov.8:13/NIV)

COMMANDMENTS OF GOD FOR US TO OBEY	REWARDS FOR OBEDIENCE/ CONSEQUENCES OF DISOBEDIENCE
1. Fear Him (Jesus Christ) who is able to destroy both your soul and body in Hell. 2. Do not fear those who kill the body but cannot kill the soul. (see Matt. 10:28) (Jesus stated, "**I and the Father are one.**" (Jn.10:30) & "**I have the keys of hell and of death.**" (see Rev.1:18/KJV))	*Blessings that follow when you fear God...* 1. **Honor, Wealth & Life...** Humility and the Fear of the Lord bring wealth and honor and life. (Prov.22:4) 2. **Rescued From Death...**The fear of the Lord is a fountain of life turning a man from the snares of death. (Prov.14:27) 3. **God's Secret & His Covenant...**The secret of the Lord is with them that fear Him and He will show them His covenant. (Ps. 25:14) 4. **Knowledge...**The fear of the Lord is the beginning of knowledge but fools despise wisdom and instruction. (Prov.1:7) 5. **Long Life...**The fear of the Lord prolongs life but the years of the wicked will be shortened. (see Prov.10:27) 6. **Security for your children...**He who fears the Lord has a secure fortress, and for his children it will be a refuge. Your children will be mighty on earth. (see Prov.14:26; Ps.112:2) 7. **Untouched by Evil...**The fear of the Lord leads to life; and he that has it will abide satisfied; he will not be touched by evil. (see Prov.19:23)

Who Is This Jesus Whom We Should Fear?

Jesus declared *"I am the Son of God."* (see Jn.10:36)

Other Declarations of Jesus Christ:

"I am The Way, The Truth and The Life...

Many saints, prophets, holy men and great religious leaders have come and gone from this earth; but no one has ever said, as Jesus said,

'I am "The Way" to Heaven;
I am "The Truth" and
I am "The Life" to your dead spirit.' Until Jesus Christ, 'The Life' comes inside of your heart, you are dead in your sins.
No one comes to the Father in Heaven except through Me' (see Jn.14:6; Eph. 2:1)

"I am the Light of the world ...

Many religions teach that God is love and God is light and point towards that light. But only the Lord Jesus Christ proclaimed "I am the true light which lights every man that comes into the world." Until Jesus Christ, the light is invited into your dead spirit, your spirit lives in the darkness of sin. (see John 1:9, 8:12)

"I am a King. (Jn.18:37)

"I am the Alpha and the Omega, the beginning and the end, the first and the last. (see Rev.1:8; 22:18)

"I am, before Abraham was. (Jn.8:58)

"I am your Lord and Teacher. (Jn.13:13-14)

"I am the Bread of Life, the right kind of food for your spirit. (see John 6:35,48)

"I am the Living Bread that came down from Heaven.(Jn.6:51)

"I am the Resurrection and the Life; for I will give you Eternal Life. (see Jn.11:25)

"I am the Door; whoever enters through Me will be saved, declared the Lord Jesus. (Jn.10:9)

"I am the Gate for the sheep. (Jn.10:7)

"I am the Good Shepherd who lays down My life for the sheep. (see John 10:11,14)"

"I am the true Vine and ye are the branches. If you abide in Me, you shall bear much fruit; for without Me, you can do nothing. (John 15:5)

"I am He that searches hearts and minds and I will repay each of you according to your deeds. (Rev. 2:23)

Jesus also said, 'I will give you *rivers of living water i.e., the Holy Spirit,* to quench your thirsty spirits. (see John 7:37-39)

Honor and Fear the Lord Jesus for who He is ...

If you honor Me, I will honor you; If you despise Me, I will despise you, says the Lord. (see 1 Sam.2:30)

Do not mock Jesus Christ as the Gentiles did. Great will be your punishment on the Judgment Day. For Jesus Christ is the *True God and Eternal Life;* (see Matt. 20:19; 1 Jn.5:20)

10. Fear Not Satan, The Wicked One

"No weapon formed against you shall prosper, and every tongue which rises against you in judgment you shall condemn. This is the heritage of the servants of the Lord, and their righteousness is from Me," says the Lord.

"I will make you into a threshing sledge, new and sharp, with many teeth. *You will thresh the mountains (of Satan) and crush them,* and reduce the hills to chaff. (see Is.54:16-17; 41:15/NIV)

COMMANDMENT OF GOD FOR US TO OBEY	REWARDS FOR OBEDIENCE
Binding Satan and His Hosts: First you bind the strong man, Satan. (see Matt. 12:29)	1. And then you will plunder his house. 2. Or else how can you enter a strong man's house and plunder his goods? (see Matt. 12:29)

What All Can You Get Back From Satan?

1. Get back your sons, daughters and your spouse from the clutches of the devil.
2. Get back your unsaved loved ones, blinded by the devil.
3. Get back your health.
4. Claim back the finances that belong to you.
5. Receive your spiritual blessings.
6. Restore your strained marriage and family life.
7. Get back your honor.

God Given Authority... If you are a true follower of Christ, God will equip you with the power of the Holy Spirit and authority to bind the strong man, Satan and his hosts. (see Luke 10:19)

The demons know who you are... It is stated in Acts 19:11-17 that when some vagabond Jews tried to cast out demons unworthily in the Name of Jesus, the demons tore them apart saying, 'Jesus and Paul we know, but who are you?' and they fled the place naked and wounded.

Can you bind Satan? You definitely can. But you must live a righteous life, have a closer relationship with the Lord and walk in obedience to His commands to have real power and authority over the devils and for the devils to tremble at your word.

COMMANDMENT OF GOD FOR US TO OBEY	REWARD FOR OBEDIENCE/ SUPPORTING SCRIPTURES
What spirits should you bind? 2. Bind on earth. (see Matt. 18:18)	1. For it will be bound in Heaven. (see Matt. 18:18) 2. For 'I give you the authority over all the power of the enemy.' (see Luke 10:19)

As true believers, we are given the authority to **bind all the spirits of darkness** which are ruling over our lives and nation. Some of the spirits you can bind are - the spirit of blindness, spirit of infirmity, spirit of adultery, spirit of idolatry, spirit of deception, spirit of pride and arrogance, spirit of unforgiveness and bitterness, etc. and be delivered in the name of Jesus. (see Luke 10:19; Eph. 6:11-16)

COMMANDMENT OF GOD FOR US TO OBEY	REWARD FOR OBEDIENCE
What should you loose? 3. Loose on earth. (see Matt. 18:18)	For it will be loosed in Heaven. (see Matt. 18:18)

1. God did not give us a spirit of timidity, but a spirit of power, of love and of self-discipline. (2 Tim.1:7/NIV)

2. We can **release the Spirit of the Lord** upon ourselves and our family members to live an abundant life, for example,
   The Spirit of truth and comfort,
   The Spirit of wisdom and understanding,
   The Spirit of counsel and might,
   The Spirit of knowledge,
   The Spirit of obedience,
   The Spirit of the fear of God,
   The Spirit of conviction and repentance (see Is.11:2; Jn.15:26)

3. You can also loose the captives from their captivity and loose the prisoners that are bound in various addictions by the power of the Holy Spirit in you. (see Is. 61:1)

10.1 Satan Trembles At The Name Of Jesus

COMMANDMENTS OF GOD	SUPPORTING SCRIPTURES
Jesus' command to the legion of devils: "Go" (Matt. 8 :32)	1. The demons called Jesus "The Son of God" for they knew who Jesus was. (see Matt.8:29) 2. The demons immediately obeyed the command of the Lord and went into the herd of swine. (see Matt. 8:32)

1. This command was given by the Lord Jesus to the "legion of devils" in the demon-possessed men, to go into the herd of swine.

2. **Hardened Hearts of men...**

   When the whole city heard that Jesus had cast out legion of devils, they pleaded with Him to leave their city. (see Matt. 8:28-34)

   Pray that God should remove your stony heart and give you a heart of flesh. (see Ezek.11:19; 36:26)

3. **Points to Ponder...**

   "Change of Heart" May Not Be By Miracles... After having witnessed a legion of demons go into the herd of 2000 swine, still the people did not invite Jesus into their city nor did they want to hear Him.

   True repentance comes only by the conviction of the Holy Spirit and may not be by witnessing miracles.

4. **Only in Jesus' Name...**Jesus Christ was the first one to cast out demons from human beings. Since Jesus has the ultimate authority over Satan, we can cast out demons only by His Name. (see Lk. 10:19)

10.2 Who Is Satan?

1. **Satan is the wicked angel who once desired God's throne and hence was cast out from Heaven by God.**

2. He is the ancient serpent who seeks "worship" that is due only unto God;

3. He is the prince and the ruler of this world.

4. Other names of Satan - Lucifer, Devil, Beast, Dragon, Old serpent.

The Evil Works Of Satan

1. Satan is the evil one who is subtle and cunning and he **blinds the minds** of them who believe not the gospel of Christ.

2. He is the murderer from the beginning who comes to **steal, kill and destroy;** he is the **enemy of our souls.**

3. There is no truth in him, for he is a **liar** and the father of lies. He makes us doubt God's love for us.

4. He is the *accuser of brethren* who accuses us before God day and night. (Job 1:6-10)

5. Your adversary the devil, as a roaring lion, walks about, seeking whom he may devour.

6. He is the **tempter** who causes us to sin. (see Is.14:12-15, 2 Cor.11:3, Gen. 3:1, Jn.8:44; 10:10; Rev. 12:9,10, Matt.4:3, 1 Pet. 5:8; 1 Jn.3:8; 2 Cor.4:4)

Our Spiritual Warfare

Ephesians 6:11-16 says,

We wrestle not against flesh and blood i.e., human beings
but against **principalities**, and
powers of darkness,
against the **rulers** of the **darkness** of this world,
against **spiritual wickedness** in high places.

Who Is Jesus?

1. God has raised up Jesus from the dead and set Him at His own right hand in the Heavenly places;

2. Jesus is **far above all principality and power**.

3. Jesus is **far above every rule and dominion**.

4. Jesus is **far above every name** that is named; not only in this world, but also in that which is to come.

5. God has put all things under His feet.

6. God has given Him to be the "Head" over all things to the Church, which is His body.

7. The fullness of **Jesus Christ fills all in all**. (see Eph.1:20-23)

The Whole Armor Of God

We must put on the whole armor of God and fight with the unseen enemy in the spiritual realm.

We must wear the **helmet of Salvation**;

The breastplate of **righteousness;**

The belt of **truth** around your waist;

The shoes shod with the **gospel of peace** for our defence; and take

The shield of **faith** in one hand;

The sword of the Spirit i.e., the **Word of God,** in the other hand in order to fight and slay the devil and his hosts.

Pause & Think... If any one of the above protective covering over you is not strong, the devil will pierce you through that area of weakness.

For example, if you are going to war, will you not want your shield to be made of bronze rather than aluminium and your "sword" made of iron rather than cardboard?

Similarly, in the spiritual warfare, the "Sword of the Spirit" i.e., the Word of God, you carry must be strong enough to slay the devil; so also the other weapons of warfare.

10.3 Ways To Overcome The Devil

Submit yourselves first to God; then resist the devil and he will flee from you. (see James 4:7)

1. **Through the Word of God**: You resist the devil by quoting Scriptures relevant to the situation. When you meditate on the Word of God daily, you will always be prepared for spiritual warfare.

2. **Through Jesus' Name,** *The Name Above Every Other Name:* You bind the devil in Jesus' Name and the devil will flee from you. For all power is given unto Jesus in Heaven and on earth. (Matt. 28:18; Phil. 2:9; Eph. 1:20-23)

3. **Through the Blood of Jesus:** We overcome the enemy by the precious blood of the slain Lamb, Jesus Christ, and by the words of our testimony. (see Rev. 12:11)

4. **Through the Power of the Holy Spirit**: Since you are the temple of the Holy Spirit, He who dwells inside of you will empower you to take authority over the devil.

5. **Through Fervent Prayer and Fasting:** Certain kind of demons cannot be cast out except through prayer and fasting. When we pray, God will send forth His angels to fight our battles. (see Matt. 17:21; Dan. 10:12-14)

6. **Through Shouts of Praise and Joy:** When you praise God with a cheerful heart, He will fight your battles, for He is the Lord of Hosts.

    You can give place to the devil and prolong the trial by talking your fears out; for life and death are in the power of your tongue. (see Josh. 6; Prov. 18:21)

7. **By Binding the evil spirits:** You must also bind the evil spirits, for example, the spirit of lust, the spirit of fornication, the spirit of bitterness and unforgiveness, etc.

10.4 Do Not Let The Devil Speak To Your Mind

COMMANDMENT OF GOD	SUPPORTING SCRIPTURES
Peter, A Disciple Rebuked: Get behind Me, Satan! For you do not have in mind the things of God but the things of men. (see Matt.16:23/NIV)	Jesus turned and said to *Peter, "Get behind Me, Satan!* You are a stumbling block to Me." (see Matt.16:23/NIV)

Lessons to Learn...

1. Jesus rebuked *Peter* when he tried to stop Him from going to the cross.

2. Jesus began to show His disciples that He must suffer many things from the elders and chief priests and scribes, and be killed and be raised again the third day. Then Peter took Him aside and began to rebuke Jesus, saying, "Far be it from you, Lord; this shall not happen to you!" But Jesus turned and said to Peter, "Get behind me, Satan! (see Matt.16:21-23)

3. **Peter, a great Servant of God, deceived...**Peter was given an awesome revelation by the Father God that *Jesus is the Christ, the Son of the Living God* and the Lord even commended him. (see Matt.16:16-17)

4. **A Man of God...Used By Satan?** But a little later, Peter let Satan speak to his mind and was rebuked by the Lord. *Peter had absolutely no idea* that the devil used him against the will of God. How scary! Peter, being a disciple of Christ for about 3 ½ years, having spent a lot of time in prayer, still could be deceived by Satan.

5. **God of Second Chances...**But the same disciple was greatly used by God after Jesus was risen from the dead. What a consolation! (see Acts 2, 3)

6. **Be Alert...**There is a lesson here for us to learn that we need to be spiritually *alert at all times,* in constant fellowship with the Lord so that we will hear only the voice of the Holy Spirit and not the devil's voice.

11. Great Commission Of Christ

COMMANDMENTS OF GOD	SUPPORTING SCRIPTURES
1. **Go and make disciples of all the Nations,** 2. **Baptize** them in the Name of the Father and of the Son and of the Holy Spirit, 3. **Teach them to observe all things** that I have commanded you. (see Matt. 28:19-20)	1. Surely, I am with you always, to the very end of the age. (see Matt. 28:18, 20/NIV) 2. Go therefore, for all authority has been given to Me in Heaven and on earth. (see Matt. 28:18)

Points to Ponder...

1. **Followers of Christ...**The "Great Commission of Christ" is **given to all His followers**.

2. **Go...** Christ expects His followers to *go to the lost souls of all nations* and teach the Word of God without any compromise.

3. **Teach...**The gospel you preach must be centred on repentance, forgiveness and remission of sins. Also preach about the power of the Holy Spirit to live a victorious life. (see Luke 24:47; Acts 2:40)

4. **Make Disciples...** The purpose is to make **not just converts but disciples,** who will observe all the commandments of Christ and follow Him with all their hearts, minds and will. (see Jn.8:31)

5. **Baptize...**Those who believe in Christ and the gospel of grace are to be baptized with water. This symbolizes that your past sinful life is buried with Christ when you are immersed in the water and when you emerge out of the water, you imply that you would live a new life in Christ.(see Rom. 6:3-4)

6. **Obey His Commands...**Christ will be with His obedient followers in the presence and the power of the Holy Spirit. (see Matt. 28:20)

7. **Authority to witness...**God's people are promised authority and boldness to proclaim the gospel around the world. Christ expects us to testify boldly about Him, not only in our neighborhood but also in our city, all over the state, nation and in other nations as well.

12. God Is Desperate For Intercessors

COMMANDMENT OF GOD	CONSEQUENCE OF DISOBEDIENCE
1. Stand in the gap before Me on behalf of the land. (see Ezek. 22:30)	1. That I should not destroy it. (see Ezek. 22:30) 2. **I sought for a man** among the people of the land who would make a wall, and stand in the gap before Me on behalf of the land, that I should not destroy it; but **I Found No one.** 3. So I will pour out **My wrath** on them and consume them with My fiery anger, bringing down on their own heads all they have done, declares the Sovereign Lord. (see Ezek. 22:30/NIV; Jer.7:17-20) 4. *O My people, put on sackcloth and roll in ashes; mourn with bitter wailing as for an only son*, for suddenly the destroyer will come upon you. (see Jer.6:26/NIV)

1. *God's perfect will...*God desires *all men to be saved* and to come to the knowledge of the truth. (1 Tim.2:4) The Lord is patient with you, *not wanting anyone to perish*, but everyone to come to repentance. (2 Pet.3:9/NIV)
2. Pray that God should raise up sincere Intercessors to stand in the gap between the perishing souls and the Hell fire.

COMMANDMENTS OF GOD	REWARDS FOR OBEDIENCE
2. "If My people, which are called by My name shall... Humble themselves, and pray, and seek My face, and turn from their wicked ways" (2 Chro.7:14/KJV)	Then... a) I will hear from heaven, b) will forgive their sin, c) and will heal their land.(2 Chr.7:14/KJV)

Qualifications Of An Intercessor:

'O Daughter of Zion,

Let **tears** run down like a river **day and night**;

give yourself no relief;

give your eyes no rest.

Arise, **cry out** in the night; at the beginning of the watches;

pour out your **heart** like water before the face of the Lord;

Lift your **hands** toward Him;

for the life of your young children, who faint from hunger (i.e., for Salvation) at the head of every street.' (Lam. 2:18-19)

As the above Scripture says, a true intercessor should have intense burden for lost souls and cry out for them.

Guess What Two Intercessors Can Do For Their Nation!

Those of you who are called to be intercessors to stand in the gap for your nation…

1. You can **form small groups** of two or three people to pray with;

2. Each group can *pray for a certain city for a month for the salvation of every person living in that city.* After that month is over, select a different city and continue to intercede for its revival until you have covered all the cities in prayer.

3. **Get the statistics book** and note down all the points that need to be prayed for each city.

4. Distribute these prayer points to all the other prayer groups as well.

5. Intercede fervently. Since you are in the will of God, Jesus will be in the midst of you to bless your work.

6. Your reward will be great in Heaven; for the scripture says that he who wins souls is wise. He will shine like stars forever and ever. (see Prov. 11:30; Dan.12:3)

7. When you carry the Lord's burden for lost souls, He will carry your burden.

God's Burden In My Heart...

** God spoke to me audibly and instructed me to start **"Prayer Groups"** to intercede for revival in every State and in every Nation. - Author*

These prayer groups will stand out like **Light Houses, in millions**, across each and every nation, bombarding Heaven, sending sweet smelling incense continually to His throne room, for God to send forth revival upon nations. Then we will see true revival breaking forth by His Spirit, even in one day. E.g. Revival in the city of Nineveh. (see Jonah 3)

I hope and pray that every church will understand this vision and implement it. - Author

Can a nation be saved in one day?

Yes. It will not be by our might or by our power
but only by His Holy Spirit. (see Zech.4:6)

13. Harvest Is Plenty But Laborers Are Few

1. Pray For Worthy Laborers

COMMANDMENT OF GOD FOR US TO OBEY	SUPPORTING SCRIPTURES
Pray ye, To the "Lord of the harvest" that **He will send** forth laborers into **His harvest**. (Matt. 9:38/KJV)	For the harvest truly is plenteous. But the laborers are few. (Matt. 9:37)

1. This is the direct command of Christ given to us to pray for more dedicated laborers to work in His vineyard.
2. For *people are destroyed* from morning to evening; they perish forever *without anyone regarding them.* (see Job 4:20/KJV)

13.2 Clay In The Potter's Hands

Our Duty is to Pray…We must pray that God should send forth the right kind of laborers whom He has called and prepared for His ministry.

Enrolled in God's School of Training…When God calls you and enrols you in His school of training, He will not settle for anything less than His standard of preparation. God is willing to wait for 10 or even 100 years to prepare that one faithful, righteous and God fearing laborer for His Kingdom. No "quick fix" will accomplish His purpose.

Once the vessel is prepared, God will do great things through him within a short time. E.g. Moses, Jonah and Joseph. After Jonah preached, all of Nineveh repented and got saved. God prepared Moses for 80 years before He called him into His service, and He prepared Joseph for 13 years to serve His purpose.

God's Prepared Vessel will be a true laborer with an intense burden for perishing souls and He will diligently work for His Kingdom. A true laborer will not work for money, his glory or to expand his ministry. He will not make God's work a business; instead his food will be to fulfil God's Will for his life, as Jesus said and did.

Prayer & Preaching Ratio (5:1)

At the age of twelve, Jesus was ready to preach but He only started His ministry at the age of 30. Jesus had spent 18 years in prayer for His 3 ½ years of ministry, which continues to impact the world for more than 2000 years. (see Luke 2:43-50)

From the example of Christ, we learn that a Minister of God needs to pray for at least 5 hours for 1 hour of preaching, to have a powerful ministry as Jesus had. Then the rebellious will begin to obey, the spiritually deaf will begin to hear; the worldly will begin to find the worldly things distasteful and the heathen will begin to truly understand the gospel and get saved.

13.3 Mission of A Worthy Laborer

COMMANDMENT OF GOD FOR US TO OBEY	SUPPORTING SCRIPTURES
Be with Me and gather (souls) with Me - Jesus. (see Matt. 12:30)	"He who is not with Me is against Me; and **he who does not gather with Me, scatters** abroad" says the Lord. (Matt.12:30)
He who does not walk with the Lord is a hindrance to others; by his lifestyle and behavior, he drags people along with him to Hell.	

COMMANDMENTS OF GOD FOR US TO OBEY	REWARDS FOR OBEDIENCE/ SUPPORTING SCRIPTURES
Parable of the Lost Sheep: Leave the ninety and nine sheep (saved souls), and go and seek that which is gone astray (lost). (see Matt. 18:12/KJV)	If the shepherd finds it, assuredly, he rejoices more over that sheep than over the ninety-nine that did not go astray. (see Matt. 18:13)

First Reach Out To The Lost...It is not the will of your Father who is in Heaven that one of these little ones should perish. For all of Heaven will rejoice over the one lost soul that receives the Lord and gets *saved*. (see Matt. 18:13-14; Luke 15:7)

13.4 Work In His Vineyard And Get Paid

COMMANDMENT OF GOD FOR US TO OBEY	REWARDS FOR OBEDIENCE
Parable of the Workers in the Vineyard: 1. You also go and work in My vineyard. (Matt. 20:4/NIV)	1. And I will pay you whatever is right. (Matt. 20:4/NIV) 2. For the Kingdom of Heaven is like a landowner who went out early in the morning to hire laborers for his vineyard. (Matt. 20:1)
2. Call the laborers and give them their wages, beginning with the last to the first. (see Matt. 20:8)	The foreman paid all the laborers, hired at various hours of the day, the same wages. (see Matt. 20:8-10/NIV)

1. The man who is hiring laborers to work in His vineyard is symbolic of Christ who is seeking for workers to labor in His harvest field.
2. ***Be Rewarded More Than You Expect...***
   You can catch up with whatever you have lost so far in your life and receive more than you have hoped for. *Even if you start right now, at the eleventh hour* and serve the Lord well, you may be equally rewarded as the others.

COMMANDMENT OF GOD	SUPPORTING SCRIPTURES
3. Take what is yours and go your way. (Matt. 20:14) 4. Don't be envious because I am generous. (see Matt. 20:15/NIV)	Pray that God should deliver you from the spirit of jealousy and fill you with the spirit of love. For Love is not envious. (see Rom. 5:5, 1 Cor.13:4)
5. Be one among the few who are chosen. (see Matt. 20:16)	For many are called, but few chosen. (Matt. 20:16)

Few are chosen... When we are called by the Lord, whether we will be chosen or not depends on how we respond to the Lord and the price we are willing to pay.

Do not be Envious... We cannot question God about His decisions, for He is a Sovereign Lord.

We should not be jealous of our brethren when the Lord, in His goodness and grace, blesses them. All believers should work in unity towards the expansion of God's Kingdom and not see our fellow brethren as competitors.

Be content knowing that your labor for Christ will not be in vain. Each man will be rewarded according to his deeds, for He is a just God. (see 1 Cor.15:58)

13.5 Eleventh Hour Laborers

1. **The Lord seeks laborers...**Our Lord, who is symbolic of the man in the parable, is also seeking to hire laborers to work in His harvest field, in these last days.

2. **The Lord neither slumbers nor sleeps...** The Lord never takes rest and is always at work, just as the man in the parable hired laborers at various hours of the day i.e., 0, 3rd, 6th, 9th and 11th hours. (see Ps 121:4)

3. **Eleventh hour laborers...**When the man hired laborers who were standing idle the whole day, how much more the Lord would be willing to hire you to serve Him, even in these last days.

4. **It is never too late** to serve the Lord if you have lost many chances in life in the past to serve Him. You can start right now! E.g. Caleb went to war at the age of 85. (see Josh. 14:10-11)

5. **God can still use you...**Do not be discouraged if you are idle and not having a job. If you fervently seek the Lord, He will reveal the purpose for your life and use you according to His will.

6. **Cursed is the man who takes God's work lightly...**If you have a willing heart to work hard, the Lord will definitely hire you to serve Him. The Lord is seeking, not loiterers but laborers, to work in His vineyard.

7. **Quality Work...**It is not the duration of service that makes you a worthy laborer but the quality of work.

14. Hunger & Thirst For The Holy Spirit

COMMANDMENT OF GOD FOR US TO OBEY	CONSEQUENCES OF DISOBEDIENCE
1. Do not **blaspheme** the Holy Spirit. (see Matt. 12:31) 2. Do not **grieve** the Holy Spirit of God, by whom you were sealed for the day of redemption. (Eph. 4:30) 3. Do not **quench** the Holy Spirit. (see 1 Thess.5:19) 4. Do not **resist** the Holy Spirit. (see Acts 7:51)	1. For all manner of sin and blasphemy shall be forgiven unto men; but the **blasphemy against the Holy Spirit shall not be forgiven unto men.** 2. Whosoever speaks a word against Jesus Christ, it shall be forgiven him but whosoever **speaks against the Holy Ghost**, it shall **not be forgiven** him neither in this world, nor in the world to come. (see Matt. 12:31-32/KJV)
Baptism of the Holy Spirit : 5. **Ask** for the Holy Spirit. (see Luke 11:13) 6. **Wait** for the Holy Spirit, the promise of the Father. 7. **Be baptized** with the Holy Spirit. (see Acts. 1:4-5)	For you will **receive Power** when the Holy Spirit comes on you and you **will be My witnesses** to the ends of the earth. (see Acts. 1:8/NIV)

Blasphemy against the Holy Spirit:

We can harden our hearts by constantly grieving, resisting and quenching the Holy Spirit, to such an extent that we will not be convicted of our sins by the Holy Spirit any more. We may end up committing blasphemy against Him.

For example, if a man of God is doing miracles under the anointing of the Holy Spirit, watch over your words and do not say that he is operating by the power of Satan. This is blasphemy against the Holy Spirit. (see Matt.12:24-32)

1. ***Power to Overcome Sin offered only by Jesus Christ:*** All religions teach good morals; for example, walk in love, forgive one another, do not steal etc., but only our Lord Jesus offers us the power and the presence of the Holy Spirit, to overcome sin, Satan and the world. Make use of the power of the Holy Spirit that is available to you to have a victorious life.

2. **"Revival" By The Holy Spirit...**If we want to have revival in our nation, it will not be by our might, nor by our power but only by the outpouring of the Holy Spirit. (see Zech.4:6)

COMMANDMENT OF GOD FOR US TO OBEY	REWARD FOR OBEDIENCE/ CONSEQUENCE OF DISOBEDIENCE
Be Committed to God: 8. Be the person who has it, to receive more and to have an abundance. (see Matt. 13:12/ NIV) ("It" could mean a little talent, a vision, the Word, the Holy Spirit, or the spirit of prayer, etc.)	Whoever has will be given more and he will have an abundance. But whoever does not have, even what he has will be taken from him. (see Matt. 13:12/NIV)

1. He who is faithful in what is least is faithful also in much. He who is unjust in what is least is unjust also in much. (see Luke 16:10/KJV)

2. For example, if you have only a little oil (Holy Spirit) in your lamp, and if you do not strive to get more, you will end up losing whatever little you have, by your careless walk before God.

3. If you have a little burden for lost souls, and you start interceding for them, then God will entrust you with a higher calling to reach out to the multitudes.

4. A believer's position and inheritance in Heaven will be based on his commitment to God on this earth.

14.1 Who Is The Holy Spirit?

I. "Person" of The Holy Spirit:

1. He is one of the three persons in the Holy Trinity and He is the One who is on the earth today after Christ ascended to Heaven. (see Jn.14:17)

2. He is a very gentle Spirit who can be easily grieved. (Eph.4:30)

3. He is a real person. He has feelings, emotions, intellect and will - power of His own.(see 1 Cor.12:11)

4. He thinks, loves, gives, receives, perceives and also *communicates* like us. He loves to have fellowship with us more   than we desire to be with Him.

5. *He imparts gifts* and talents to the children of God according to His will. (see 1 Cor.12:11)

6. *He gives us power* to live a successful Christian life.

7. The Holy Spirit is as powerful as Father God and Jesus Christ but He functions differently.

II. Holy Spirit, The Comforter...
As Jesus promised, He sent us the Comforter, the Holy Spirit who teaches us all things and brings all things to our remembrance. (see Jn.14:26/KJV)

The word "Comforter" when translated from Greek to English takes up a sevenfold meaning :

1. Comforter - (see Jn.14:16/KJV; Luke 2:25-27)

2. Counselor - (see Jn.14:26, 15:26/NIV)

3. Strengthener - (see Acts 1:5, 8)

4. Intercessor - (see Rom. 8:26-27)

5. Helper - (see Rom. 8:26)

6. Advocate - (see Rom. 8:16; Jn.15:26/NIV)

7. Standby - (see Rom.8:26)

14.2 The Holy Spirit Makes You An Overcomer

Our Lord has promised, "In the last days I will pour out My Spirit upon all flesh." God is willing to anoint us with His precious Holy Spirit, not only up to our ankles or knees or waist but to the overflowing of our hearts.

All we need to do is to desperately cry out for the power of the Holy Spirit to be an overcomer. (see Ezek. 47:1-12; Joel 2:28)

Eternal Rewards For An Overcomer

1. The Overcomer will **eat of the Tree of Life** which is in the midst of the paradise of God and will also receive a **Crown of Life.** (see Rev.2:7, 10)

2. The Overcomer will **not** be hurt of the **second death.**(see Rev. 2:11)

3. The Overcomer will eat of the **hidden manna** and will receive a **white stone** that has a **new name** written on it which no man knows but he who receives it. (see Rev. 2:17)

4. The Overcomer will receive the **morning star**, Jesus as well as **power over nations.** (see Rev. 2:26-28)

5. The Overcomer will be clothed in **white raiment** and his **name** will not be blotted out of the **Book of Life** but Jesus will confess his name before His Father and His angels. (see Rev. 3:5-6)

6. The Overcomer will be made a **pillar in the temple of God** and Jesus will write upon him the **Name of His Father** and the name of the city of God which is **New Jerusalem** and the **new Name of Jesus Christ.** (see Rev.3:12)

7. The Overcomer will **sit with Jesus on His throne** even as Jesus sat with His Father on His Father's throne.

   What an honor it would be for us, Overcomers, on that Final Day, to receive all these rewards !

14.3 Will Your Lamp Burn Until The Bridegroom Comes?

You are the light of the world. Let your light so shine before men, that they may see your good works, and glorify your Father in Heaven. (see Matt. 5:14,16)

COMMANDMENT OF GOD FOR US TO OBEY	REWARDS FOR OBEDIENCE
The Parable of the Ten Virgins: 1. Be like the five wise virgins who took burning lamps along with oil in jars to meet the bridegroom. (see Matt. 25:1,4/ NIV)	1. The Kingdom of Heaven will be like ten virgins who took their lamps and went out to meet the bridegroom. 2. When the bridegroom came the five wise virgins, who were ready, went in with him and the door was shut. (see Matt. 25:1,10/ NIV)
2. Watch and be ready always. (see Matt.25:13/NIV)	For you know neither the day nor the hour in which the Son of Man is coming. (Matt. 25:13)

1. In this parable, the virgins represent believers who are expecting their bridegroom, Jesus Christ.
2. The burning lamp is symbolic of the virgin's intimate relationship with the Lord. The oil is symbolic of the Holy Spirit.

Why were they called wise virgins?

1. **Burning lamps with extra oil…**The wise virgins acted prudently and took extra oil along with their burning lamps.

2. **Wise counsel…**They did not show any compassion towards the other five virgins who wanted to borrow some oil but asked them to get the oil from the seller. They acted wisely because if they had lent some oil to them, it would not have been sufficient for all of them.

3. **Readiness…**They were expecting the Bridegroom and were fully prepared to meet Him.

Are you ready like the five wise virgins to meet your Bridegroom, Jesus Christ?

Is The Church Ready To Meet Her King?

Christ indicates in this Parable that He will not wait until all Churches are prepared for His coming.

It is sad that a large portion of the "Church" may not be ready at the time of His return. (see Matt. 25:8-13)

COMMANDMENT OF GOD FOR US TO OBEY	CONSEQUENCES OF DISOBEDIENCE
3. Do not be like the five foolish virgins who took their burning lamps but took no oil with them. (see Matt. 25:3)	The Bridegroom Jesus said to them, "I do not know you" and they could not go in with Him and the door was shut. (see Matt.25:11)

1. **Foolish Virgins, Not Fully Prepared...** The foolish virgins also anticipated the bridegroom's coming but were not fully prepared.
2. **Last minute preparation will not help you...** You should be in the will of God at all times to receive the extra oil of the Holy Spirit to meet your bridegroom as His worthy bride unlike the foolish virgins.
3. **Intimacy With The Lord...** If you are not careful in your daily personal relationship, you are in danger of being excluded from His Kingdom.

Why The Foolish Virgins Were Rejected By The Bridegroom?

Burning lamps but no extra oil... The virgins met the basic criteria to be the brides of Christ. They found out the place and the day of His coming. They went out to meet the bridegroom with burning lamps but did not take extra oil with them.

Desire and persistence... The virgins did not go back home when the bridegroom delayed His coming. They had the desire to meet with the bridegroom. They paid the price by waiting until midnight. But the price they paid was not enough to be chosen by the bridegroom.

Not fully prepared... The virgins did not anticipate that their lamps would go out. They could only meet their bridegroom with the burning lamps. They slept along with the wise virgins. While the wise virgins slept, they could have gone out to buy oil.

Too late... They returned a little later with burning lamps but it was too late and they were rejected by the Bridegroom.

Are you a wise virgin or a foolish virgin?

15. His "Great Commandments" On Love

*God's Unfailing Love Towards Us...*God is Love. His love is a selfless love that embraces the entire world of sinful mankind. The chief expression of that love was His sending of Jesus, *His only son, to die for us*, while we were yet sinners. (see 1 Jn.4:8-10; Jn.3:16)

Christ's love for humanity is so deep and enduring that **He does not want anyone to perish** but everyone to come to repentance. We must be rooted and grounded in His love to comprehend what is the **breadth and length and depth and height of the love of Christ.** (see 2 Peter 3:9; Eph. 3:17-19)

COMMANDMENT OF GOD FOR US TO OBEY	REWARDS FOR OBEDIENCE
The First Great Commandment of Christ: 1. **Love the Lord** your God, with all your **heart,** 100% with all your **soul,** 100% with all your **mind,** 100% with all your **strength,** 100% (see Matt. 22:37; Mark 12:30/NIV)	Jesus says, 'Whoever has My commands and obeys them, he is the one who loves Me. **'He who loves Me will be...** 1. Loved by My Father and 2. I too will love him and 3. Show Myself to him and 4. We will come to him and 5. Make our home with him.' (see Jn.14:21,23/NIV)

1. **God Tests Your Love**...God may test your love for Him. For example, He will give you a choice - between Him and your education; your job or His calling, etc. Get back to your first love if you have backslidden from God. (see Rev. 2:4,5)

2. **Do we Love the Lord as He expects us to?**
   We often sing songs to the Lord without even understanding the meaning of the songs. For example, we sing "All to Jesus, I surrender..." when we still hold on to the things of the world.

15.1 Ways To Express Our Love For God

1. The Lord expects us to have a devoted love for Him. (see Deut. 6:5)

2. We can reveal our love for Him by longing for His friendship. (see Jn.15:14-15)

3. We can express our love for Him through our obedience. (see Jn.14:21)

4. We can show our love for Him by seeking *His Honor and Glory* in everything we do and say. (see 1 Cor.10:31)

5. We can exhibit our love by being faithful in our commitment to Him. (see Col. 3:17)

6. If we truly love Him, we will not deny Him at any cost; even at the point of death.

7. We must love Him wholeheartedly because He first loved us. (Jn.3:16)

Where do you stand in your love for the Lord?

15.2 The Second Great Commandment Of Christ

COMMANDMENTS OF GOD FOR US TO OBEY	REWARDS FOR OBEDIENCE/ CONSEQUENCES OF DISOBEDIENCE
1. Love your neighbor as yourself. (Matt. 22:39/NIV)	1. For all the law and the prophets hang on these two commandments. (Matt. 22:39-40/NIV)
2. 'Love one another. (see Jn.13:35/NIV)	2. By this all men will know that you are **My disciples.**' (see Jn.13:35/NIV)

1. **Blessing…**On the judgment day, our King Jesus will say to those on His right hand,
   "Come, you blessed of My Father, inherit the Kingdom prepared for you from the foundation of the world." (see Matt. 25:34/NKJV)
   For whatever you did for one of the least of My brothers, you did it for Me. (see Matt. 25:40/NIV)

2. **Curse…**The King will say to those on His left hand,
   "Depart from Me, you cursed, into the **Everlasting Fire,** prepared for the devil and his angels." (see Matt. 25:41/NKJV)
   'For whatever you did not do for one of the least of My brothers, you did not do for Me.' (see Matt. 25:45/NIV)

How Can We Love Our Neighbours?

- By feeding those who are hungry.
- By providing clothes to the needy.
- By helping strangers like the Good Samaritan.
- By visiting the sick.
- By visiting those in prison. (see Matt. 25:31-46)

15.3 Love Your Neighbour As Jesus Loved You

Jesus says "A new commandment I give unto you, that you love one another as I have loved you. By this all men will know that **you are My disciples** if you love one another."(Jn.13:34-35)

The characteristics of true love -

1. Love is **patient.**
2. Love is **kind.**
3. Love does **not envy.**
4. Love does **not boast.**
5. Love is **not proud.**
6. Love is **not rude.**
7. Love is **not self-seeking.**
8. Love is **not easily angered.**
9. Love **keeps no record of wrongs.**
10. Love **thinks no evil.**
11. Love does not delight in evil but rejoices in the truth.
12. Love **bears all things.**
13. Love **believes all** things.
14. Love **endures all** things
15. Love **always trusts**
16. Love always hopes.
17. Love **never fails.**
18. Though we **give all** we possess to the poor but **have not love**, we gain **nothing in Heaven.**
19. God values genuine love greater than ministry, faith or spiritual gifts. Love is the greatest of faith, hope and love. (see 1 Cor.13:3-8,13)
20. **Love covers all sins.** (Prov.10:12)

How do we receive this "Christ-like love"?

It is poured out into our hearts **by the Holy Spirit** as we wait on Him. (see Rom. 5:5)

16. "I Am The Lord That Healeth Thee"

Jesus healed the lepers, the blind, the crippled, the deaf and the dumb and even set free the demon-possessed when He walked on earth. You too can experience the same miracle working power of Jesus today, simply by following the principles brought out in the healings given below:

16.1 Touch Of Jesus Cleanses The Leper

COMMANDMENTS OF GOD	REWARDS FOR OBEDIENCE
Specific Commands To The Leper: 1. Be cleansed. 2. See that you tell no one. 3. Go your way. 4. Show yourself to the priest. 5. And **offer the gift that Moses commanded**, as a testimony. (see Matt. 8:1-4)	Jesus put out His hand and touched the leper, saying, I am willing; be cleansed. And immediately his leprosy was cleansed. (see Matt. 8:3)

How Did The Leper Receive His Healing?

1. The leper approached Jesus, the Living God, for his healing.
2. The leper worshipped Jesus and honored Him as "Lord".
3. The leper **believed** in Jesus' ability to heal him; for he said "Lord, if You are willing, You can make me clean" which exhibits the leper's faith.
4. The leper had to offer a gift of thanksgiving to God after he received his healing.

16.2 Faith Makes You Whole

Command to the woman with the issue of blood: Daughter, be of good comfort. (see Matt. 9:22; Mark 5:22-43/KJV)	For thy faith has made thee **whole**. (see Matt. 9:22; Mark 5:22-43/ KJV)

The woman who had been subject to bleeding for 12 years came up behind Jesus and touched the edge of His garment saying to herself, If only I touch His cloak, I will be -healed. This woman plugged her faith into the unlimited power of Jesus and drew her healing from the Lord. The woman was made well from that hour. (Matt. 9:22)

16.3 Great Faith Of A Gentile

COMMANDMENT OF GOD	REWARD FOR OBEDIENCE
Specific Command to the Centurion: Go your way; and **let it be done for you as you have believed.** (see Matt. 8:13/ NIV)	Jesus marvelled at the centurion's great faith and said to those who followed, "Assuredly, I say to you, I have not found such great faith, not even in Israel! Then Jesus said to the centurion, "Go your way; and as you have believed, so let it be done for you." And **his servant was healed** that same hour. (see Matt. 8:10-13/NIV)

The characteristics of the Roman centurion that brought about his servant's healing:

1. *Approached The Living God…*The Roman centurion came to Christ, the True and Living God, pleading for help.

2. *Honored Jesus as Lord…*The centurion, a Gentile, called Jesus "Lord" giving Him the honor that is due unto Him.

3. *Humility Manifested…*He counted himself unworthy of having Jesus into his house thereby displaying his humility.

4. *Great Faith Expressed…* The centurion exhibited great faith in Christ by saying, "Lord, just speak a word and my servant will be healed."

5. *Acted On His Faith…*The centurion believed Christ's words and undoubtedly held on to the Lord's *promise* on his way back home.

6. *Love For His Servant…*The centurion showed such loving concern for another person even though he was just a servant.

16.4 Sickness Can Be Due To Unconfessed Sins

COMMANDMENT OF GOD	REWARDS FOR OBEDIENCE
Jesus' Command To The Man With Palsy: Son, be of good cheer. Arise, take up your bed, and go to your house. (see Matt.9:2,6/NIV)	1. Arise, because *your sins are forgiven.* (see Matt. 9:1-2/NIV) 2. He immediately obeyed the Lord, *arose and departed* to his house. (see Matt.9:7/NIV)

1. *The paralytic was healed because of the following reasons:*
   The *faith* of his four good friends.

   Their *act of kindness* to bring him to Jesus.

   *Persistence...*They did not give up when the crowd blocked their entrance. They persisted in their faith and reached out to Jesus through the roof. (see Matt.9:1-7)

2. *Steps to follow to receive your healing:*
   Confess your trespasses to one another, and pray for one another, that you may be healed.

   The effective, fervent **prayer of *a* righteous** man avails much.

   The **prayer of faith** will save the sick, and the Lord will raise him up. And if he has committed sins, he will be forgiven. (see James 5:15-16)

16.5 Jesus Will Not Take Responsibility For Our Stupidity

Resist the spirit of infirmity... Scripture says that *every good and perfect gift comes from the Father of lights* and sickness is not a good and perfect gift. Sicknesses, diseases and infirmities are not from God but from Satan. Therefore, every time you are sick, you must rebuke the spirit of infirmity. (see James 4:7)

Bear the consequences... Take good care of your health, for your body is the temple of the Holy Spirit. If you abuse the natural laws of health, you may get sick, for example, by not taking timely meals and vitamins, lack of exercise, etc. Jesus will not take responsibility for your foolishness. (see 1 Cor.6:19)

16.6 Jesus Still Heals The Blind

Believer's Healing, only through His Covenant…God may heal the unbelievers out of His mercy but He heals the believers because of His covenant with them; for they are the spiritual children of Abraham, the father of faith.

God expects *faith and obedience* from us so that we can receive His covenant blessings.

COMMANDMENTS OF GOD	REWARD FOR OBEDIENCE
Healing of the 2 Blind Men: 1. Believe that I am able to do the miracle. (see Matt. 9:28/KJV) 2. *According to your faith, be it to you.* (see Matt. 9:29)	Jesus touched the blind men's eyes and said "According to your faith will it be done to you." And their *sight was restored*. (see Matt. 9:29-30/NIV)
1. The two blind men followed Jesus, crying out, "Have mercy on us, O Son of David." 2. The blind men sought the Lord for His mercy but Jesus still expected them to show at least a mustard seed like faith, to receive their healing from Him.	

COMMANDMENT OF GOD	CONSEQUENCES OF DISOBEDIENCE
Specific Command To The Blind Men: 3. See that no one knows about the miracle. (see Matt. 9:30/NIV)	1. You are those who justify yourselves before men, but God knows your hearts. 2. For what is highly esteemed among men is an *abomination in the sight of God*. (see Lk.16:15)
Jesus never wanted to receive fame from people. He only appreciated the testimony which He received from His Father. (see Jn.8:17-18)	

16.7 Why Trust Jesus For Our Healing?

1. **Jesus' Sacrifice on the Cross** - By **His stripes** we are healed. (see Is.53:5)

2. **Jesus' Mercy & Compassion** - While on earth, Jesus was moved with compassion and healed the great multitude of people who came to Him.

3. **Jesus' Unchanging Nature** - Jesus will do the same for us today. For He is the same yesterday and today and forever. (see Heb.13:8)

4. **Jesus' Will** - It is His will that we be healed and live in good health. (see James 1.17)

5. **Jesus' Word** – For He sent His Word and healed their diseases. (see Ps.107:20)

6. **The Spirit of the Lord** -The anointing of the Holy Spirit breaks the yoke of bondage of infirmity; The Lord is that Spirit. (Is. 10:27; 2 Cor.3:17)

16.8 The Lord's Ways of Healing

Our Lord Jesus is very creative. He used different methods to heal the blind in three separate instances.

First Method of Healing - by Faith: Jesus said to the two blind men who approached Him for healing, "According to your faith, it shall be done unto you." He touched and instantly healed the eyes of the blind men. (see Matt.9:27-31)

Second Method - by Faith and Obedience: In another instance, Jesus spat on the ground, made clay of the spittle and anointed with the clay the eyes of the man who was born blind; Jesus said to him, **Go, and wash** in the pool of Siloam. The man went his way, washed, and came seeing.

Here, the blind man had to believe Jesus' Word and **act on it** in obedience to receive his healing. (see John 9:1-12)

Third Method: Step-by-Step Healing by His Grace: In Mark 8:22-26, when the people asked Jesus to touch and heal the blind man, instead,

i. Jesus **took** the blind man by the hand and **led** him out of the town;

ii. and **spat** on his eyes;

iii. and **put His hands** upon his eyes,

iv. and **asked** him, Do you see anything? The man looked up and said, I see men **as trees**, walking.

v. Again, Jesus **put His hands** on the blind man's eyes,

vi. and made him **look up**;

vii. he was **restored** and saw every man clearly.

Jesus did not heal everyone instantaneously. In this case, it was a gradual healing.

Hear & Follow The Holy Spirit:

You need to wait on the Lord in prayer to **find out the specific method** He chooses for your healing. Obey His instructions to receive your healing.

For example,

(i) if the Lord asks you to just "Rest" for a while, you do the same.

(ii) If Jesus asks you to take medicines, you obey Him. There is nothing wrong in taking medicines.

(iii) If the Lord asks you to go for surgery, listen to Him and use the medical technology that is available, for the wisdom of the doctors is from the Lord.

(iv) If the Lord asks you to rely on His Word, *His promises of healing*, then stand firm in faith, never doubting. Be still and see the salvation of the Lord. Our Lord will never test you beyond your level of faith.

(v) Remember, it is the Lord who is the Healer, our Jehovah Rapha and He must get all the Glory.

Do not choose your own method of healing.

17. Is Your Marriage Ordained By God?

COMMANDMENT OF GOD FOR US TO OBEY	REWARDS FOR OBEDIENCE
Be united to your spouse: 1. Leave your father and mother and be united to your wife. (see Matt. 19:5/NIV)	1. The husband and the wife will ***become one flesh***. 2. Therefore, what God has joined together, ***let not man separate***. (see Matt. 19:5-6/NIV)

1. **Who Ordained Marriage?**
   Marriage was instituted and designed by God Himself. (see Gen.2:18-25)

2. **Purpose of Marriage:** The very purpose of marriage ordained by God is for companionship and intimacy. (see Gen. 2:18)

3. Do not neglect your parents but make sure their basic needs are met.

COMMANDMENT OF GOD	CONSEQUENCES OF DISOBEDIENCE
Unbelieving spouse may bring God's wrath on you: 2. Do not be unequally yoked together with unbelievers. (2 Cor.6:14-16)	1. For we are the temple of the living God. (2 Cor.6:14-16/NIV) 2. Do not intermarry with unbelievers for they will turn you away from following Me to serve other gods. 3. Then **the Lord's anger will burn against the believer** and will quickly destroy him. E.g. King Solomon. (see Ex. 34:16; Deut. 7:3-4; 1 Kings 11:1-10)

If you are already married to an unbeliever...

1. If any brother has a wife who is not a believer and she is willing to live with him, he must not divorce her. And if a woman has a husband who is not a believer and he is willing to live with her, she must not divorce him.

2. But if the unbeliever leaves, let it be so. The believer is not bound in such circumstances; God has called us to live in peace. (see 1 Cor.7:12-13, 15/NIV)

Advice to the Unmarried... Partner of God's choice: It is better to pray and find a life partner of God's choice, for it is a turning point in your life. But you must be willing to accept whoever God chooses for you regardless of his/her financial status, qualification, family background, etc.

Believe that God will only give you what is best for you. When you accept God's choice joyfully, then He will bring the best out of your life; for He knows the end from the beginning. For example, Abraham's servant prayed to find a suitable bride for his master's son, Isaac and God answered his prayer favorably. (see Gen.24:12-14)

Husband's Commitment In Marriage

1. **Love as Christ loved...**Husbands must love their wives even as Christ loved the church and died for the church. (see Eph.5:25)

2. **Love as you love Your Own Body...**Husbands ought to love their wives as their own bodies and not be harsh with them. (see Eph.5:28; Col.3:19)

3. **Nourish and Cherish your Wife:** He that loves his wife loves himself. For no man ever yet hated his own flesh; but nourishes and cherishes it even as the Lord nourishes the church. (see Eph.5:28-29).

4. **Treat Her with Respect...**Husbands ought to treat their wives with respect and as equal heirs of God's gifts so that their prayers are not hindered. (see 1 Pet.3:7)

5. **Treat Her as Equal...**Since Eve was taken not from the head nor from the feet of Adam but from his side (rib), the wife should be treated as equal with her husband and not above him or under his feet.

6. **Appreciate** the noble character and the goodness of your wife. (Prov.31:10-31)

7. **Praise the woman who Fears the Lord;** for charm is deceptive and beauty is vain. (Prov.31:30)

Wife's Commitment In Marriage

1. **Be a Helper...**The wife should be a help-mate to her husband. (see Gen.2:18)

2. **Submit in Love...**The wife should love her husband and submit to him in everything, as unto the Lord; as the church submits to Christ. (see Eph.5:22-24)

3. **Good attitude...**The wife can win her unsaved husband for the Lord, by her good behavior without any talk.

4. **Be Gracious...**Who can find a wife of **noble character**? She is **worth far more than Rubies**. A wife should be a woman of noble character.

5. **Be God-Fearing...**A wife must have the fear of God to be worthy of her husband's praise. (see Prov.31:10-31)

18. Jesus Christ Still Does Miracles

The principles brought out from the following miracles are applicable to our lives even today.

18.1 Obedience Brings God's Favor

COMMANDMENT OF GOD FOR US TO OBEY	REWARDS FOR OBEDIENCE
Specific Command To His Disciples: 1. Depart to the other side of the sea.' (see Matt. 8:18) **2. *Do not be afraid*, you of little faith. (Matt. 8:26/NIV)**	*Calming the Storm:* 1. The disciples immediately obeyed the Lord's command and kept the boat ready. Jesus got into the boat with His disciples; and said to them, Let us go over to the other side of the sea. And they launched out. 2. Suddenly, a great tempest arose on the sea, so that the boat was covered with the waves. But Jesus was asleep. 3. The disciples came to Him and awoke Him, saying, Lord, save us! We are perishing! 4. Then He arose and ***rebuked the winds and the sea, and there was a great calm***. (see Matt. 8:18, 23-27)

Points To Ponder ...

1. **Obeyed But Still Faced Storms...**Though we walk in the path of obedience, sometimes, the Lord may still allow problems in our lives, to teach us to trust Him and also to display His Power.

2. Are you in trouble in spite of being obedient to the Lord? Then, Jesus' help is at hand. *When Jesus is with you in the boat of life, you need not be afraid of any storm* that passes your way. For He has the authority to rebuke the strong winds that blow in your life.

3. **Rebuke the Natural Calamities...**Christ rebuked the winds and the sea and there was a great calm. We should also rebuke the natural calamities like thunderstorms, cyclones, tsunamis, etc., for only the good and perfect gifts come from God and the rest are from the devil. (see James 1:17)

18.2 The Creative Power Of Christ

COMMANDMENT OF GOD	REWARDS FOR OBEDIENCE
Jesus' Specific Command To His Disciples: 1. You give the multitudes something to eat. (Matt. 14:13, 16) 2. 'Bring the five loaves and two fish to Me.' (see Matt. 14:17-18) *Jesus' Specific Command To The Multitudes:* 3. Sit down on the grass. (see Matt. 14:19)	Jesus took the five loaves and the two fish and looking up to Heaven, He blessed and broke, and gave the loaves to the disciples; and the disciples gave to the multitudes. So **they all ate and were filled**. And they were **about five thousand men**, besides women and children. (see Matt. 14:19-21)

1. **Jesus Feeds The Five Thousand...** The creative power of Christ was wonderfully displayed when He multiplied five simple barley loaves and two fish to feed 5000 men, besides women and children.

2. **Jesus, The Bread of Life...** This miracle points to Jesus as the "Bread of Life" for both body and soul.

    For Jesus said "I am the Bread of Life - He that comes to Me shall never hunger; He that believes on Me shall never thirst." (see Jn.6:35)

Lessons To Learn...

1. Show compassion towards the needy as Jesus did.

2. We ought to give ***thanks to God at every meal***, as Christ did before multiplying the loaves.

3. By involving the disciples in this miracle, the Lord teaches us that ***we should do our part and He will do His part.***

4. When we willingly hand over to Jesus the little (money/talents) we have, He will multiply it manifold.

5. We cannot out-give our Lord, for the boy who willingly gave his meal to the Lord, probably went back with the twelve baskets of fragments of bread. (see Matt. 14:19)

18.3 Raise The Dead As Jesus Did

COMMANDMENTS OF GOD	REWARD FOR OBEDIENCE/ SUPPORTING SCRIPTURES
Jesus' Command to Jairus: **1. Do not be afraid; only believe.** (see Mark 5:36) *Jesus' Commands to the People and to the Dead Girl:* 2. "Make room, for the girl is not dead, but sleeping." "Little girl, I say to you, arise." (see Matt. 9:24- 25; Mark 5:41)	Jesus came to Jairus' house and saw the people weeping because the little girl was dead. Then Jesus took the child by the hand and said to her, Little girl, arise. **Immediately the girl arose and walked** and the people were overcome with great amazement. (see Matt. 9:23-25; Mark 5:41)

Pause & Think!

1. **Jesus Conquered Death...**Jesus has the ultimate authority and power over death. For *He is the resurrection and the Life.* (see Jn.11:25)

2. Jesus expects us to use the same authority that is in His Name to raise the dead. (see Matt. 10:8)

3. **Brief but Powerful Prayer...**Jesus did not have to say a long prayer or fast for days even to raise the dead. Since Jesus had close communion with Father God through His intense prayer life, all He had to say in public was "Little girl, arise" just a few words to raise the dead girl up.

    Jesus expects His disciples to follow His example.

18.4 Step Out In Faith

COMMANDMENTS OF GOD	SUPPORTING SCRIPTURES
Jesus' Specific Commands to His Disciples: 1. 'Get into the boat and go to the other side before Me.'(see Matt.14:22) 2. Be of good cheer! **Do not be afraid.** (see Matt. 14:27)	*Jesus Walking on the Sea:* The boat was in the middle of the sea, tossed with waves; for the wind was contrary. In the fourth watch of the night, **Jesus went to the disciples, walking on the sea.** (see Matt.14:24-25)

Power Over Nature…This fascinating miracle brings out the awesome power of God over nature.

Overcome Fear…We fear many things in life but if we keep our focus on Jesus, we can overcome fear; for God has not given us the spirit of fear but of power and of love and of a sound mind. (see 2 Tim.1:7)

COMMANDMENT OF GOD	SUPPORTING SCRIPTURES
Peter walks on Water: 3. "Come." (Matt. 14:29)	And Peter said, "Lord, if it is You, command me to come to You on the water." So He said, "Come." And when Peter had come down out of the boat, he walked on the water to go to Jesus. (see Matt. 14:28-29)

1. This is a specific command to Peter to step out of the boat in the middle of the sea and walk on water in faith, as Jesus did.
2. Remember, our Lord Jesus Christ is **Omnipotent** (all powerful), **Omniscient** (all knowing) and **Omnipresent** (present everywhere) (see Ps.139)
3. When we obey His commands in faith, nothing will be impossible for us to achieve, even if it is "walking on water" as Peter did.

COMMANDMENT OF GOD FOR US TO OBEY	REWARD FOR OBEDIENCE/ SUPPORTING SCRIPTURES
4. O you of little faith, do not doubt. (see Matt.14:31)	When Peter saw that the wind was boisterous, he was afraid; and **beginning to sink**, he cried out, saying, "**Lord, save me!**" And **immediately Jesus stretched forth His hand and caught him**. When they got into the boat, the wind ceased. (see Matt. 14:30-32)

Focus on Jesus & Not on the Problem: When Peter took his eyes away from Jesus and focused on the raging waves, only then he began to sink in the sea.

Jesus Rescues: The Lord immediately responded to Peter's shortest plea for help. Similarly, when we face problems in life, we should not focus on the problems but fix our eyes only on the Lord. Just as He rescued Peter, He will also deliver us from our troubles.

19. Jesus Christ Is Coming Soon!

19.1 Are You Ready To Meet Him?

The **Gospel of Christ shall be preached in all the world** for a witness unto all nations; and **then shall the end come.** (see Matt. 24:14/KJV)

COMMANDMENTS OF GOD	CONSEQUENCES OF DISOBEDIENCE
Behold, I Come Quickly! 1. Take heed that no one deceives you. (Matt. 24:4, 5) 2. Do not be troubled.(Matt. 24:6)	1. For many will come in My Name, saying, I am the Christ, and will deceive many. (Matt. 24:4, 5) 2. When you hear of wars and rumours of wars. (see Matt. 24:6)

Watch Out For The Signs of the Last Days...

1. **False Messiah & Deception:** Many will come in My Name, saying, I am the Christ, and will deceive many. (Matt. 24:5)

2. **Wars:** You will hear of wars and rumors of wars; for all these things must come to pass; but the end is not yet.
   For nation will rise against nation and kingdom against kingdom

3. **Famines:** There will be famines.

4. **Plagues:** There will be pestilences (E.g. AIDS, Mad Cow disease, Bird Flu, etc.)

5. **Earthquakes:** There will be earthquakes in various places.

6. **Sorrows:** All these are the beginning of sorrows.

7. **Afflictions:** They will deliver you up to tribulation.

8. **Murders:** They will kill you.

9. **Persecution for Christ:** You will be hated by all nations for My Name's sake.

10. **Betrayal:** Then many will be offended. And will hate and betray one another.

11. **False Prophets:** Many false prophets will rise up and deceive many.

12. **Iniquity:** Lawlessness will abound in the last days. E.g. Adultery, homosexuality, murders, etc.

13. **Lack of Love:** And the love of many will grow cold. (see Matt. 24:4 -14)

14. **Preaching of the Gospel:** The gospel of Christ will be preached in all the world as a witness to all the nations, and then the end will come.

15. **Endurance:** Only he who endures to the end shall be *saved*. The saved will be those who stand firm in their *faith* through all the end time misery.

Watch Out For the People of the Last Days...	The Believers of the last days should have the "Fruit of the Holy Spirit" i.e.,
There will be terrible times in the last days. People will be...	
1. Lovers of themselves.	1. Love
2. Lovers of money.	2. Joy
3. Boastful.	3. Peace
4. Proud.	4. Patience
5. Abusive.	5. Kindness
6. Disobedient to their parents.	6. Goodness
7. Ungrateful.	7. Faithfulness
8. Unholy.	8. Gentleness
9. Without Love.	9. Self-control (see Gal.5:22-23)
10. Unforgiving.	
11. Slanderous.	
12. Without Self-Control.	
13. Brutal.	
14. Not lovers of the Good.	
15. Treacherous.	
16. Rash.	
17. Conceited (haughty).	
18. Lovers of pleasure rather than lovers of God.	
19. Having a form of godliness but denying its power and	
20. Opposing the Truth – men of depraved minds.	
Have nothing to do with them. (see 2 Tim 3-1-5,8)	

19.2 Flee To The Mountains
(When You See The Antichrist In The Holy Place)

There will be great tribulation, such as has not been since the beginning of the world until this time, no, nor ever shall be. And unless those days are shortened, no flesh would be saved; but for the elect's sake those days will be shortened. (see Matt. 24:21-22)

COMMANDMENTS OF GOD FOR US TO OBEY	CONSEQUENCES OF DISOBEDIENCE/ SUPPORTING SCRIPTURES
1. Let the reader understand - when you see the abomination of desolation, i.e., the antichrist, standing in the Holy place; then let those who are in Judea *Flee to the mountains.* (see Matt. 24:15-16; Dan. 9:27) 2. Let no one on the roof of his house go down to take anything out of the house, but flee. (see Matt 24:17/NIV) 3. Let him who is in the field not go back to get his clothes, but flee. (see Matt. 24:18) 4. Pray that your flight will not take place in winter or on the Sabbath. (see Matt. 24:20/NIV) 5. Do not be deceived by the great signs and miracles done by the false christs and false prophets. (see Matt.24:24/NIV) 6. Do not go out to look for Christ; 7. Do not believe it if anyone says to you, "Look, here is the Christ!" or "There." (see Matt.24:23, 26)	***Signs that will occur during the Great Tribulation:*** 1. False christs and false prophets will appear, and perform great signs and miracles, **to deceive even the elect.**(see Matt. 24:23-24/NIV) 2. *Jesus Christ Comes like the Lightning...*If anyone tells you "There he is, out in the desert" Do not go out; or "Here he is, in the inner rooms," do not believe it. (Matt. 24:26/NIV) For as the lightning comes from the east and flashes to the west; so also will the coming of the Son of Man be. (Matt.24:27)

19.3 Events That Will Take Place When Jesus Christ Returns...

1. The gathering of His faithful saints by the angels. (see Mark 13:27)

2. God's judgment on the wicked. (see Rev. 19: 11-21)

3. **The 1000-year reign of Christ on earth**. (see Rev. 20:4-6)

4. God's judgment on the antichrist and the false prophet. (see Rev. 19:20; 20:1-3)

5. **God's Judgment on Satan** who will be cast into the bottomless pit for a thousand years.

6. Later on, Satan will be thrown into the Lake of Fire and brimstone, to be tormented day and night forever and ever. (see Rev. 20:1-3, 10)

7. **God's Great White Throne Judgment:** If anyone's name is not found written in the Book of Life, he will be thrown into the lake of fire. (see Rev. 20:11-15)

19.4 Signs Of Christ's Coming After The Tribulation

1. The sun will be darkened.

2. The moon will not give it's light.

3. The stars will fall from the sky.

4. The Heavenly bodies will be shaken.

5. Then the sign of the Son of Man will appear in the sky.

6. All the tribes of the earth will mourn.

7. They all will see the Son of Man, the Lord Jesus Christ coming in the clouds of Heaven with power and great glory.

8. Christ will send His angels with a great sound of a trumpet.

9. The angels will gather together *His elect* from the four corners of the earth.

10. The generation which sees the fig tree putting forth it's leaves (i.e., restoration of Israel) will by no means pass away till all these things are fulfilled. (See Matt. 24:29-35)

19.5 The Day & Hour Unknown

COMMANDMENT OF GOD	SUPPORTING SCRIPTURES
1. Watch. (see Matt. 24:42)	1. For you do not know what hour your Lord is coming. (see Matt. 24:42) **2. *The Unexpected Coming of Christ:*** No one knows about that day or hour of Christ's coming, not even the angels in Heaven but only the Father. (see Matt. 24:36/NIV)

*You Be The One Who will be Taken Home...*Two men will be in the field; one will be taken and the other left. Two women will be grinding with the hand-mill; **one will be taken and the other left.** (Matt. 24:40-41/NIV)

We must be ready to meet Christ, as though He is going to come today, yet we should continue with whatever we are good at, as though the Lord will come after a hundred years. Christ's return for the Church is feasible any day since all the prophecies concerning His coming are already fulfilled.

Parable of a Wise & a Faithful Servant: 2. Be a wise and a faithful servant who is ready to meet the Lord. (see Matt: 24:44-45)	**1. Blessed is that servant.** 2. And the Lord will make him **"Ruler"** over all His goods. (see Matt.24:45-47)
3. Do not be an evil servant who is not ready to meet the Lord. (see Matt.:24:48)	For the Lord will come on a day when he does not expect him and **cut him to pieces and assign him a place with the hypocrites;** There will be **weeping and gnashing of teeth.** (Hell) (see Matt.24:51/NIV)

Jesus will come at an hour when you do not expect Him. Be ready at all times. (see Matt.24:44/NIV) If the evil servant lives as he likes, eating and drinking, smiting his fellowmen, saying in his heart, **My Lord delays His coming,** then the Lord will come suddenly and punish him swiftly. (see Matt. 24:48-51)

20. Jesus Christ, The Morning Star Will Guide You

COMMANDMENT OF GOD	REWARDS FOR OBEDIENCE/ SUPPORTING SCRIPTURES
Specific Command to the Wise Men: Do not return to Herod. (see Matt 2:12)	Being divinely warned in a dream that they should not return to Herod, they departed for their own country another way. (see Matt.2:12)

God's Guidance Is Always Complete

Follow God's Direction Till The End... The star which the wise men saw in the East went before them till it came and stood over where the child was. When they saw the star, they rejoiced with exceeding great joy.

And when they were come into the house, they saw the young child with Mary His mother, and fell down and worshipped Him. (see Matt. 2:9-11)

"I will never leave you nor forsake you."
"I am with you always, even to the end of the
age" says Jesus Christ. (Matt.28:20)

21. Life & Death Are In Your Words

The tongue is a fire, a world of iniquity. Therefore, we should pray like the Psalmist, "Set a guard over my mouth, O Lord; keep watch over the door of my lips." (see James 3:6; Ps. 141:3)

COMMANDMENT OF GOD FOR US TO OBEY	SUPPORTING SCRIPTURES
Speak Good Words: 1. Speak good things; 2. Be like the good man who brings forth good things out of the good treasure of his heart. (see Matt. 12:34-35)	For out of the abundance of the heart the mouth speaks. (Matt. 12:34)

1. If you are evil, you cannot speak good things. Jesus calls such people, brood of vipers. (see Matt.12:34)
2. If our hearts are filled with the love of God, then we will be able to speak only kind and encouraging words to others. (see Rom. 5:5)

COMMANDMENTS OF GOD FOR US TO OBEY	CONSEQUENCE OF DISOBEDIENCE
Speak Not Evil Words: 3. Do not be like the evil man who brings forth evil things out of the evil treasure of his heart. (see Matt. 12:35)	**For death and life are in the power of the tongue.** (see Prov.18:21)

Points to Ponder...

1. There are *only two options* given in the Scriptures. The words that we speak will bring forth either death or life. So watch over your words! (see Prov.18:21)

2. *Reckless words pierce like a sword,* but the tongue of the wise brings healing. If any man offends not in word, the same is *a perfect man.* (see Prov.12:18/NIV; Jam. 3:2/KJV)

3. When we don't have the love of God in our hearts, only then we speak hurtful, criticizing and condemning words to reproach others. Sometimes, without our knowledge, we crush their spirit leaving them in depression.

COMMANDMENT OF GOD	CONSEQUENCES OF DISOBEDIENCE
Speak Not Vain Words: 4. Do not speak idle words. (see Matt. 12:36)	1. For ***every idle word*** men may speak, they will ***give account of it*** on the day of judgment. (see Matt. 12:36) 2. By your words you will be **justified**; and by your words you will be **condemned**. (Matt. 12:37)

When words are many, sin is not absent but he who holds his tongue is wise. Prov.10:19/NIV) Let every man be swift to hear, slow to speak, and slow to anger. (see James 1:19)

| *Words Can Defile You:*

5. Hear and understand; do not defile yourself with the words of your mouth. (see Matt.15:11) | 1. "Not what goes into the mouth (i.e., food) defiles a man; for it goes into the stomach and is eliminated.

2. But what comes out of the mouth, from the heart this defiles a man."

3. ***For out of the heart proceed*** evil thoughts, murders, adulteries, fornications, thefts, false witness, and blasphemies. (see Matt. 15:10-11, 17-19) |

1. "Defiling yourself" means corrupting yourself with the wickedness of your heart.
2. An impure heart will defile one's thoughts, words and actions. The heart of the righteous weighs its answers, but the mouth of the ***wicked gushes evil.*** (Prov.15:28/NIV)
3. When we allow Christ to abide in our hearts, then He will transform our hearts into His own image by His Spirit.

| *No Corrupt Speech:*

6. Let your 'Yes' be 'Yes,' and your 'No' be 'No.' (see Matt.5:37) | 1. For ***whatever is more than these is from Satan,*** the evil one. (see Matt.5:37)

2. The **Lord detests** lying lips.

3. But He **delights** in men who are truthful. (Prov.12:22/NIV) |

The Psalmist confessed, 'My tongue shall ***speak of Your Word.*** I open my lips to speak what is right, for my lips detest wickedness.'(Ps.119:172)

22. Possess The Kingdom Of God

22.1 Seek His Kingdom As A Priceless Treasure

COMMANDMENT OF GOD FOR US TO OBEY	REWARDS FOR OBEDIENCE/ SUPPORTING SCRIPTURES
Parable of the Hidden Treasure: 1. Be like the man who found the treasure hidden in a field. (see Matt.13:44)	The man who found the hidden treasure in a field went and sold all he had and bought that field with joy. (see Matt.13:44)
The Kingdom of Heaven is like the treasure hidden in a field. Therefore, we should seek the Kingdom of Heaven as we would seek the hidden treasure. (see Matt. 13:44)	

COMMANDMENT OF GOD	REWARD FOR OBEDIENCE
Parable of the Goodly Pearl: 2. Be like the merchant who sought and found the goodly pearl. (see Matt.13:45)	The merchant, when he had found *the pearl of great price*, he went and sold all that he had and bought it. (see Matt.13:44-46)

These two parables bring forth the following Truth:

1. The Kingdom of God is like the priceless treasure and like the goodly pearl that are to be desired above all else.

2. The Kingdom of God is to be possessed by giving up everything that would prevent our being part of it.

3. To give up everything or sell all you have means that you must transfer your whole heart from other interests to the one supreme interest, i.e., Christ.

4. Possess the Kingdom of God like the man who sold all he had to buy the goodly pearl.

22.2 Believers In The Kingdom Of God

Phil.3:20 says that *our citizenship is in Heaven.* It cannot be bought or handed down to us, but is obtained only by accepting Jesus Christ as our Lord and Savior.

We are aliens in this world. We are in the world but not of the world. We represent Jesus, our King, on earth. So we, through our behavior, attitude, values, morals and concepts of life, must bring the culture of Heaven to earth.

Kingdom Code... In a democratic country, we, the people elect the President to rule over us. But in the Kingdom of God, the King, Jesus Christ is the ultimate authority and He decrees the Law.

As citizens of God's Kingdom, it is mandatory for us to obey the King's Law, the Word of God.

The Bible is called the "Law of God." None of God's Words are for debate but for obedience. This is the Kingdom code.

Angels fight our battles... As the military soldiers fight for their nation, angels who are the warriors in the Kingdom of God fight our battles while we, citizens, just have to petition the King through prayer.

God hears our prayers and deploys His ministering angels to battle with the demonic forces on our behalf. This is called pulling down strongholds. – *Paraphrased from a message heard on TBN.*

22.3 The Kingdom Of God Is Like A Dragnet

Everlasting Kingdom of God...God of Heavens will set up a Kingdom which shall never be destroyed; and the Kingdom shall not be left to other people. It shall break in pieces and consume all the other kingdoms, and it shall stand forever. (see Dan. 2:34-45)

COMMANDMENT OF GOD FOR US TO OBEY	REWARD FOR OBEDIENCE/ CONSEQUENCE OF DISOBEDIENCE
Parable of the Net: Be like the good fish in the net that are collected in baskets. (see Matt. 13:48/NIV)	1. For the Kingdom of Heaven is like a net that was let down into the lake and caught all kinds of fish. 2. When it was full, the fishermen pulled it up on the shore. Then they *collected the good fish in baskets but threw the bad away.* 3. This is how it will be at the end of the age. *The angels will come and separate the wicked from the righteous* and throw them into the *fiery furnace*, where there will be weeping and gnashing of teeth. (see Matt. 13:47-51/NIV)

1. In this parable, a true believer in Christ is symbolic of the good fish in the net.
2. A believer in Christ is the one who lives in true faith and the righteousness of God. Sadly, all professed Christians are not true believers.

22.4 Do Not Despise Small Beginnings

COMMANDMENT OF GOD FOR US TO OBEY	REWARD FOR OBEDIENCE
Parable of the Mustard Seed and Leaven: Be like a grain of mustard seed and the leaven.	1. For the Kingdom of Heaven is like a grain of mustard seed which indeed is the least of all seeds: but when it is grown it is greatest among herbs, and becomes a tree, so that the birds of the air come and lodge in its branches. (Matt. 13:31-32/KJV) 2. For the Kingdom of Heaven is like leaven, which a woman took and hid in three measures of meal till it was all leavened. (Matt. 13:33)

1. The mustard seed and the leaven may appear to be small and insignificant, but they can bring forth great results. (see Matt.13:31-35)
2. **When we are in God's Kingdom...** Believers may have a small and a humble beginning but in the long run, we can impact the world on a large scale, as Christ's twelve disciples did.

23. Praise Him, All Ye Nations

God dwells amongst the praises of His people. (see Ps.22:3)
Whoever offers praise glorifies Me. (Ps. 50:23)

COMMANDMENTS OF GOD FOR US TO OBEY	REWARD FOR OBEDIENCE/ SUPPORTING SCRIPTURES
1. Praise the Lord, all ye nations. 2. Praise Him, all ye people. (see Ps. 117:1/KJV)	For His *merciful kindness* is great towards us; and *the truth* of the Lord endures forever. (see Ps. 117:2)
3. Praise Him like children and infants. (see Matt. 21:16/ NIV)	From the lips of children and infants you have ordained praise because of your enemies, *to silence the foe and the avenger.* (see Ps 8:2/NIV)

Ways to Praise God... We can praise our God with musical instruments, songs, hymns, in the spirit, etc.

When Jesus did many wonderful things in the temple of God, the children and the multitudes cried out, saying, 'Hosanna to the Son of David. Blessed is He who comes in the Name of the Lord. Hosanna in the Highest.' (see Matt.21:15; Mark 11:9-10)

23.1 Worship The Lord & Him Only You Shall Serve

1. Worship the Lord your God and Him only you shall serve. (see Matt. 4:10) 2. Do not worship Me, in vain. (see Matt. 4:7,9; Is. 29:13)	*Worshipping God In Vain...*The Lord says "These people *draw near to Me with their mouth*, and honor Me with their lips, but *their heart is far from Me.* They worship Me in vain; their teachings are but rules taught by men." (see Matt. 15:8-9)

1. Do not worship God in vain, as the Pharisees did. (see Matt. 15:1,7-8) But worship the Lord as His *disciples worshipped Him as the "Son of God"* when they saw Him walking on the sea. (see Matt. 14:33)
2. Do you give all your worship to the Lord or do you give your worship to other idols such as, TV, money, spouse, children, career, sports and movie stars?

23.2 Praise & Worship Takes You Into The Presence Of God

Entering the Outer Court…As you offer thanksgiving to God, you enter into the gates of His Temple. Whenever you begin to pray, you always start in the flesh in the outer court where the devil will try to divert you from praying.

Moving into the Inner Court…Here, you focus your mind on the Lord and as you offer praises to Him, you move from the outer court into the inner court of His Temple.

Into the Holy of Holies…As you worship Him with all your heart, you move from the inner court into the Holy of Holies where the Lord Jesus Himself will lay His hands on you and fill you with His Holy Spirit.

What you could not do for a year on your own, the presence of the Holy Spirit will accomplish it in minutes. Here, your spirit interacts directly with the Spirit of God.

As you make it a practice to *follow this pattern daily,* the Spirit of God will keep cleansing your heart and empowering you for His service. (see Ex.26; 27:9-19

23.3 He Is Worthy Of Your Worship

All of our worship is due only unto Him, for He is the Most Holy God. In Heaven, millions of angels and saints of God, along with the twenty-four elders and the four living creatures, fall prostrate before our God's throne and worship Him that lives forever and ever.

They do not rest day or night, saying, *"Holy, Holy, Holy, Lord God Almighty,* who was and is and is to come!" (see Rev.4:4 -11; 7:9-11)

God Will Never Share His Glory With Anyone... Satan desired God's throne and the worship that is due only to Him and therefore, was cast out of Heaven. (see Matt. 4:9; Is. 14:12-17)

How Do You Worship Him?

God is Spirit, and those who worship Him must *worship in spirit and truth."* (Jn.4:24)

"Worshipping in spirit" means that the Holy Spirit in us intercedes *for* us and *through* us, with much groaning and agony, for we do not know what we ought to pray. (see Rom. 8:26)

"Worshipping in truth" means that we worship God in our own native language with the understanding of the mind; for Jesus Christ is The Truth. (see Jn.14:6)

24. Sabbath, The Sanctified Day

COMMANDMENTS OF GOD FOR US TO OBEY	REWARD FOR OBEDIENCE/ SUPPORTING SCRIPTURES
1. Do good on the Sabbath Day. (see Matt.12:12) 2. Do not forsake the assembling of yourselves together. (see Heb.10:25) 3. Remember the Sabbath day, to keep it Holy. (Ex.20:8)	For the Son of Man is Lord even of the Sabbath. (see Matt. 12:8)

Keep the Sabbath Day Holy... God Almighty sanctified the seventh day to be the day of rest, worship and blessings.

Every believer must observe the Sabbath as a day of worship and as a *sign to the world that we belong to Christ and that He is our Lord and Savior.* (see Gen.2:3)

Since God has set apart the Sabbath day as a holy day, we should not spend time in the worldly things like watching movies, sports, TV. etc., but set apart that one day in a week for the Lord, praying and reading the Word of God.

COMMANDMENT OF GOD	REWARD FOR OBEDIENCE/ SUPPORTING SCRIPTURES
Jesus' command to the man with the withered hand: *4.* Stretch out your hand. (Matt. 12:13)	1. He obeyed immediately and his **hand was restored as whole** as the other. 2. The Pharisees were furious with Jesus because **He did this miracle on the Sabbath day.** (see Matt. 12:13)

1. The Pharisees in Jesus' time misinterpreted the Sabbath laws and became legalistic about observing the Sabbath and would not even show kindness to someone who was in need on that day.

2. But Jesus rebuked the Pharisees by saying, **"It is lawful to do good on the Sabbath."** And He taught them a lesson by healing the man on the Sabbath day.

25. Step By Step Counsel Of God

COMMANDMENT OF GOD	SUPPORTING SCRIPTURES
Specific Commands to Joseph: 1. Do not be afraid to take Mary as your wife. (see Matt.1:20/ NIV)	Because what is conceived in her is from the Holy Spirit. (see Matt. 1:20/ NIV)
2. You shall call His name Jesus. (see Matt.1:21)	For He will save His people from their sins. (Matt.1:21)
3. Arise, and take the young child and His mother, flee to Egypt, and stay there until I bring you word. (Matt.2:13)	For king Herod will seek the young child to destroy Him. (see Matt. 2:13)
4. Arise, take the young child and His mother, and go to the land of Israel. (Matt. 2:20)	For those who sought the young Child's life are dead. (Matt. 2:20)
5. Turn aside into the region of Galilee. (see Matt. 2:22)	When he heard that Archelaus was reigning over Judea instead of his father Herod, he was afraid to go there. And being warned by God in a dream, he turned aside into the region of Galilee. (Matt. 2:22,23)

Points to Ponder:

1. **Do Not Try To Figure Out God's Ways, Just Obey...**Sometimes, God will reveal the reasons why you ought to obey Him; other times, *He may not reveal the reasons but you still have to obey Him because He says so.* For example, God asked Abraham to sacrifice his son, Isaac, without giving him any reason. (see Gen. 22:2) If you disobey God by trying to figure out His ways, you may end up bearing the consequences.

2. *God may not reveal all the details of His plan in the beginning.* But as you obey Him, He will counsel you step by step like He counselled Mary, Joseph, Abraham etc.

3. By his "step-by-step" obedience to all of God's commands, *Joseph absolutely fulfilled the will of God for his life*. Great will be his reward in Heaven for Eternity. What about you?

26. Teachers of God's Word

The Lord Jesus was displeased with the religious leaders of His time and rebuked them for being self-righteous, hypocritical, proud, greedy, self-indulgent, etc.

The following Commandments that Jesus expected the religious leaders to obey are still applicable to the present day teachers of God's Word.

26.1 Jesus' Power To Forgive Sins

An angel of the Lord appeared to Joseph in a dream saying that Mary would bring forth a Son, and Joseph should **call His name JESUS, for He will save His people from their sins.** (see Matt. 1:20-21)

COMMANDMENT OF GOD FOR US TO OBEY	SUPPORTING SCRIPTURES
Do not entertain evil thoughts in your hearts. (see Matt. 9:4/NIV)	1. Some men brought to Jesus a paralytic, lying on a bed. Jesus, seeing their faith, said to the paralytic, "Son, be of good cheer; **your sins are forgiven**. 2. Arise, take up your bed, and go to your house." And **he arose and departed** to his house. (see Matt. 9:2-8)

1. The Lord Jesus stated this to the teachers of the law who questioned His authority to forgive sins.
2. Jesus proved to the unbelieving teachers of the law that He had power on earth to forgive sins by first forgiving the sins of the paralytic and then healing him.

26.2 "I Desire Mercy & Not Sacrifice"

COMMANDMENT OF GOD FOR US TO OBEY	SUPPORTING SCRIPTURES
Be Kind & Not Legalistic: Go and learn what this means: I desire mercy and not sacrifice. (Matt. 9:13/NIV)	For Jesus says, I did not come to call the righteous but sinners, to repentance. (see Matt. 9:13)

1. The Lord stated this to the Pharisees who thought they were perfect.
2. The Pharisees believed that by their offerings, they could please God.
3. Jesus taught the Pharisees that ***He would rather show kindness and lead a sinner to Salvation*** than be legalistic and stay away from sinners by judging them.
4. For example, Jesus chose Matthew, a tax collector as one of His disciples when others disliked him. (see Matt. 9:9)

26.3 Honor God, Not With Your Lips But With Your Heart

COMMANDMENT OF GOD FOR US TO OBEY	SUPPORTING SCRIPTURES
God Sees Your Heart: Be ye not hypocrites. (see Matt. 15:7)	Jesus called the Pharisees "hypocrites" saying, "These people draw near to Me with their mouth, and ***honor Me with their lips, but their hearts are far from Me.*** In vain they worship Me, teaching *as doctrines the commandments of men.*" (see Matt. 15:7-9)

1. The Lord detests the sacrifice of the wicked but the prayer of the upright pleases Him. (Prov.15:8/NIV)
2. The Lord is pleased with the worship that comes from a pure heart. God abhors the worship of the hypocrites. For **they preach whatever the people like to hear** - the commandments of men as God's commandments.

26.4 Gospel Not To Be Corrupted By Tradition

COMMANDMENT OF GOD FOR US TO OBEY	SUPPORTING SCRIPTURES
1. Do not transgress the Commandment of God by your tradition. (see Matt. 15:3/KJV) 2. Honor your father and mother; and he who curses father or mother, let him be put to death. (Matt.15:4)	Jesus stated, You Pharisees say, 'whoever says to his father or mother, "whatever profit you might have received from me has been dedicated to the temple" - is released from honoring his father or mother.' (see Matt.15:5-6) Thus *you nullify the Word of God for the sake of your tradition*.(see Matt.15:6/NIV)

Pause & Think!

1. The Pharisees changed the Commandment of God according to their convenience.

2. John's disciples once asked Jesus, "why do we and the Pharisees fast often, but your disciples not fast?" Jesus said to them, **Men do not pour new wine into old wineskins. For the wineskins break and the wine will spill.**

3. The new wine is fresh unfermented grape juice. It is symbolic of the saving message of Jesus Christ. **This Gospel of Grace should not be corrupted by the teachings of the Pharisees. (i.e., the old wineskins)** Here Jesus was trying to teach the disciples how the Pharisees put the heavy yoke of needless fasting upon their followers.

4. Jesus says, "Take My yoke upon you and learn from Me, for I am gentle and humble in heart, and **you will find rest for your souls. For My yoke is easy** and My burden is light. (see Matt. 9:17; 11:29)

5. Therefore, Teachers of God's Word, be warned! Do not put heavy yoke of unnecessary rules upon people.

Witchcraft Is An Abomination To The Lord

We should not misinterpret the Word of God based on tradition, superstition, popular opinion or present day cultural standards, as the Pharisees did. For example, Christians doing witchcraft against others and observing auspicious days based on the sun, stars, etc., are forbidden by God. Scripture says,

There shall not be found among you...

Anyone who makes his son or his daughter pass through the fire,

or one who practices *witchcraft*,

or a soothsayer,

or one who interprets omens,

or a sorcerer,

or *one who conjures spells*,

or *a medium*,

or *a spiritist*,

or one who calls up the dead.

For all who do these things are an abomination to the Lord.

The Gentiles listen to soothsayers and diviners. But as for you, the Lord your God has not appointed such for you. (see Deut.18:10-14)

It is our responsibility to *teach people not to practice witchcraft or go to psychics for counselling* but rather turn to God in times of need; so that we do not transgress the commandment of God.

26.5 Beware Of The Doctrine Of The Teachers Of Law

COMMANDMENT OF GOD FOR US TO OBEY	SUPPORTING SCRIPTURES
Take heed and beware of the leaven of the Pharisees and the Sadducees. (Matt. 16:6)	The disciples understood that Jesus was not telling them to guard against the yeast used in bread, but against the teaching of the Pharisees and Sadducees. (see Matt. 16:12/ NIV)

Pause & Think!

1. The leaven (yeast) is symbolic of evil and corruption. It refers to the teaching of the Pharisees and Sadducees.

2. Jesus calls the teaching of the Pharisees and the Sadducees "leaven" because even a small wrong teaching can influence a large group of people to believe the wrong doctrine.

3. Hence, when you hear a message through any preacher, you should *always check whether it is in line with the Word of God*.

4. *Only The Holy Spirit of God in you can help you understand the Word of God* as He intends to. (see 2 Tim. 3:16-17; Jn.14:26;16:13)

26.6 Do Not Follow The Works Of The Pharisees

COMMANDMENT OF GOD FOR US TO OBEY	SUPPORTING SCRIPTURES
Let Christ Be Your Role Model: Observe and do whatever the teachers of the law tell you, but do not do according to their works. (see Matt. 23:3)	Jesus spoke to the multitudes and to His disciples about the ***Works of the Pharisees,*** saying: 1. The Pharisees do not practice what they preach. 2. They ***put heavy loads*** on men's shoulders, but they themselves will not lift a finger to move them. 3. All their works they do ***to be seen by men.*** 4. **They desire the most important seats in the temple of God.** 5. They love the place of honor at banquets. 6. They expect greetings and honor from people. (see Matt. 23:3-7/ NIV)

Points to Ponder...

1. *The Words of the Lord are pure words; as silver tried in a furnace of earth, purified seven times.* (Ps. 12:6/NIV)

2. The Holy Word of God, although preached by an unclean vessel, a Pharisee like teacher, is purified seven times, as silver is purified in a furnace, before it reaches the hearts of the hearers and produces fruits in their lives.

3. **God pities the innocent** *and ignorant people and does miracles for them* out of His mercy, and not because of the preacher. Be careful to give all the glory to God alone and not to any preacher.

4. **Be warned...**Jesus warns us not to follow the works of the Pharisee like preachers. Do not model your life according to their lifestyle, for you may backslide and may even lose your Salvation.

26.7 Discern The Signs Of Jesus' Coming

COMMANDMENT OF GOD FOR US TO OBEY	SUPPORTING SCRIPTURES
Living in end times: Discern the signs of the times. (see Matt.16:3)	O ye hypocrites, you can discern the appearance of the sky; but can you not discern the signs of the times? (see Matt.16:3/KJV)
In the last days, people will live selfish lives, as in the days of Noah, eating and drinking, marrying and giving in marriage. (see Matt. 24:37-39) Please refer to chapter 19 on "Jesus Christ Is Coming Soon!" for the signs of the last days.	

God Will Make You Accountable For the Lost Souls; For The End Is Near

The Lord says, "On your clothes is found the blood of the lives of the poor innocents, I have not found it by secret search, but plainly on all these things.

Yet you say, 'because I am innocent, surely His anger shall turn from me.'

Behold, *I will plead My case against you, because you say, 'I am innocent.'*" (see Jer. 2:34-35)

So, do not live in luxury and in your comfort zone lost in your own world, not caring about the things of God, when souls around you are perishing and going to hell without knowing their Messiah, Jesus Christ.

Redeem your time. Time lost cannot be regained. Be alert, watch and pray. *Jesus is coming back sooner than you expect.*

26.8 Do Not Be An Adulterous Generation

COMMANDMENT OF GOD	SUPPORTING SCRIPTURES
Do not be a wicked and an adulterous generation; for they seek after a sign.(see Matt. 16:4)	You, my brothers, are called to be free. But ***do not use your freedom to indulge in the sinful nature***. (Gal. 5:13/NIV)

Pause & Think!

Jesus called the teachers of the law "a wicked and an adulterous generation."

It is sad to see that some servants of God who should be role models to others, have lost reverential fear of God and are living in adultery. If they continue to live in sin, ignoring the convictions of the Holy Spirit, then the Lord may judge some of them on this earth while others await judgment till the final day.

26.9 God Opposes The Proud

COMMANDMENTS OF GOD	REWARD FOR OBEDIENCE/ CONSEQUENCE OF DISOBEDIENCE
1. Do not exalt yourself, for you will be humbled. 2. Be humble, for you will ***be exalted***. (see Matt. 23:12)	1. "God opposes the proud but gives grace to the humble." 2. When ***pride comes, then comes disgrace,*** but with humility comes wisdom. (Prov. 11:2/NIV) 3. Pride goes before destruction, and a ***haughty spirit before a fall.*** 4. Better to be of a humble spirit with the lowly, than to divide the spoil with the proud. (Prov. 16:18-19) 5. If anyone thinks he is something when he is nothing, he deceives himself. (Gal.6:3) 6. God gives ***more grace to the humble***. (see 1 Pet.5:5/NIV; James 4:6)

For example, God crushed Haman's pride by judging him to death on the same gallows that he had prepared for Mordecai. (see Est.7:9-10)

26.10 Honor From Men Is An Abomination Before God

COMMANDMENTS OF GOD FOR US TO OBEY	CONSEQUENCES OF DISOBEDIENCE
1. Do not work to be seen by men. (see Matt. 23:5) 2. Love not the place of honor at banquets. (see Matt. 23:6/NIV) 3. Do not love chief seats in the temple of God. (see Matt. 23:6/KJV)	Jesus said to the Pharisees, "You are those who justify yourselves before men, but God knows your hearts. For *what is highly esteemed among men is an abomination* in the sight of God." (Luke 16:15)

1. Jesus Christ, our Master was oblivious to the praises of men. He never worked miracles to draw crowds to Himself.

2. *Jesus often commanded the demons to be quiet* and did not even allow the demons to reveal who He was because they knew that He was the "Son of God." (see Mark 1:32-39)

3. **What About Us?**

   Many of us may feel happy and proud to be introduced by the demons as true servants of God.

   Men-pleasers will not receive rewards in Heaven, for they receive rewards and honor from people on earth. So be quick to give glory to God.

26.11 Jesus, The Only One "Rabbi"

Jesus declared, "*My teaching is not My own. It comes from Him who sent Me.*

If anyone chooses to do God's will, he will find out whether My teaching comes from God or whether I speak on My own.

He who speaks on his own does so to gain honor for himself, but he who works for the honor of the one who sent him is a man of truth; there is nothing false about him." (Jn. 7:16-18/NIV)

COMMANDMENTS OF GOD FOR US TO OBEY	REWARDS FOR OBEDIENCE/ SUPPORTING SCRIPTURES
1. Do not be called "Rabbi." (see Matt.23:8)	For you have only one Master, the Christ and you are all brothers. (see Matt. 23:8/NIV)
2. Do not call anyone on earth "your Father." (see Matt.23:9)	For you have one Father, and He is in Heaven. (see Matt.23:9)
3. Do not be called "teachers."(see Matt. 23:10/NIV)	For you have one Teacher, the Christ. (see Matt. 23:10/NIV)

1. Jesus Christ is the only one who is worthy to be called "Rabbi" and "Teacher" for He is perfect.
2. Nicodemus, a Pharisee and a ruler of the Jews, came to Jesus and said to Him, 'Rabbi, we know that you are a *teacher come from God*; for no one can do these signs that You do unless God is with him." (see Jn. 3:2)

26.12 Serve Others To Be Great In Heaven

COMMANDMENTS OF GOD FOR US TO OBEY	REWARD FOR OBEDIENCE
1. Be a servant to others. (see Matt. 23:11) 2. Serve one another in love. (see Gal.5:13/NIV)	For you will be the **greatest** among others. (see Matt. 23:11)

Pause & Think...

1. We have different gifts, according to the grace given to us. *If a man's gift is serving,* let him serve. (see Rom. 12:7)

2. Each one should use whatever gift he has received to serve others, faithfully administering God's grace in its various forms. If anyone serves, he should do it with the strength God provides so that in all things God may be praised through Jesus Christ. (1 Peter 4:10-11/NIV)

3. *Be Shepherds of God's flock* **that is under your care,** *serving as overseers -*

   not because you must, but because you are willing, as God wants you to be;

   not greedy for money, but eager to serve;

   not lording it over those entrusted to you, but being examples to the flock;

   When the Chief Shepherd, the Lord Jesus Christ appears, you will receive the *crown of glory* that will never fade away. (see 1 Pet.5: 2-4/NIV)

26.13 Jesus' Woes Upon The Religious Leaders

COMMANDMENT OF GOD FOR US TO OBEY	CONSEQUENCES OF DISOBEDIENCE
1. Do not shut up the Kingdom of Heaven against men. (see Matt. 23:13)	1. **Woe to you**, teachers of the law, you hypocrites! 2. For you neither go to Heaven yourselves nor will you let others who are trying to go in. (see Matt. 23:13)

Jesus condemned the religious leaders of His time who had rejected/misinterpreted the Word of God. They had replaced the Word with their own ideas and interpretation.

COMMANDMENTS OF GOD	CONSEQUENCES OF DISOBEDIENCE
2. Do not devour widows' houses. (Matt. 23:14) 3. Do not take advantage of a widow or an orphan. (Exo.22:22/NIV)	1. **Woe to you**, teachers of the law, you hypocrites! For you devour widows' houses, and for a pretence make long prayers. Therefore you will receive *greater damnation.* (Matt. 23:14) 2. God defends the cause of the fatherless and the widow. (Deut. 10:18; Ps. 68:5)

Pure and undefiled religion before God, our Father is this: to *look after orphans and widows* in their trouble and to keep oneself unspotted by the world. (see James 1:27)

When you go to the house of a grieving widow to console her, do not expect anything in return.

26.14 Woe To The Worthless Shepherd

Scripture says, "Woe to the worthless shepherd, who **deserts the flock.**" (Zech. 12:17)

"Woe to the shepherds who are destroying and scattering the sheep of my pasture!" declares the Lord.

Therefore, this is what the Lord says to the shepherds:

"Because you have **scattered my flock** and driven them away and have **not bestowed care on them**, I will bestow punishment on you for the evil you have done." (Jer. 23:1-2/NIV)

COMMANDMENT OF GOD FOR US TO OBEY	CONSEQUENCES OF DISOBEDIENCE
Do not make a convert (new believer) **twice as much a son of hell as you are.** (see Matt. 23:15/ NIV)	1. Woe to you, teachers of the law, you hypocrites! For you travel land and sea to win a single convert. 2. When he becomes a believer, **you make him two fold more the child of hell than yourself** by your lifestyle. (Matt. 23:15)

A new believer tends to look up to the religious leaders for guidance until such time he has grown strong in the Word of God.

Therefore, a shepherd should nurture the believers and guide them in the right path according to the Word of God.

The shepherd's life should be a good example to them, especially to the new converts.

A Religious Leader Must Be...

1. Blameless,

2. the husband of one wife,

3. vigilant,

4. sober minded,

5. of good behavior,

6. hospitable,

7. able to teach (the Word of God);

8. not given to wine,

9. not violent,

10. not greedy for money,

11. but gentle,

12. not quarrelsome,

13. not covetous;

14. one who rules his own house well,

15. having his children in submission with all reverence,

16. not a novice; lest being puffed up with pride he fall into the same condemnation *as the devil.*

17. Moreover, he must have a good testimony among those who are outside, lest he fall into reproach and the snare of the devil.

18. He must be reverent,

19. not double tongued,

20. Holding the mystery of the faith with a pure conscience.

(see 1 Tim. 3:1-9)

26.15 Do Not Be A Blind Guide

COMMANDMENT OF GOD FOR US TO OBEY	CONSEQUENCES OF DISOBEDIENCE
Do not be a blind guide. (see Matt. 23:16)	1. Woe to you, teachers of the law, you hypocrites! 2. For you say, if anyone swears by the temple, it means nothing; but if anyone swears by the gift on the altar or gold of the temple, he is guilty and is bound by his oath. **3. He who swears by the temple swears by it and by the One who dwells in it.** 4. The temple where the presence of God abides is what makes the gift or the gold sacred. (Matt. 23:16-21)

The Pharisees were blind leaders of the blind and if the blind lead the blind, both shall fall in the ditch. (see Matt. 15:13)

Do not be like the Pharisees who were blind to the ways of God. They were so blinded in their self-righteousness that they missed out on the Messiah, Jesus Christ and eventually lost their souls to Hell.

They held honourable positions on the earth but yet did not make it to Heaven. How sad!

26.16 Do Not Strain Out A Gnat & Swallow A Camel

COMMANDMENT OF GOD FOR US TO OBEY	CONSEQUENCES OF DISOBEDIENCE
Do not neglect the more important matters of the Law - justice, mercy and faithfulness.(see Matt. 23:23/NIV)	1. Woe to you, teachers of the law, you hypocrites! 2. For you give a tenth of your spices - mint, dill and cumin. But **you have neglected the more important matters of the Law - justice, mercy and faithfulness.** 3. You should have practiced the latter, without neglecting the former. 4. **You blind guides**! You strain out a gnat but swallow a camel. (see Matt. 23:23-24)

*Tithes...*The Pharisees were obedient to God in paying tithes even in their spices. Since our righteousness should exceed that of the Pharisees, *how much more we need to be faithful in paying tithes to God* to expand His Kingdom.

At the same time, God expects us not to disregard the weightier matters of the Law, i.e., justice, mercy and faithfulness.

26.17 Let The Inside Of Your Heart Be Clean

COMMANDMENT OF GOD	CONSEQUENCES OF DISOBEDIENCE
1. Do not be full of greed and self-indulgence. (see Matt. 23:25/NIV)	1. *Woe to you,* teachers of the law, you *hypocrites!* 2. You clean the outside of the cup and dish, but inside you are full of greed and self-indulgence. 3. *You blind guides,* first clean the inside of the cup and dish, and then the outside also will be clean. (see Matt. 23:25-26/NIV)
2. *Put to death* whatever belongs to your earthly nature: sexual immorality, impurity, lust, evil desires and *greed*, which is idolatry. (see Col. 3:5-6/NIV)	Because of these the *wrath of God* is coming upon you. (see Col. 3:5-6/NIV)
The outward conduct of the Pharisees appeared righteous but their hearts were full of hypocrisy, greed, pride, lust and wickedness.	

26.18 Escape The Damnation Of Hell

COMMANDMENT OF GOD FOR US TO OBEY	CONSEQUENCES OF DISOBEDIENCE
Do not outwardly appear righteous to men and be full of hypocrisy and lawlessness inside. (see Matt. 23:28)	1. Woe to you, teachers of the law, you hypocrites! 2. **For you are like whitewashed tombs** which appear beautiful outwardly, but inside are full of dead men's bones and all uncleanness. 3. Jesus condemned the Pharisees, saying, **You snakes!** You Brood of Vipers! How can you escape the damnation of hell? (see Matt. 23:27,33)

The teachers of God's Word in Jesus' time were so blinded in their self-righteousness that **they interpreted the Word of God with their own reasoning and not by the anointing of the Holy Spirit.**

They could not see the Messiah, Jesus Christ who was in their midst and eventually lost their souls to Hell.

27. 'This Is My Beloved Son, Hear Ye Him'

COMMANDMENT OF GOD FOR US TO OBEY	SUPPORTING SCRIPTURES
1. "This is My beloved Son; in whom I am well pleased. Hear ye Him!" (see Matt. 17:5/KJV)	1. When Jesus was transfigured before His disciples, *His face shone* like the sun, and His clothes became as white as the light.
	2. And behold, *Moses and Elijah* appeared to them, talking with Him.
	3. Behold, a *bright cloud* overshadowed them;
	4. And suddenly a *voice* came out of the cloud, saying, "This is my beloved Son; **in whom I am well pleased.** Hear Him!" (see Matt. 17:1-13)

This was a confirmation by Father God that Jesus is His only true Son in whom He is well pleased.

Peter, James and John had the privilege to see Christ's heavenly glory as He really was - God in human flesh.

COMMANDMENT OF GOD	SUPPORTING SCRIPTURES
2. Arise, and be not afraid. (Matt. 17:7/KJV) 3. Tell the vision to no man until the Son of man is risen from the dead. (see Matt. 17:9)	When the disciples were given this supernatural vision by God, they fell on their faces and were greatly afraid. And Jesus comforted them.(see Matt.17:6-7)

Points to Ponder...

Please Father God, as Jesus did... Our Heavenly Father declared that Jesus is His only true Son in whom He is well pleased. In fact, Father God was so pleased with His Son, Jesus, that every time Jesus prayed, Father God answered His prayers.

For example, before Jesus raised Lazarus from the dead, He lifted up His eyes and said, "Father, I thank You that You have heard Me. And I know that *You always hear Me.*" God will be pleased with us too as He was with Jesus, when we hear Jesus and obey Him. (see Jn.11:41-42)

Be the Privileged Ones... Out of the twelve disciples, only Peter, James and John, received this special revelation from God and saw Jesus being transfigured. We must also desire and pray to be among the privileged ones who receive such divine revelations, the hidden treasures of His Kingdom.

Hunger for Heavenly Visions... The Psalmist prayed, "Open my eyes that I may see wonderful things in Your Law."

The Lord promises us, "Call to Me, and I will answer you, and show you great and mighty things which you do not know." Therefore, desire for the things of the above. (see Ps.119:18/NIV; Is. 45:3; Jer.33:3)

28. Well Done, Good & Faithful Servants!

COMMANDMENT OF GOD FOR US TO OBEY	REWARD FOR OBEDIENCE/ CONSEQUENCE OF DISOBEDIENCE
The parable of the talents: Be like the good and faithful servants who multiplied their (five and two) talents. (see Matt. 25:16-17)	1. The Lord commended the faithful servants and said, 'Well done, good and faithful servants; 2. You have been faithful over a few things; **I will make you Ruler** over many things; 3. Enter into the joy of your Lord i.e., *Heaven.* (see Matt. 25:21,23) **4. Blessings of the Faithful…**A faithful man will abound with blessings. (Prov.28:20) The Lord's eyes are upon the faithful of the land. (see Ps.101:6) The Lord **preserves** the faithful. (Ps. 31:23)

Faithful Men of God…

1. "Moses was faithful in all My house", said the Lord.
2. Timothy was another faithful servant of the Lord. (see Heb. 3:2; Num. 12:7; 1 Cor.4:17)

COMMANDMENT OF GOD FOR US TO OBEY	REWARD FOR OBEDIENCE/ CONSEQUENCE OF DISOBEDIENCE
The Wicked & Lazy Servant Judged: Do not be like the wicked and lazy servant who hid his one talent in the ground. (see Matt. 25:18)	1. The Lord called him a wicked and lazy servant and said, Take the talent from him, and give it to him who has ten talents. *2. Cast the unprofitable servant into the outer darkness,* where there will be weeping and gnashing of teeth. 3. For to everyone who has, more will be given, and he will have abundance; 4. but *from him who does not have even what he has will be taken away.* (see Matt. 25:28-30)

Pause & Think...

1. The Lord did not spare the lazy servant who brought back his talent to the Lord without multiplying it.

2. The wicked servant had the wrong perception about the Lord as a hard man, reaping where He has not sown. He did not have the right kind of relationship with the Lord and therefore did not understand His ways.

3. This wicked and lazy servant was cast into Hellfire for not using his talent for the Lord; for he was not saved in the eyes of the Lord. If he had truly understood the sacrifice the Lord had done for him and if he had made Jesus his Savior and the Lord of his life then he would have definitely multiplied his talents.

4. If you don't use it, you lose it.

What Are Your Talents?

Talent...A talent symbolizes our abilities, resources, time and opportunities to serve God.

Be faithful in small things... He that is faithful in the least is also faithful in the much. The Lord usually tests us and watches carefully to see what we do with a few talents that we have. If we are faithful in small things, He will entrust us with greater responsibilities. So, do not despise small beginnings. (see Luke 16:10)

Use your talents for the Lord... Do you have a lot of time at hand? Think about what you can do for the Lord in your free time?

Can you sing or write songs or lead the worship? Then, use your talents for the Lord. Do not wait for a big opportunity to come your way to make a name for yourself. Seek only God's glory so that God can lift you up at the right time.

Do you have the spirit of prayer and intercession? Then, join with someone and pray for your city or nation. You can raise up intercessors or start prayer groups, etc. *If you are into construction business*, use your talent to build churches for the Lord across your nation, especially in remote villages.

The Holy Spirit knows our potential and accordingly imparts different gifts to us. Gifts and talents are given to us by God to be used for others. The anointing of the Holy Spirit in us must constantly flow to others and not be stagnant. Where there is a will, there is a way. God will make a way to use your talents for His Kingdom if you are available for His service.

29. Why Good & Wicked Live Together On Earth?

COMMANDMENT OF GOD FOR US TO OBEY	REWARD FOR OBEDIENCE/ CONSEQUENCE OF DISOBEDIENCE
The Parable of the Good Seed & Weeds : Be ye like the good seed in the parable that is symbolic of the righteous children of God. (see Matt.13:37, 43)	1. **Final Judgment**...At the end of the age, our Lord will send His angels and they will **gather out** of His Kingdom all things that offend, and those **who practice lawlessness.** 2. And they will cast them into the **furnace of fire**: there will be wailing and gnashing of teeth on that day. 3. **Then the righteous will shine forth as the sun** in the Kingdom of their Father. (see Matt.13:37- 43)

This parable of the good seed and the weeds emphasizes that Satan will sow alongside those who sow the Word of God.

God allows the good and the wicked to live together on this earth until the very end.

The Lord Waits Till The End To Judge The Wicked

1. **Deceivers Vs Righteous**...The good seed represents the true children of God. The weeds represent the followers of Satan, sometimes disguised as believers. It is difficult to distinguish between the righteous and those who pretend to be the children of God. Therefore, the Lord waits till the end to weed out all those who do evil;

   just as it is explained in the parable that if the reapers pull out the weeds when they are growing, they might accidentally root up some of the wheat with the tares/weeds.

   The wicked will be punished and God's children will be rewarded on the final Judgment day. It is a great consolation to those of us who live a righteous life for the Lord.

2. **Jesus' Longsuffering**...The Lord is patient with us, not wanting anyone to perish, but everyone to come to repentance. (see 2 Pet. 3:9)

30. Youth, The Valiant Soldiers Of The Lord

Remember your Creator in the days of your youth, before the days of trouble come and the years approach when you will say, "I find no pleasure in them." (Eccl. 12:1/NIV)

The youth of this generation are not bound by tradition or superstition of the days of old. Since they are open to the truth, they will readily accept the Good News of Jesus Christ when it is given to them.

The knowledge of Christ, the Savior of the world, will penetrate homes through the youth of the nations. This is the promise of the Lord given to this present generation.

God has tremendously used a lot of youth in the past *to fulfil His will on earth*, for example, Joseph, David, Daniel, Jeremiah, etc. Remember, even Jesus was a young man when He was mightily used by Father God.

30.1 Remember Your Creator

COMMANDMENT OF GOD FOR US TO OBEY	SUPPORTING SCRIPTURES
Walk with God: Remember your Creator in the days of your youth. (see Eccl.12:1/NIV)	*Who is your Creator?* Jesus is the image of the invisible God and by Him all things were created that are in Heaven and that are on earth. All things were **created through Him and for Him.** And He is before all things, and in Him **all things consist.** (see Col.1:15-17)
Jesus is not only the Creator but also the Director of the Universe and He longs to have fellowship with you. He is the King of Kings and the Lord of Lords. So walk with your Creator as Enoch did. (see Gen. 5:22; Rev.19:16)	

195

30.2 "Do Not Forget My Law"

COMMANDMENT OF GOD FOR US TO OBEY	REWARDS FOR OBEDIENCE/ CONSEQUENCES OF DISOBEDIENCE
Be Rooted in His Word: My son, do not forget my law, but let your heart keep my commands. (see Prov.3:1/NIV)	**Blessings...** 1. Let your heart keep my commands, for they will ***prolong your life*** many years. 2. They will bring you ***prosperity.*** 3. You will win ***favor and good name*** in the sight of God and man. (see Prov.3:2-4/NIV) *Consequences...* 4. He who ***despises the Word will be destroyed,*** but he who fears the commandment will be rewarded. (Prov.13:13)

1. **How can a young man cleanse his way**; by taking heed according to His Word. (see Ps. 119:9)

2. The Psalmist states, "I will ***delight myself in Your statutes***; I will not forget Your Word.

3. King David declares, "The law of the Lord is perfect, **rejoicing the heart**; the Commandment of the Lord is pure; enlightening the eye; more to be desired are they than gold, yea, than much fine gold; sweeter also than honey and the honeycomb." Therefore, God called David, "The man after My own heart." (see Ps. 119:16;19:7-12/NIV)

30.3 Trust In The Lord & Be Blessed

COMMANDMENTS OF GOD FOR US TO OBEY	REWARDS FOR OBEDIENCE/ CONSEQUENCES OF DISOBEDIENCE
Trust in the Lord with all your heart, Lean not on your own understanding. (see Prov.3:5)	1. "You will keep in **perfect peace** him whose mind is steadfast, because he trusts in you." (Is.26:3-4) 2. The Lord is good, a refuge in times of trouble. He **cares** for those who trust in Him. (Nah.1:7/NIV) 3. *Blessed* is the man who trusts in the Lord, whose confidence is in Him. (Jer.17:7/NIV) 4. *Cursed* **is the one who** *trusts in man* **and whose heart turns away from the Lord. (see Jer.17:5/NIV)**

The Lord is...

i.   The everlasting God,

ii. The Creator of the ends of the earth.

iii. He will not grow tired or weary.

iv. He gives strength to the weary and

v.   He increases the power of the weak.

Even youths grow tired and weary and young men stumble and fall;

But *those who hope in the Lord...*

i.   They will *renew* their strength.

ii. They will *soar on wings* *like eagles.*

iii. They will run and *not grow weary.*

iv. They will walk and not be faint.

   (see Is. 40:29-31/NIV)

30.4 God's Way Or Your Way?

COMMANDMENT OF GOD FOR US TO OBEY	REWARDS FOR OBEDIENCE
Acknowledge Him in all your ways. (see Prov.3:6)	1. And He will make your paths *straight*. (see Prov.3:6) 2. **God's Ways...**God's Way is **Perfect.** All His ways are Just. *All His ways are Just.* (Ps. 18:30; Deut. 32:4) 3. **Our Ways...** There is a way that seems right to the man, but in the end it **leads to death.** *(*Prov.14:12) 4. **Commit your way to the Lord;** trust in Him and He will make your **righteousness shine** like the dawn. 5. **Light to your path...** "Your Word is a lamp to my feet, and a light to my path." (see Ps. 119:105) 6. **Walk according to the Law of God...** Blessed are they whose *ways are* **blameless,** who walk according to the law of the Lord. (see Ps. 119:1/NIV)

When you surrender your ways to the Lord, then He promises you, "I will go before you and make your crooked places straight." (see Ps. 37:5-6/NIV; Is.45:2)

30.5 Avoid The Path Of The Wicked

COMMANDMENTS OF GOD FOR US TO OBEY	CONSEQUENCES OF DISOBEDIENCE
1. My son, if sinners entice you, do not give in to them. (see Prov.1:10) 2. Do not set foot on the path of the wicked or walk in the way of evil men. **Avoid it.** Do not travel on it; turn from it and go on your way. (see Prov.4:14-15) 3. Flee the evil desires of youth, and pursue righteousness, faith, love and peace. (see 2 Tim. 2:22)	1. Bad company ***corrupts good character.*** Do not be misled. (see 1cor.15:33) 2. ***Friendship with the world*** *is* ***enmity with God.*** (James.4:4)

1. Avoid bad friends: When friends entice you to…

    smoke cigarettes,
    drink alcohol,
    watch filthy movies,
    commit sexually immoral acts,
    do drugs,
    gamble,
    live a gay lifestyle, etc.,

then it indicates that they are of the world. Therefore stay away from them and avoid their path.

2. How do you avoid bad company?

Seek The Holy Spirit, Your Helper…Earnestly seek for the power of the Holy Spirit that is always available to you to overcome sin and the world. For He helps you in your weaknesses. (see Rom. 8:26)

For God has not given us a spirit of fear, ***but of Power,*** *and of Love and of a Sound mind.* (see 2 Tim.1:7)

Serve the Lord…Stand firm. Let nothing move you. *Always* ***give yourselves fully to the work of the Lord.***

Because you know that your labor in the Lord is *not in vain.* (see 1 Cor.15:58)

30.6 Are You A Friend Of God Or Of The World?

1. *To be carnally minded is enmity against God...*Do not make any human being your idol, for example, Movie and Sports stars. For the Lord says, "I am the Lord, your God. *You shall have no other gods (idols) before Me.*(see Rom. 8:7; Ex. 20:1-2)

   *Imitate Jesus...*Whoever claims to live in Him, must walk as Jesus did. Make Jesus Christ your role model. (see 1Jn.2:6/NIV)

2. *Do not love the world or anything in the world...*For everything in the world - the cravings of sinful man, the lust of his eyes and the boasting of what he has and does - comes not from the Father God but from the world.

   Do the will of God... The world and its desires pass away, but the man who does the will of God lives forever. (see 1 Jn.2:15-17)

3. *Have God fearing friends...He who walks with the wise, grows wise* but a companion of fools suffers harm. (see Prov.13:20)

   Have good believer friends, fellowship with them and pray with them.

4. *Develop Clean Hobbies...*You can keep yourself occupied with a sports activity, learn to play a musical instrument, develop a creative or productive non-sinful hobby, etc.

   Check yourself. Choose to be a friend of God.

30.7 The Lord Disciplines Whom He Loves

COMMANDMENT OF GOD FOR US TO OBEY	SUPPORTING SCRIPTURES
Do not despise the Lord's discipline and do not resent His rebuke. (see Prov.3:11)	Jesus says, "Those whom I love I rebuke and discipline, so be earnest, and **repent.**" (see Rev.3:19)
The Psalmist said, "Before I was afflicted I went astray, but *now I obey Your Word.* It was good for me to be afflicted so that I might *learn Your decrees." (see Ps. 119:67,71/NIV)*	

God Disciplines Us For Our Good

1. **Share in His Holiness...**God disciplines us for our good that we may share in His Holiness.

2. **Righteousness and Peace...**No discipline seems pleasant at the time, but painful. Later on, however, it produces a harvest of righteousness and peace for those who have been trained by it. (Heb. 12:10-11)

3. **The Lord Loves You...***Do not despise* the chastening of the Lord, nor detest His correction; for whom the Lord loves, He corrects. (see Prov.3:12)

4. **The Lord Receives You...** *Do not be discouraged* when you are rebuked by Him.

   For the Lord chastens and scourges every son whom He loves and receives.

5. **God Treats You As Sons...** Endure hardship as discipline; God is treating you as sons. For what son is not disciplined by his father?

6. **If you are not disciplined,** then you are *illegitimate* children and not true sons. (see Heb.12:5-7)

7. **Prayer...**"May Your unfailing love be my comfort." (see Ps. 119:67-76)

30.8 Place Christ Above Your Wealth

COMMANDMENTS OF GOD FOR US TO OBEY	REWARDS FOR OBEDIENCE
A Rich Young Ruler: 1. Obey the Commandments of God. (see Matt. 19:17/NIV) 2. Go, sell what you have and give to the poor. (see Matt. 19:21)	1. For you will have **Eternal life.** (see Matt.19:16-17) 2. For you will have **treasure in Heaven**. (see Matt. 19:21) 3. You will be **perfect** in God's eyes. (see Matt.19:21)

Points to Ponder...

1. **Young and rich...**The man was rich, young and held a powerful position yet he was not satisfied with all that the world could give him.

2. **Most vital question asked...**He asked Jesus, What shall I do to inherit Eternal life? At that young age, he asked the most important question in life, to Jesus, the Messiah Himself.

3. **Place Christ above Money...** Since money must have become an idol for him at that point, he refused to part with it. His pride and self-righteousness could have blinded him from the truth. He was not able to put Christ above his wealth. So he went away sorrowful.

4. **No Negotiations with the Lord...** If the Lord had allowed him to keep even a small portion of his wealth such as 10-25% for himself and give the rest to the poor, he might have still followed Jesus. Surprisingly, Jesus never called him back and negotiated with him, about selling a part of his assets.

5. "Assuredly, I say to you that **it is hard for a rich man to enter the Kingdom of Heaven.**"

It is easier for a camel to go through the eye of a needle (a gate with the smaller arch) than for a rich man to enter the Kingdom of God. It is impossible for a rich man or any man in that case, to be saved on his own.

But **with God all things are possible**, for it is the work of the Holy Spirit which draws people to Christ. (see Matt.19:16-26)

PART II

GOD'S WAYS HIGHER THAN OUR WAYS

"My thoughts are not your thoughts, neither are your ways My ways. As the heavens are higher than the earth, so are My ways higher than your ways, and My thoughts than your thoughts."(Is.55:8-9/NIV)

What Are God's Ways?

1. God's way is **perfect.** (Ps. 18:30)

2. The Lord is **righteous** in all His ways.(Ps.145:17)

3. The Lord is the rock; His works are perfect and all His ways are **just.** (Deut.32:4)

4. The way of the Lord is **strength** to the righteous; but it is the ruin of those who do evil. (Prov.10:29)

5. Great and marvellous are Your works, Lord God Almighty; **just and true** are Your ways.

   May God's ways be made known upon the earth. (Ps. 67:2)

What Are Our Ways?

1. There is a way that seems right to the man, but in the end it **leads to death**. (Prov.14:12)

2. A man's heart devises his way but the Lord directs his steps. (Prov.16:9)

3. The way of the wicked is an abomination unto the Lord. (Prov.15:9)

4. The Lord knows the way of the righteous; but the way of the ungodly will **perish.** (Ps. 1:6)

How Do We Learn God's Ways?

1. Through the Word of God (see Ps. 18:30; 119:1)

2. Through the Life of Jesus Christ; for Jesus is "The Word of God" and Jesus declared, *"I Am The Way."* (see Rev.19:13; Jn.14:6)

3. Through Prayer

4. Through the Holy Spirit's guidance in our day to day life.

Our Ways Based On God's Ways...

1. God will teach us His ways so that we may **walk in His paths**. (Micah 4:2)

2. The steps of a good man are ordered by the Lord and *He delights* in his way. (Ps.37:23)

3. When a man's ways please the Lord, He makes even his **enemies to live at peace** with him. (Prov.16:7)

So let us examine our ways and test them, and let us return to the Lord. (Lam.3:40)

Attributes Of The Holy Spirit

1. Love The Lord Your God

Commandment of God:

The first great commandment of Christ:

Love the Lord your God,

with all your **heart,** 100%

with all your **soul**, 100%

with all your **mind**, 100%

with all your **strength,** 100%

(see Matt. 22:37; Mark 12:30/NIV)

God's Way: *Did Jesus love His Father God with all His heart, soul, mind, and strength?*

Jesus' Profound Love for His Father God: While on earth, Jesus' deep love was expressed through His *obedience* to His Father's will even unto death.

For Jesus said, "My food is to do the will of Him who sent Me and to finish His work."(see Phil.2:8; Jn.4:34)

Our Way Based On God's Way: The Lord said, *"If you love Me, you will obey what I Command."* We can express our love for Him through our obedience. (see Jn.14:15/NIV)

Our obedience to God is directly proportional to our love for Him. For example, If you love Him 10%, you will obey only 10% of His Commandments.

2. Second Great Commandment On Love

<u>Commandment of God:</u> **Love your neighbor** as yourself; for this is the second great commandment. (see Matt. 22:39/NIV)

God's Way: *Jesus' Love for His Neighbor:* The Lord cared for the Samaritan woman who was living an immoral life. Jesus, the Holy One, loved her enough to reveal Himself as her Messiah. (see Jn.4:5-26)

When we were yet sinners, *Jesus loved us all,* to die in our place. He accepts us just as we are. (see Jn.3:14-16)

Our Way Based On God's Way: We can love our neighbors by providing for those who are hungry, thirsty or sick, at the point of their need. (see Matt. 25:31-46)

Do unto others what you want them to do to you. (see Matt. 7:12)

3. Love Your Enemies & Be God's Children

<u>Commandment of God:</u>

Love your enemies,

bless those who curse you,

do good to those who hate you, and *pray* for those who spitefully use you, and persecute you.

So that you may be the children of your Father who is in Heaven; for God is Love. (see Matt. 22:37-39; 5:44-45; Deut. 6:5)

God's Way: *Jesus' Love for His Enemies:* While hanging on the cross in agony, Jesus, out of love for His enemies, forgave those who brutally crucified Him. He did not desire the wrath of God to come upon them. (see Luke 23:34)

Our Way Based On God's Way: It is extremely hard to love our enemies, to bless them and to pray for them. But it is not impossible when we *seek the help of the Holy Spirit* who dwells in us.

The Holy Spirit will pour out His divine love into our hearts for our enemies. (see Rom. 5:5)

Attributes Of The Holy Spirit

4. Dependence On God

Commandment of God: **Be poor in spirit;** for you are blessed and yours is the Kingdom of Heaven. (see Matt. 5:3)

(To be poor in spirit is to depend on God for everything rather than on your own abilities.)

God's Way: When Jesus lived on this earth, He was totally dependent on His Heavenly Father for _His Words, Teachings and Deeds;_ for He knew Him. (see Jn.7:29)

Jesus declared, "I have not spoken of Myself. (see Jn.12:49/KJV)

Whatever I speak, _just as the Father has told Me, so I speak."_ (see Jn.12:50)

"My teaching is not My own. It comes from Him who sent Me." (see Jn.7:16/NIV).

"I do nothing on My own. Whatever I see Him doing, the same I do.

The Father who dwells in Me, He does the works." (see Jn.8:28;14:10)

Our Way Based On God's Way: We too should entirely depend on God for our thoughts, words and actions by constantly being in fellowship with Him.

Depend on the Lord in whatever you do, and your plans will succeed. (Prov.16:3)

5. Humility

<u>Commandment of God:</u> **1. Be humble**; for you are blessed and you will inherit the earth. (see Matt.5:5)

2. Humble yourselves under God's mighty hand, that He may lift you up in due time. (see 1Pet. 5:6/NIV)

God's Way: Jesus always walked in humility. After washing His disciple's feet, Jesus said to them, If I, your Lord and Master, have washed your feet; you also ought to wash one another's feet, thereby teaching them to walk in humility. (see Jn.13:14)

"Take My yoke upon you and learn from Me, for *I am gentle and humble in heart,* and you will find rest for your souls." (Matt.11:29/NIV)

Our Way Based On God's Way: All of you, clothe yourselves with humility toward one another, because, God opposes the proud but gives grace to the humble. (see 1 Pet. 5:5/NIV)

In humility *consider others better than yourselves.* He that shall humble himself shall be exalted. (see Phil.2:3; Matt.23:12/KJV)

Pray to God for the Spirit of humility; for *God dwells with him* that is of a contrite and humble spirit and revives him. (see Is. 57:15)

6. Compassion

<u>Commandment of God:</u> **Be merciful**; for you are blessed and you will obtain mercy. (see Matt.5:7)

God's Way: Whenever Jesus saw a great multitude, He was moved with compassion towards them. He healed their sicknesses, setting aside His own personal needs. (see Matt. 9:36; 14:14)

Jesus, out of compassion, *touched the leper* and healed him when lepers were not accepted in the society. (see Matt. 8:1-3)

Our Way Based On God's Way: We should always be kind and compassionate towards those who are suffering.

The Lord does not expect us to help all the poor and needy in the world but *when He sends a needy person in our path,* He expects us to help that person.

Attributes Of The Holy Spirit

7. Holiness

Commandment of God: **Be pure in heart;** for you are blessed and you will see God. (see Matt.5:8)

God's Way: Jesus came in the flesh and dwelt among us as an ordinary human being. *He was tempted in every way,* just as we are - yet He kept Himself pure and *without sin.* (see Heb. 4:15).

He boldly asked His accusers who were ready to find fault in Him, *"Can any of you prove me guilty of sin?"* And nobody could point an accusing finger at Him. (see Jn.8:46)

Even the Roman governor, Pilate who judged Jesus said, *"I find no fault in Him. I am innocent of His blood."*(see Matt. 27:24)

Our Way Based On God's Way: The God whom we worship is the Most Holy God who cannot tolerate sin. Just as He who called you is Holy, so *be holy in all you do;* for it is written: *"Be ye holy, because I am Holy."* (1 Peter 1:15)

Prayer: Make me so pure that I will be able to see You, Lord.

8. Peace

Commandment of God: **Be peacemakers**; for you are blessed and you will be called children of God. (see Matt.5:9)

God's Way: Scripture says that Jesus Christ is *"The Prince of Peace."* The one who loves *violence His soul hates.* (see Is.9 :6)

Jesus prevented His disciples from fighting with those who came to arrest Him. When Peter tried to attack one of the men with the sword, Jesus commanded him to put his sword back in its place, saying to him, *"For all who draw the sword will die by the sword"* and allowed the men to arrest Him peacefully.(see Matt. 26:52/NIV)

Our Way Based On God's Way: We ought to be at peace with God through the cross and be at peace with one another. (see Rom.5:1; Rom.12:18)

The Lord expects us to *reconcile* with our brothers and sisters *if they* have any *offense* against us before we offer our gift unto Him. (Matt. 5:23-24)

9. Forgiveness

Commandment of God: 1. Forgive men their trespasses. If you do not forgive men their trespasses, neither will your Father forgive your trespasses. (see Matt.6:14,15)

2. Forgive each other, just as in Christ God forgave you. (see Eph. 4:32)

3. Forgive your brother who sins against you seven times in a day and **seven times in a day returns to you,** saying, I repent. (see Luke 17:4)

God's Way: Jesus forgave the woman caught in adultery when everyone around her wanted to stone her to death, according to their Jewish law. (see Jn.8:2-11)

Even while hanging on the cross in agony, Jesus was willing to forgive those who whipped Him, spat on Him, mocked at Him and finally crucified Him. He said, **_Father, forgive them, for they know not what they do._** (see Luke 23:34/KJV).

Our Way Based On God's Way: When God has freely forgiven all our past sins, being the children of God, it should not be difficult for us to forgive those who hurt us. _Forgiveness is the best gift we can give to one another._

10. Greatness Measured By Your Service

Commandment of God: 1. Be ye a minister unto others; Whoever desires to be _great_ among you, let him be your minister;

2. Be a servant to others; and whoever desires to be _chief_ among you, let him be your servant. (see Matt. 20:25-27/KJV)

God's Way: In the Kingdom of God, _greatness is measured not by our authority over others but by our service to others._

Jesus, having come from the Heavenly atmosphere, always served the people in humility when He was on the earth. **_For the Son of Man, Jesus Christ, did not come to be served, but to serve,_** and to give His life as a ransom for many. (see Matt. 20:28)

Our Way Based On God's Way: In this world, those who have power and authority are considered great. But it is written, **_"The servant is not greater than his Lord."_** We, His servants, ought to follow our Master's example and find opportunities to serve others rather than be served. (Jn.13:16)

11. The Most Gracious God We Serve

Commandment of God: **The Lord is merciful and gracious,** slow to anger, and abounding in mercy.

He will not always strive with us, nor will He keep His anger forever. He has not dealt with us according to our sins, Nor punished us according to our iniquities. (Ps.103:8-10)

Judgment, if you take God's grace in vain... Never take God's grace in vain. God is not mocked.

If you keep ignoring the convictions of the Holy Spirit and continue sinning, then surely His judgment will fall upon you. For example, God gave 120 years of grace period during Noah's time before destroying the earth with floods. (see Gal. 6:7; Gen.6-9)

God's Way: 1.God was so _gracious upon mankind_ that when Adam, the first man disobeyed God's command, He provided us with the last Adam, Jesus Christ, His only begotten son, the obedient of the Lord to redeem us from our sins. (see 1 Cor.15:45)

2. God showered His _grace upon Cain, the first murderer,_ when he pleaded for His mercy. The Lord put a mark on Cain so that no one who found him would kill him. (see Gen.4:14-15/NIV)

3. God's grace was abundant _on King David_ when he sincerely repented for his sin of adultery with Bathsheba. God forgave David and _chose Solomon, the son of David and Bathsheba_ as the next king of Israel and Jesus Christ came through that lineage. (see Ps. 51; Matt.1:6-17)

4. Jesus forgave the _thief on the cross_ when he cried out, "Lord, remember me when You come into Your kingdom." Immediately, Jesus extended His grace upon him by promising him a place in Paradise. (see Luke 23:42-43)

Our Way Based On God's Way: _We are Saved by God's Grace._ God rained down His abundant grace upon us by giving us the free gift of Salvation which we do not deserve at all, when millions around us are perishing without knowing their Messiah, Jesus Christ. (see Titus 2:11)

Pray for His grace to fall upon you... "I will be gracious to whom I will be gracious, and I will have compassion on whom I will have compassion," says the Lord God Almighty. Pray, therefore, that God would shower His grace upon you. (see Ex.33:19)

12. Rest In Him, You Who Are Heavy Laden

Commandment of God: 1. "Come to Me, all you who are weary and burdened, and I will give you Rest.

2. Take My yoke upon you and **learn from Me.** For I am gentle and humble in heart, and you will find rest for your souls. **My yoke is easy** and My burden is light." (Matt. 11:28-30/NIV)

God's Way: 1. Jesus granted peace and *"rest"* to the man with palsy by *forgiving his sins.* (see Matt. 9:2-6)

2. He gave *"rest"* to the woman suffering with the issue of blood for 12 years, *by healing her sickness.* (see Matt. 9:20-22)

3. The Lord gave *"rest"* to the Canaanite woman by *casting a demon* out of her daughter. (see Matt. 15:22-28)

4. He **restored** joy to Lazarus and his family **by raising him from the dead.** (see Jn.11:17-44)

5. Jesus granted *"rest"* to the troubled disciples *by calming the storm;* for nothing is impossible with Him. (see Matt. 8:23-27)

Our Way Based On God's Way: Will He not give you *"rest"* when you come to the Lord? Indeed, He is able to deliver you from all your problems.

Jesus will give rest to your troubled hearts as you wait on Him; for He says, "My peace I give unto you; I do not give as the world gives." (see Jn.14:27)

13. Jehovah Jireh - Your Provider

Commandment of God: **Do not worry** about your life, what you will **eat or drink; or** about your body what you will **wear**; *for is not life more important than food* and the body more important than clothes. (Matt.6:25/NIV)

God's Way: While on earth, Jesus ate very simple food like fish and bread, wore a simple robe and had no fixed place to lay His head. (see Matt. 8:20)

He neither worried nor did He do miracles to fulfil His basic needs but always trusted His Father God to provide for Him.

Our Way Based On God's Way: Do not be anxious about anything; for *your Father God knows* that you have need of all these things. Cast all your anxiety on Him because *He cares* for you. (1 Pet.5:7/NIV;Matt.6:32)

Your Heavenly Father feeds even the birds of the air. Are you not of more value than the birds of the air? Which of you by worrying can add one cubit to his stature? (Matt. 6:26-27)

As children of God, we are entitled to have our basic needs met by our Heavenly Father who loves us so much. Trust in Him..(see 1Tim.5:8)

When we obey Him joyfully, He will fulfil all our desires. (see Ps 37:4)

14. Serving God Or The World?

<u>Commandment of God:</u> 1. You shall **worship the Lord your God, and Him only you shall serve**.

2. Do not worship the Lord in vain.

3. Do not serve two masters: God and money. For no one can serve two masters. (see Matt. 4:10; 6:24; 15:9)

4. Do not store up for yourselves treasures on earth rather store up treasures in Heaven; for where your treasure is, there your heart will be also. (see Matt. 6:19-21/NIV)

God's Way: *"I Honor My Father"* said Jesus. Everything He did in His lifetime was to bring glory to His Father. Jesus' whole life was a worship unto His Father through His obedience and good deeds. (see Jn.11:4; Jn.8:49)

Jesus overcame the world, sin and Satan...The Lord declared, "Satan, the prince of this world is coming, and he has *no hold on Me."* Jesus, as a perfect human being, had overcome the world, sin and Satan through much prayer. (see Jn.14:30)

Our Way Based On God's Way: **1.** He who sins is of the devil. (1 Jn.3:8)

2. Friendship with the world is enmity with God. (see James 4:4)

3. If you are a slave to sin or to the world, then you are a slave to the devil, serving the kingdom of Satan and not the Kingdom of God.

4. Rather walk in the Spirit and you will not fulfil the lust of the flesh. (Gal. 5:16)

5. Is Jesus your No.1 priority or do you have other idols such as, TV, money, spouse, children, career, etc. God will never share His glory with anyone or anything.

15. Do Not Fight For Power & Position

Commandment of God: Jesus stated, Whoever desires to be great among you, let him be your servant. (see Matt. 20:26)

(Do not be moved with indignation against your brethren.

When the disciples got angry with James and John for desiring prominent positions in Heaven, Jesus intervened and said to them that only the rulers of the **gentiles will fight** for power and position. **But it shall not be so among you.** (see Matt 20:24-26))

God's Way: _Did Jesus seek high positions on the earth?_

The Lord declared that He did not come into the world to be served, but to serve. (see Matt. 20:28)

Jesus, being the King of Kings, left the glorious Heaven and came to the earth. He chose to be born in a _stable_ instead of a palace and was raised up in a _poor carpenter's family._ He rode on a humble _donkey_ and not on a horse like the Roman soldiers did. (see Luke 2:7; Matt. 13:55; Jn.12:13-15)

Seeing Jesus' mighty miracles, the Jews wanted to make Him a King, But Jesus did not desire a kingdom for Himself on this earth but only wanted _to establish the Kingdom of God in people's hearts._(see Jn.6:15)

Our Way Based On God's Way: Our lifestyle, character and behavior should be totally different from that of an unbeliever, a Gentile. (see 2 Cor.5:17)

We should not envy and compete with our brothers and sisters in the Lord. _A true believer should help his brother fulfil his calling._

We believers must not desire top positions to exercise power over others because of pride.

16. Take Authority Over Satan -

Set The Captives Free

Commandment of God: First you bind the strong man, Satan, and then you can plunder his house. Or else how can you enter a strong man's house and plunder his goods? (see Matt. 12:29).

God's Way: Jesus often cast out devils by the Spirit of God while He was on earth. E.g., 1. Jesus cast out a legion of demons from the man who lived in the tombs at Gadarenes. (see Matt.12:28; Mark 5:3,8)

2. Jesus rebuked Satan who spoke through Peter, to prevent Him from going to the cross in accordance to the will of God. (see Matt.16;23)

Our Way Based On God's Way: "Behold, I have *given you* **authority** to trample on snakes and scorpions and *to overcome all the power of the enemy;* nothing will by any means harm you" says the Lord. (Luke 10:19)

Therefore, we must take authority over all the power of the enemy and claim everything that the devil has stolen from us, especially our unsaved loved ones for Christ. For greater is He that is in us than he that is in the world. (see Luke 10:19; Matt. 12:29; 1 Jn.4:4)

17. Take Authority Over Satan -

Deliverance From Infirmities & Debts

Commandment of God: First you bind the strong man, Satan, and then you can plunder his house. Or else how can you enter a strong man's house and plunder his goods? (see Matt. 12:29)

God's Way: 1. Jesus delivered the woman who was bound by Satan for eighteen years. He set her free by casting out the _spirit of infirmity_ from her.

2. Jesus healed a man who was blind and dumb by casting the devil out of him.

3. Jesus rebuked and cast the demon out of the lunatic boy and healed him. (see Luke 13:12; Matt.12:22;17:15-18)

Our Way Based On God's Way : Be wise about what is good and be innocent concerning evil and then the **_God of Peace will crush Satan under your feet,_** says apostle Paul to the obedient children of God.

If you are bound with sickness, first cast out the spirit of infirmity and then speak forth healing Scriptures to keep your healing.

Similarly, for a financial problem, bind the devil and quote Scriptures concerning prosperity to claim your miracle. (see Rom. 16:19-20)

18. Take Authority Over Satan -

Prevent Natural Calamities

Commandment of God: 1. First you bind the strong man, Satan, and then you can plunder his house. Or else how can you enter a strong man's house and plunder his goods? (see Matt. 12:29)

2. Bind anything on earth; for it will be bound in Heaven. (see Matt. 18:18)

3. Loose anything on earth; whatever you loose on earth will be loosed in Heaven. (see Matt. 18:18)

God's Way: The Lion of Judah, our Lord Jesus Christ has crushed Satan's head under His feet. E.g., When His disciples faced a raging storm, *Jesus rebuked the winds and the sea* and then came a great calm. (see Matt. 8:18; 23-27)

Our Way Based On God's Way: Every good and perfect gift comes from the Father of lights. (see James 1:17)

Since every natural calamity like earthquakes, volcano eruptions, tsunamis, floods, droughts, etc., are from the devil, we must use the God given authority and rebuke the devil as Jesus did, to **nullify Satan's plans over nature**.

19. Overcome Temptation With "The Word"

Commandment of God: 1. Man shall not live by bread alone; but by every word that proceeds from the mouth of God. (Matt. 4:4)

2. You shall not tempt the Lord your God. (Matt. 4:7)

(Jesus quoted these verses to Satan, when Satan, by using the Word of God, tried to divert Jesus from the path of perfect obedience to His Father's will.)

God's Way: Jesus fasted and prayed for 40 days in the wilderness. When the devil came to tempt Him, Jesus was physically without food but very much alive in the Spirit; because He was full of God's Word.

Since Jesus knew the Scriptures well and also the ways of His Father God, He did not fall for the devil's snare.

Each time Satan tempted Jesus with the Word of God, He quoted another Scripture to the devil and overcame the temptations. (see Matt. 4:1-11)

Our Way Based On God's Way: If we know the Scriptures well, we will also understand God's ways and we will not be deceived by the devil when he misleads us using the Scriptures. (see Ps. 119)

We too should quote appropriate Scriptures to the devil to overcome temptations. (see Rev.12:11)

20. Watch & Pray Lest You Fall Into Temptation

Jesus' Command to His disciples at Gethsemane: Stay here and watch with Me. The Son of Man is betrayed into the hands of sinners. (see Matt. 26:38)

Watch and pray that you enter not into temptation; for the spirit indeed is willing but the flesh is weak.(see Matt. 26:41/KJV)

God's Way: As a perfect human being, Jesus cried out, "O My Father, if it is possible, let this cross pass from Me; yet not as I will but as You will." (see Matt. 26:39)

In the Garden of Gethsemane, Jesus, anticipating His crucifixion, **_prayed more earnestly_** that His sweat was like great drops of blood falling to the ground. That powerful prayer enabled Him to endure the sufferings of the cross till the end, for our redemption. (see Luke 22:44)

Our Way Based On God's Way: 1. Since Peter ignored Christ's repeated warnings to pray, he could not overcome the temptations and denied the Lord thrice.

2. Be alert in prayer so that when trials come your way, you will be equipped with His power to overcome the enemy.

3. No prayer, no power; little prayer, little power; more prayer, more power.

21. Despise Not The Little Ones

Commandment of God: Take heed that you do not despise one of the little ones. For their angels always see the face of My Father in Heaven. (see Matt.18:10)

(The little one represents a child or a child like believer.)

God's Way: Jesus did not despise the illiterate fishermen or the unfortunate ones like the lepers and the blind. (see Matt.4:18-22; 8:2-3)

He did not look down upon those who led immoral lives like Mary Magdalene. (see Luke 7:36-39)

Jesus treated everyone alike, the ordinary as well as the wealthy, like Zacchaeus and Matthew. (see Luke 19:1-10)

Our Way Based On God's Way: You should not despise any believer or a child who is created in the image of God, based on their qualifications or social status.

They are so valuable to the Lord that He has bought them with His own precious blood. (see Matt.18:10)

When we believe in Christ...

We become the _"children of the Almighty God"_ whereby we call Him, "Abba Father." (see Jn.1:12; Rom. 8:15)

We did not choose Him but He chose us and made us _citizens of Heaven._ (see Jn.15:16; Phil. 3:20)

We are the _ambassadors of Christ_ and _fellow workers_ with Him. (see 2 Cor.5:20; 6:1)

We are _seated in Heavenly realms with Christ Jesus._ (see Eph. 2:6)

Jesus calls us _"friends"_ and _not servants_ any longer. (see Jn.15:15)

When we receive Christ, we are _"a new creation"_ and our bodies become the _"Temple of the Holy Spirit."_ (see 2 Cor.5:17; 1 Cor.6:19-20)

22. 'Receive A Little Child In My Name'

Commandment of God: 1. Receive a little child in My Name. Whoever receives a little child in My Name, receives Me, says the Lord. (see Matt. 18:5)

2. If anyone causes one of the little ones who believe in Me to sin, it would be better for him to have a large millstone hung around his neck and to be drowned in the depths of the sea.(see Matt. 18:6/NIV)

God's Way: Jesus loved the little children and spent His precious time with them. He loved to embrace them and bless them.

He said to His disciples, Let the little children come to Me; forbid them not; for the Kingdom of Heaven belongs to such as these little children. (see Matt. 19:14)

Our Way Based On God's Way: We should spend time with our children, listen to their problems and try to solve them, since children are a reward from the Lord. (see Ps.127:3)

Fathers, do not provoke your children to anger lest they be discouraged; instead bring them up in the instruction and training of the Lord.(see Eph. 6:4; Col. 3:21)

Discipline your son and he will give you peace; he will bring delight to your soul. (Prov.29:17)

23. Shine Your Light Before Men

Commandment of God: 1. Be ye the light of the world. (see Matt.5:14/KJV)

2. Do not light a lamp and put it under a basket, but on a lamp stand; and it gives light to all who are in the house. (see Matt.5:15)

3. Shine your light before men; for people may see your good works and glorify your Father in Heaven. (see Matt.5:16)

God's Way: Jesus proclaimed, "I am the Light of the world; He that follows Me will not walk in darkness, but will have the light of life". (see Jn.8:12)

Jesus, as a young man _went about doing good all His life._ His life was so fruitful that within 3½ years of ministry, He impacted the whole world and even today, 2000 years later, He is still changing lives.

Our Way Based On God's Way: We must radiate Jesus Christ to the world through our good deeds and good conduct.

Each of you should look not only to your own interests, but also to the interests of others. (see Phil.2:4)

Let us not be weary in doing good; for in due season we shall reap if we do not give up. As we have, therefore, opportunity, let us do good unto all men, especially unto believers.(see Gal. 6:9-10)

24. Be Slow To Anger & Quick To Reconcile

<u>*Commandment of God:*</u> 1. Do not be angry with your brother without a cause; whoever is angry without a cause will be in danger of the judgment.

2. Do not say to another "You fool!" For you will be in danger of **Hell Fire**. (see Matt.5:22)

3. First be reconciled to your brother who has something against you. (see Matt.5:23)

God's Way: **1.** In the eyes of God, anger is equivalent to murder.

2. Though Judas betrayed Jesus with a kiss, yet the Lord was not angry with him but called him a friend. (see Matt.26:50)

3. The Lord lets the wicked live together with the righteous until the day of judgment, as explained in the parable of wheat and tares; for He is a God of long suffering. (see Matt. 13:24-30)

Our Way Based On God's Way: Be slow to anger and slow to speak; for man's anger does not bring about the righteous life that God desires. Do not sin in your anger.   (see James. 1:19,20; Eph. 4:26)

Be quick to reconcile with the person who holds bitterness against you. (see Matt. 5:23)

It is possible to overcome anger by the anointing of the Holy Spirit. (see Gal. 5:22-25)

25. What Will Keep Your Soul From Troubles?

Commandment of God: 1. Do not speak idle words; for every idle word men may speak, they will give **account of it** on the day of judgment. (see Matt. 12:36)

2. Speak only good things; for out of the abundance of the heart the mouth speaks. (see Matt. 12:34)

3. Let your "Yes" be "Yes" and your 'No' be 'No'; for whatever is more than these is from Satan, the evil one. (see Matt.5:37)

God's Way: When Jesus was accused by the chief priests and elders, He answered nothing. *He never spoke a word* to them in defence.

Jesus committed no sin, and **no deceit was found in His mouth.** When they hurled their insults at Him, He did not retaliate; when He suffered, He made no threats.

Instead, Jesus entrusted Himself to the Father who judges justly. (see Matt. 27:12-14; 1 Pet. 2:22-23)

Our Way Based On God's Way: 1. Whoever guards his mouth and tongue keeps his soul from troubles.

2. By your words you will be justified, and by your words you will be condemned. (see Matt. 12:37)

3. A wise man spares his words; even a fool is thought wise if he keeps silent.

4. The tongue that brings healing is a tree of life; but a deceitful tongue crushes the spirit. So think before you speak. (Prov.17:27-28; 21:23; 15:4)

---

26. Do Not Delay In Fulfilling Your Vow

Commandment of God: 1. Do not break your oath, but keep the oaths you have made to the Lord. (see Matt.5:33/NIV)

2. Do not swear at all; neither by Heaven nor by the earth; neither by Jerusalem nor by your head; for Heaven is God's throne;

The earth is His footstool. (You should not swear even by your head because you cannot make one hair black or white. (see Matt.5:34-36)

God's Way: God has no pleasure in fools who do not keep their vows. Do not say before the angels that the vow you made was an error. Do not allow your mouth to cause your flesh to sin.

God will be angry at your words and destroy the work of your hands. (see Eccl. 5:2-7)

Our Way Based On God's Way: 1. When you make a vow to God, do not delay in fulfiling it.

2. Do not be quick with your mouth to utter anything before God. Let your words be few when you are in His presence.

3. It is better not to vow than to make a vow and not fulfil it. (Eccl. 5:2-7)

---

27. Behold The Beam In Your Eye

Commandment of God: 1. Do not judge, or you too will be judged. For with what judgment you judge, you will be judged. With the same measure you use, it will be measured back to you. (Matt.7:1,2)

2. You hypocrite, do not behold the mote in your brother's eye; first cast out the beam out of your own eye. (see Matt.7:1-5/KJV)

God's Way: Jesus did not judge and condemn the Samaritan woman who led an immoral life. He gently made her confess her sins and then revealed Himself as her Savior. (see Jn.4:1-26)

The Lord did not judge Zacchaeus, the chief tax collector who was despised by all people, but went and stayed in his house and led him to repentance and Salvation.(see Luke 19:1-10)

Our Way Based On God's Way: 1. Jesus disapproves the habit of criticizing others while ignoring one's own faults. We must first examine ourselves before attempting to judge and influence our brothers and sisters in the Lord. (see Matt.7:1-5)

2. When we have *pride, jealousy or when we think too highly of ourselves* and look down upon others, we begin to judge people.

3. When we are confident about who we are in Christ, then we will never compare ourselves with others nor judge them.

28. Short Prayers Can Bring Forth Miracles

<u>*Commandment of God:*</u> 1. When you pray, do not be like the hypocrites, who love to be seen by men. (see Matt.6:5)

2. When you pray...

Go into your room;

Shut your door;

Pray to your Father.

Do not use vain repetitions as the heathen do.

For your Father who sees in secret will **reward** you openly.

The heathen think that they will be heard because of their many words. (see Matt.6:6,7)

God's Way: Jesus was always full of the Holy Spirit because of His constant fellowship with His Father. Therefore, He often prayed very short prayers in public but they were so powerful that they brought forth miracles.

For example, Jesus said, "Talita Kumi" meaning **"little girl, arise"** and she immediately rose up from the dead. (see Mark 5:41)

Jesus said, **"Peace, be still"** and the raging storms calmed down at once. (see Mark 4:39)

Our Way Based On God's Way: The Lord longs for your fellowship more than you long for Him. As you spend more time with Him alone, you will receive more of His Holy Spirit.

And if you pray long enough in secret, all you have to do is to say a couple of words in public to bring forth miracles.

For the anointing of the Holy Spirit destroys the yoke of bondage. (see Is.10:27)

29. Total Dependence On The Holy Spirit

Commandment of God: 1. Do not blaspheme the Holy Spirit. For all manner of sin and blasphemy shall be forgiven unto men. But the blasphemy against the Holy Spirit shall not be forgiven unto men neither in this world, nor in the world to come. (see Matt.12:31,32 /KJV)

2. Ask for the Holy Spirit. (see Luke 11:13)

3. Be baptized with the Holy Spirit and Fire. (see Matt 3:11; Acts 1:4-5)

God's Way: Jesus & The Holy Spirit...

1. Jesus was miraculously _conceived_ by the Holy Spirit and was born of a virgin. (see Matt. 1:18,23; Luke 1:35)

2. Jesus was _baptized_ and as He was praying, Heaven was opened and the Holy Spirit descended upon Him like a dove.

(see Luke 3:21-22/NIV)

3. Jesus, full of the Holy Spirit, was able to _overcome_ Satan's temptations in the wilderness. (see Luke 4:1-2)

4. Jesus was anointed with the Power of the Holy Spirit that He went about _doing good, and healing_ all that were oppressed of the devil. (see Acts. 10:38)

5. Jesus was _raised up_ from the grave as the true Son of God by the Power of the Holy Spirit. (see Rom.8:11)

Our Way Based On God's Way: If our Master and Savior, as a human being, had to rely on the Holy Spirit all the time in His life, how much more, we need to depend on the Holy Spirit to live a victorious life. (see Rom 8:14)

Jesus said, When I go away, I will send the _Helper_ to you to be with you forever; who is the Spirit of Truth. (see Jn.14:16-20; 6:7-9, 14)

Since the Lord has promised, "I will pour out My Spirit upon _all flesh,_" anyone who is thirsty, needs to wait on the Lord daily for the infilling of the Holy Spirit. (see Joel 2:28; Jn.7:37)

30. Obedience Unto Death

Commandment of God: 1. Obey His Commandments and teach others so; for you will be called **great** in the Kingdom of Heaven. (see Matt.5:19)

2. Do not break even the least of God's Commandments and teach men so. Or else, you will be called **least** in the Kingdom of Heaven. (see Matt.5:19)

3. Blessed are those who hear the Word of God and obey it; for obedience is the **way to joy**. (see Luke 11:28; Ps. 19:8)

Those who obey and do the will of God will have **Eternal Life**. (see Matt. 7:21-23)

We will come to **know Him**, if we obey His Commands. And God's love will be made complete in us. (see 1 Jn.2:3-6)

God's Way: 1. Though Jesus was the Son of God, yet He learned obedience from what He suffered.

2. Jesus humbled Himself and became obedient to death-even death on a cross. (see Heb. 5:8; Phil. 2:8/NIV)

3. Jesus was put on a trial all through the night, betrayed and deserted by His own disciples, mocked, spat upon the face, whipped and humiliated by the Gentiles. He finally hung naked on the cross, forsaken by His Father, yet He was determined to finish His Father's will, to be a ransom for many.

4. His goal was set by His Father God and no amount of pain, torture or humiliation could deter Him from fulfiling His Father's will for His life. (see Is.53)

Our Way Based On God's Way: 1. What about you? Will your obedience be unto death to accomplish God's will for your life?

2. Jesus says, *"If you love Me, you will keep My Commandments."* (see Jn.14:15)

3. The Psalmist said, It is good for me to be afflicted so that I might learn Your Commandments. Sometimes God takes us through a difficult path to teach us obedience. (see Ps. 119:71)

4. Obedience is better than sacrifice, in the eyes of God. (1 Sam.15:22-23)

31. *Healing According To Your Faith*

Commandment of God: 1. Go your way. It will be done just as you believed it would. The Roman centurion's servant was healed that very same hour. (see Matt. 8:13 see Matt. 8:13/NIV)

2. Daughter, be of good comfort; for thy faith has made thee whole. (see Matt. 9:22; Mark 5:22-43/KJV)

God's Way: Jesus always expected "faith" from people who came to Him for healing. When they plugged their faith into the unlimited power of Jesus, they received their healing.

The Lord asked the blind men who came to Him for healing, Do you believe in My ability to do the miracle? When they replied, "Yes, Lord," then Jesus touched their eyes and restored their sight, saying, "**According to your faith**, be it unto you." (see Matt. 9:28-30)

Our Way Based On God's Way: Faith cometh by hearing and hearing by the Word of God. (see Rom. 10:17)

Our Father God is seated on the throne as the King of kings. We, being His dear children should know how to go into His throne room and take anything we need from His hands, by faith.

We don't need to beg Him; for an obedient child knows his or her rights. If we cry, God will also cry with us; His face will move but not His hands. Only by our faith we can receive our miracles.

Our Lord will never test us beyond our level of faith. Even faith, as small as a mustard seed, can bring forth miracles for us.

We must not only express our faith in the Lord's ability to do a miracle but also act upon it, as the centurion did. (see Matt. 8:8-13)

If you believe, you will receive anything you ask in prayer. (see Matt. 21:22)

32. Seek Not Your Own Will But God's Will

Commandment of God: 1. Do not say to Me 'Lord, Lord' but do the will of My Father in Heaven to enter His Kingdom.

2. Do the _will of My Father_ in Heaven to enter the Kingdom of Heaven. (see Matt. 7:21)

You can **prophesy** accurately in Jesus' Name.

You can **cast out demons** in His Name.

You can **do many wonders** in His Name.

And you can say to **Jesus, 'Lord, Lord.'**

After having done these things, if you have still not done the will of the Father, you will **not enter into Heaven;**

for Jesus will say to you, "I never knew You; depart from Me, you who practice lawlessness!" (see Matt.7:22-23)

God's Way: 1. Jesus declared, "My food is to do the will of Him who sent Me and to finish His work.

2. I do not seek My own will but the will of the Father who sent Me." (see Jn.4:34; 5:30)

3. It was the Father's will that Jesus should suffer as a ransom for us. Though Jesus was exceedingly sorrowful unto death, He prayed, "O My Father, if it is possible let this cross pass from Me; yet not as I will but as You will."

4. He totally surrendered His will to His Father and died on the cross in our place. (see Is.53:5-12; Matt. 26:38-39)

Our Way Based On God's Way: As Jesus always did those things that pleased His Father, you too must first find out what God's perfect will is for your life. (see Jn.8:29; Eph.5:17)

Ask God to fill you with the knowledge of His will and then commit yourself to fulfil it. (see Col. 1:9)

God's "Perfect Will" Revealed in His Word...

1. It is the will of your Father that none of the souls should perish. (see Matt. 18:14; 1Tim.2:4)

2. It is the will of the Father that we be not drunk with wine but be filled with His Spirit. (see Eph. 5:18)

3. It is the will of God that everyone of you should know how to possess his vessel in sanctification and honor. (see 1 Thess.4:3-7)

33. My Church, The House Of Prayer

Commandment of God: 1. Call My House, a House of Prayer. Do not make My house a den of thieves. Do not make My Father's House a house of merchandise. (see Matt. 21:13; Jn.2:16)

2. Guard your steps when you go to the House of God. Go near to listen rather than to offer the sacrifice of fools. (see Eccl. 5:1/NIV)

God's Way: Jesus & Prayer...

Lord Jesus is our role model in prayer. He always chose to be in the House of God. He often departed into solitary places and _prayed._ (see Mark 1:35)

1. The Lord spent _all night in prayer_ before choosing His twelve disciples. (see Luke 6:12-16).

2. Jesus, while being baptized, _prayed_ and received the power of the Holy Spirit to have an effective ministry. (see Luke 3:21-22)

3. Jesus, being a man of prayer, and knowing that His house ought to be a _"House of Prayer,"_ cleansed the temple by casting out all those who sold and bought in the temple. Out of zeal for God's house, He overthrew the tables of the money-changers and the seats of those who sold doves. (see Jn.2:17)

Our Way Based On God's Way: In these last days, there is no "Fear of God" in many Churches; but only an outward form of godliness. Christ expects His House, "The Church" to be a place of unceasing prayer.

Let us not profane the House of God by making it a means for social advancement, entertainment and financial gain.

We believers are also the temple of the Holy Spirit i.e., the house of God. So we should keep our hearts pure and consecrated and resist sin. (see 1 Cor.6:19; Heb.12:4)

34. Follow Christ & Become His Disciple

<u>*Commandment of God:*</u> **"Follow Me,** and I will make you fishers of men." (Matt.4:19; 9:9)
God's Way: Jesus called the disciples to follow Him first, before making them fishers of men. (see Matt.4:19; 9:9)
Our Way Based On God's Way: 1. Jesus expects us to follow Him first to become His disciples.
2. We must place Him above everything and learn from Him to be efficient soul-winners.

35. Jesus Calls His Disciples - To Be Fishers of Men

<u>*Commandment of God:*</u> "Follow Me, **and I will make you fishers of men."** (Matt.4:19; 9:9)
God's Way: Jesus made His disciples "Fishers of Men" by being a role model to them; in prayer, through His obedience to His Father's will, and by His simple lifestyle and good deeds. (see Mark 1:35; Jn.4:34)
Our Way Based On God's Way: 1. Similarly, we should **live as Christ lived** and be an example for others to follow. A disciple can prepare another disciple only up to his spiritual level. (see 1Jn.2:6; Lk.6:40)
2. Hence, we should be fishers of men first and then train other believers to be fishers of men who will win lost souls to Christ. (see 2 Tim.2:1-2)
3. He that wins souls is wise. (see Prov.11:30)

36. Jesus Calls His Disciples - To Live A Purpose Driven Life

Commandment of God: Follow Me, and I will make you fishers of men. (see Matt.4:19; 9:9)

God's Way: Jesus called the disciples out of their earthly jobs and family ties, not to keep them idle but to give them **a new job** of fishing for men. (see Matt.4:19)

Our Way Based On God's Way: 1. We are so caught up with our worldly jobs and chores that we don't have time to think about the God given purpose our lives.

2. God has saved us and called us with a holy calling, not according to our works, but according to His own purpose and grace. (see 2 Tim 1-9) for

3. As we follow Christ, we receive the mind of Christ to reach out to the lost which is the very purpose of our lives. (see 1 Pet.3:9; 1 Tim.2:4)

4. For we believers are a chosen people, **a *royal priesthood*** that we may declare the praises of Him who called us out of darkness into His marvellous light. (see 1 Pet.2:9)

37. Jesus Calls His Disciples - To Have One Vision

God's Way: 1. As Jesus began His ministry, He chose 12 disciples after spending a whole night in prayer. He delegated His vision to them.

2. Among His disciples were illiterate fishermen, a tax collector and brothers from the same families, etc., but the only reason why Father God chose them was because of their devoted love for Jesus and that they all would die for Him. (see Luke 6:12-13)

3. Though His disciples came from different backgrounds, they all were given one vision to become fishers of men i.e., to reach out to the lost which is God's perfect will. (see 1 Pet.3:9; 1 Tim.2:4)

Our Way Based On God's Way: If you are chosen by God to be a leader with a specific vision for ministry, you should also, after much prayer, **make a team of disciples.**

Share your vision with the team and work together in unity and love, for the expansion of His Kingdom.

38. The Cost Of Discipleship
The Narrow Way - Path Of Our Savior

Commandment of God: 1. Follow Me; and let the dead bury their own dead. (Matt. 8:21-22)

2. Carry neither gold, nor silver, nor money in your purses. Do not take any bag for your journey nor two coats, neither shoes, nor yet knives.

God's Way: 1. Our Savior's path is a path of suffering. During His 3 ½ years of ministry on earth, Jesus walked long distance from city to city preaching the gospel of the Kingdom of God. (see Mark 1:14)

2. His priority was to accomplish the will of His Father on this earth.(see Jn.4:34)

3. Jesus said to one of the scribes who wanted to be His disciple, "Foxes have holes and the birds of the air have nests; but the Son of Man has nowhere to lay His head." (see Matt. 8:20)

4. Jesus did not look for comfort all through His life. The climax of His suffering was that He died on the cross to deliver us from this present evil world. (see Gal.1:4)

Our Way Based On God's Way: 1. We are **God's elect, but strangers** in this world; for our citizenship is in Heaven. Therefore, we should passionately serve the Lord fulfiling His will, without seeking comfort in life; for our rewards are stored in Heaven. (see 1 Pet.1:1)

2. Endure hardship like a good soldier of Christ. Be faithful, even to the point of death, and Jesus will give you the **Crown of Life.** (see 2 Tim.2:3; Rev. 2:9-10)

3. When God calls you for His ministry, He will meet all your needs. Trust in God at all times. For the worker is worthy of his food. (see Matt. 10:9-10)

39. The Cost Of Discipleship
Deny Yourself To Be Worthy Of Christ

Commandment of God: 1. Do not love your father or mother more than Me. Do not love your son or daughter more than Me. For then, you are **not worthy of Me.** (see Matt. 10:37)

2. Deny yourself, take up your cross and follow Me; And he who does not take his cross and follow after Me is **not worthy of Me.** (see Matt. 10:38; Matt. 16:24)

3. He who finds his life will lose it. He who loses his life for My sake will find it.(see Matt. 10:39)

4. For what good will it be for a man if he gains the whole world, yet loses his own soul? (see Matt. 16:26/NIV)

God's Way: 1. Jesus denied Himself by putting His Father's will above His mother and brothers when they came to see Him. He did not go out to see them but continued to teach the Word to the crowd.

2. Then pointing to His disciples, Jesus said, 'Here are My mother and my brothers; for whoever does the will of My Father in Heaven is My brother and sister and mother.'(see Matt. 12:46-50)

3. Jesus was filled with the Holy Spirit without measure because of the price He paid on the earth by denying His own interests. (see John 3:34)

Our Way Based On God's Way: 1. God must be your priority, even above your parents or your children. But it is your responsibility to make sure their needs are met. (see Matt.10:37)

2. Put to death, whatever belongs to your earthly nature; sexual immorality, lust, evil desires, greed for money etc. (see Col. 3:5)

3. The higher the price we pay in denying ourselves, the greater will be the anointing of the Holy Spirit we receive for His service. (see Heb.1:8-9)

40. Preach "Repentance" To All Nations

Commandment of God: 1. Repent; for the Kingdom of Heaven is near. (see Matt. 3:2; 4:17)   2. Repent, or else you will all perish. (see Luke 13:3,5)

God's Way: Jesus began His ministry with the first message of repentance because He knew that there can be "No Salvation without Repentance." Hence, Jesus said to His disciples that repentance and remission of sins should be preached in His Name to all nations.(see Matt. 4:17; Luke 24:47)

Our Way Based On God's Way: 1. Jesus has already paid the price for the redemption of our souls. Now that we know this truth, how much more we need to preach the message of repentance to the lost souls around us.

2. Since Jesus has finished all that is to be done on the cross for the Salvation of mankind, all we have to do now is to say "Sorry" to Him and accept the free gift of salvation by faith.

3. _Prayer of Repentance_: "Lord Jesus, forgive my sins and cleanse me with your precious blood. Come into my heart and be the Lord and Savior of my life."

41. Go & Preach -The Kingdom Of Heaven Is Near

Commandment of God: Go, preach this message: The Kingdom of Heaven is near. And heal the sick, cleanse the lepers, raise the dead, cast out devils. (Matt. 10:7, 8/KJV)

God's Way: 1. Jesus went into Galilee and proclaimed, The Kingdom of God is near. Repent and believe the good news. (see Mark 1:14)

2. Jesus often spent time alone with His Father in prayer that empowered Him with the Holy Spirit, to preach with authority and to do miracles.

3. He was filled with God's Spirit in abundance because of His **obedience** to the will of God. (see John 3:34)

Our Way Based On God's Way: 1. We too should wait on the Lord in prayer to have the guidance and the power of the Holy Spirit in ministry.

2. Jesus stated that we will do greater works than what He did. The same anointing that was upon Jesus is available to us as well.

3. He will also equip us with the gifts of the Holy Spirit, for example, gift of healing, gift of miracles, etc. (see Jn.14:12; 1 Cor.12:9-10)

42. Freely Give; For Freely You Have Received

Commandment of God: Freely give; for freely you have received. (Matt.10:8)

God's Way: 1. Jesus' heart was so burdened for lost souls that He did not care about financial matters; He entrusted the money bag to Judas, knowing that he was a thief. (see Jn.13:29)

2. Jesus never expected earthly benefits, like houses, chariots, boats, horses, etc., in return for the mighty miracles He did.

3. He did not even seek honor and fame from people. He only treasured the testimony which He received from His Father. (see Matt. 9:30/NIV; Jn.8:17-18)

Our Way Based On God's Way: 1. Since Jesus has given us _Salvation, His Word and the anointing of the Holy Spirit for free,_ He commands us not to expect anything in return when we serve Him.

2. Do not even expect honor from people, for what is highly esteemed among men is an abomination in the sight of God. But Jesus says if any man serve Me, him will My Father honor. (see Luke 16:15; Jn.12:26)

3. As we do His will, He will make sure our needs are met; for a laborer is worthy of his wages. (see 1 Tim. 5:18)

4. A true laborer will have a deep burden for perishing souls and will tirelessly work to reach out to the lost.

5. He will not work for money, his own fame or to expand his own ministry. He will not make God's work a business. (see 1 Tim.6:6)

6. Godliness with contentment is great gain. But only men of corrupt mind, who have been robbed of the truth, will think that godliness is a means to financial gain.(see 1 Tim. 6:5-6)

PART III

ETERNAL LIFE OR ETERNAL DAMNATION? YOU DECIDE!

The Word of God says that there is only one life to live and then there is judgment awaiting us after our death. You must decide here on earth where you want to spend your Eternity - in Heaven or in Hell. (Heb 9:27)

To inherit Eternal Life, it is vital that we accept Jesus Christ as our Lord and Savior and continue to abide in Him. For Jesus Christ is the true God, and Eternal Life. Only those who endure till the end in true faith, purity and love will be saved. (see 1 Jn.5:20; Matt. 10:22)

Place Of Eternal Rest

Glorious Heaven	Fiery Hell
1. The Kingdom of Heaven is ruled by the Father God, Son and the Holy Spirit. (Matt. 28:18; Dan.7:9)	1. The Kingdom of Hell is ruled by Satan - the God of this age, assisted by principalities, powers and rulers of the dark world. (see 2 Cor.4:4; Eph. 6:12)
The Heaven, even the **Heavens are the Lord's** and they cannot be measured. (see Ps. 115:16; Jer.31:37)	2. Hell is a **fiery furnace** where there is **weeping** and **gnashing of teeth**. (Matt.13:41-42)
2. "Heaven is My throne and I make all things new", says the Lord God Almighty. (see Is.66:1, Rev. 21:5)	3. Hell is a **place of eternal damnation** where sinners will be tormented with unquenchable fire and burning sulphur. (Matt.25:46; Luke 16:23; Rev.14:10)
3. Heavens are the works of God's fingers. There are millions of glorious angels in His mighty presence. (see Jn.1:51; Ps. 8:3)	

Glorious Heaven	Fiery Hell
4. The Kingdom of Heaven is a peaceful place where there will be no tears, no crying and **no more death.** (see Rev.21:4)	4. The Kingdom of Satan is a place of darkness where men gnawed their tongues in **agony** and their **worms** die not. They curse the God of Heaven because of their pain and their **sores** and they will have **no rest** day and night. (see Rev. 14:11; 16:10; Jude 13; Mark 9:48)
5. Heaven is a joyful place where there is **no more sorrow and pain**. (see Rev.21:4)	
6. Heaven is a magnificent place where our Lord Jesus is preparing "**Mansions**" for us. (see Jn.14:1)	5. In "Divine Revelation of Hell" Kathryn Baxter describes Hell as a **foul smelling place** where ugly looking evil, demonic creatures fly everywhere.
7. Heaven is such a wonderful place from where every spiritual blessing comes to the children of God. (see Eph. 1:3)	6. This dreadful place of hell was originally **created for Satan**, his fallen angels and for the antichrist. (see 2 Pet. 2:4; Rev. 19:20)
	Make sure that you don't end up in Hell.

The Holy City of Heaven

(New Jerusalem)

The beautiful **city** of new Jerusalem, the Holy city comes down from God out of Heaven, prepared as a Bride adorned for her husband.(Rev.21:10, 21)

The **wall** of the city is made of jasper and the city is **pure gold**, like unto clear glass.

The **foundations** of the city walls are decorated with every kind of precious stones. The first foundation is **jasper**, the second **sapphire**, the third chalcedony, the fourth emerald, the fifth sardonyx, the sixth is carnelian, the seventh chrysolite, the eighth beryl, the ninth topaz, the tenth chrysoprase, the eleventh jacinth and the twelfth amethyst.

The city has **12 gates** which are made of **12 pearls**; each gate is made of a single pearl. The gates shall not be shut at all by day.

The **street** of the city is made of pure gold like transparent glass.

There is no need for the sun or the moon to shine. There shall be no night there; for the *glory of God illuminates it*, and the Lamb of God, **Jesus, is its light.** (see Rev. 21:23)

Who will dwell in the Holy city of Jerusalem?

The nations of those who are saved shall walk in its light.

There shall be nothing impure that will ever enter it, nor will anyone that works abomination, or makes a lie will enter, but **only those whose names are written in the Lamb's Book of Life**. (see Rev.21:24, 27)

Make sure you make it to Heaven!

IN JESUS, WE LIVE!

How can you inherit Eternal Life?

God's Command is Everlasting Life. So obey and inherit Eternal Life. (see Jn.12:50)

We have listed below all the Commandments pertaining to Eternal Life and Eternal Damnation, from the Gospel of Matthew. A few Commandments from the other books of the Bible have also been included.

1. Eternal Life In Jesus Christ, The Savior

COMMANDMENT OF GOD FOR US TO OBEY	REWARD FOR OBEDIENCE/ CONSEQUENCE OF DISOBEDIENCE
Believe in Him, the Lord Jesus Christ, our Savior. (see Jn.3:16; Matt.1:21)	**1. Believe in Jesus & Receive Everlasting Life...** For God so loved the world that He gave His Only begotten Son. Whoever believes in Him should *not perish* but have *Everlasting Life*. (Jn.3:16)
	2. Jesus Came To Save the World... God did not send His Son into the world to condemn the world, but *to save* the world through Him. (Jn.3:17/NIV)
	3. Believe & Not Be Condemned... Whoever believes in Jesus is not condemned. (see Jn.3:18/NIV)
	4. Unbelief Brings Condemnation... Whoever does not believe stands condemned already because he has not believed in the Name of God's one and only Son, Jesus. This is the Verdict. (see Jn.3:18,19/NIV)

Believe in Him, the Lord Jesus Christ, our Savior. (see Jn.3:16; Matt.1:21)	**5. God's Wrath for Rejecting Jesus...** "Whoever believes in the Son has Eternal Life, but whoever rejects the Son will not see life, for God's wrath remains on him." (Jn.3:36/NIV))
	6. Believe & Live... Jesus said, "I am the Resurrection and the Life. He who believes in Me will live, even though he dies." (Jn.11:25/NIV)
	7. Believe & Never Die... Whoever lives and believes in Me will never die. (Jn.11:25-26)
	Do You Believe In Jesus Christ Now?

Why Don't People Come To Christ?

1. ***Men Love Darkness...***The light, Jesus Christ, has come into the world, but men loved darkness instead of light because their deeds were evil. (see Jn.3:19/NIV)

2. ***Evil Deeds will be Exposed...*** "Everyone who does evil hates the light, and will not come into the light for fear that his deeds will be exposed. But whoever lives by the truth comes into the light." (Jn.3:20-21/NIV)

3. ***Not My Sheep...***You do not believe because you are not My sheep; for My sheep listen to My voice. (see Jn.10:26-27/NIV)

Why Should We Believe In Jesus Christ?

1. ***Jesus Must Be Lifted Up In Our Place...*** Jesus declared, As Moses lifted up the serpent in the wilderness, even so the Son of Man must be lifted up; that whosoever believes in Him should not perish but have Eternal Life. It was ordained by God that Jesus should die on the cross in our place. (see Jn.3:14-15)

2. ***Jesus Was Slain For Our Sins...*** Jesus Christ, the unblemished Lamb of God, was slain for our sins. The Lord has laid on Him the iniquity of us all. (see Is.53:6)

3. ***We are Sanctified by His Blood...*** The wages of our sin is death; but the gift of God is Eternal life through Jesus Christ, our Lord. (Rom.6:23)

When we believe in Him, and truly repent of our sins, we are sanctified by His precious blood. Our sins are erased from our record. Therefore, we don't need to pay the penalty for our sins but enjoy the free gift of Eternal life in Heaven. (see Heb. 9:14; 13:12)

2. Eternal Life In Jesus By Being Born Again

COMMANDMENT OF GOD FOR US TO OBEY	REWARD FOR OBEDIENCE/ CONSEQUENCE OF DISOBEDIENCE
1. Be Born Again. (see Jn.3:3)	For Jesus declared, "I tell you the truth, *no one can see the Kingdom of God unless he is born again."* (John 3:3/NIV)

1. Salvation is found in no one else, for there is **no other name** under Heaven but the Name of Jesus, given to men by which we must be saved. (see Acts 4:10, 12/NIV)
2. If you confess with your mouth the Lord Jesus and believe in your heart that God has raised Him from the dead, you will be saved. (Rom.10:9)

COMMANDMENT OF GOD FOR US TO OBEY	REWARD FOR OBEDIENCE/ SUPPORTING SCRIPTURES
2. Repent. (see Matt 4:17)	"For the Kingdom of **Heaven** is near." (Matt 4:17/NIV)

Why should you repent?

1. For your iniquities will *separate you* from your God.(see Is.59:2)
2. Your sins will *hide His face* from you and He will *not hear.*
3. Your sins will *withhold good things* from you. (see Jer.5:25/KJV)
4. So be quick to repent.

COMMANDMENT OF GOD FOR US TO OBEY	REWARD FOR OBEDIENCE/ SUPPORTING SCRIPTURES
3. Confess Me before men - Jesus. (see Matt. 10:32)	Jesus says, Whoever confesses Me before men, I will also confess him before My Father who is in **Heaven.** (see Matt. 10:32)

We should boldly acknowledge Christ before those who oppose the Lord, His ways and His standards. Ask God to give you wisdom what to say in difficult times.

How To Be Born Again?

Steps to follow - as simple as A, B, C...

Admit that you are a sinner before God, and truly repent for your sins. (see Rom.3:23)

Ask God to forgive you; and He is faithful and just to forgive. (see Prov.28:13)

Accept His forgiveness by faith; for it is a *free gift*. (see 1 Pet.1:9)

Believe in your heart that Christ died for your sins and rose up from the dead.

Confess with your mouth Jesus Christ as your Savior and Lord; and then you shall be *saved* and be *born again*. (see Rom. 10:9)

Pray... Invite Jesus into your heart and ask Him to wash your heart with His precious blood and fill you with the *peace* that the world cannot give you. (see Rev.3:20; Jn.14:27)

Reward... You will be rewarded with *"Eternal Life"* for being born again. (see Jn.3:3, 16)

3. Eternal Life In Jesus By Being Born of Water & Spirit

COMMANDMENT OF GOD FOR US TO OBEY	REWARD FOR OBEDIENCE/ CONSEQUENCE OF DISOBEDIENCE
Be ye born of water and the Spirit. (see Jn.3:5)	For Jesus stated, "I tell you the truth, **no one can enter** the Kingdom of God **unless he is born of water and the Spirit.**" (Jn.3:5/NIV)

4. Eternal Life Through Jesus, The Way

COMMANDMENT OF GOD FOR US TO OBEY	REWARD FOR OBEDIENCE/ CONSEQUENCE OF DISOBEDIENCE
Know the way to the Father's house.(Heaven) (see Jn.14:2,5,6)	1. For *"I am the Way*, the Truth and the Life; *No one comes to the Father except through Me"* says Jesus Christ. (Jn.14:6)
	2. For I am the Son of God. (see Jn. 10:36)
	3. I am the gate for the sheep. (Jn.10:7/NIV)
	4. "I am the gate; whoever enters through Me will be **saved**" declares the Lord Jesus. (Jn.10:9/ NIV)

Declaration of Jesus Christ...

Many religions teach that "God is Love and God is Light" and point towards that light. But the Lord Jesus Christ proclaimed:

1. "I am the light of the world." This was the true light which gives light to every man who comes into the world. (see John 1:9; 8:12);

2. I am "The Way" to Heaven;

   I am "The Truth;"

   I am "The Life" to your dead spirit.

   And no one comes to the Father in Heaven except through Me. (see Eph. 2:1)

5. Eternal Life In Jesus, The Bread of Life

COMMANDMENT OF GOD FOR US TO OBEY	REWARD FOR OBEDIENCE
Eat the Bread of Life, Jesus Christ and live forever.	1. Jesus declared, *I am the Bread of Life* that came down from Heaven; if anyone eats of this living bread, he will not die but *live forever.* (see Jn.6:48-51) 2. "Whoever eats My flesh and drinks my blood has *Eternal Life,* and I will raise him up at the last day." (Jn.6:54) 3. Jesus said, "He who eats my flesh and drinks my blood *abides in Me,* and I in him." (Jn.6:56) 4. The bread that I shall give is my flesh, which I shall give for the **life of the world.** (see John 6:48-51)

Pause & Think!

1. Jesus relates the **Bread of life i.e., His flesh, to the Word of God.** Jesus is the living Word and the Bible is the written Word. Therefore when we meditate and obey the Word of God, it is symbolic of eating His flesh and abiding in Him. (see Jn.1:1-5; 6:48; Rev.19:13; 2 Tim.3:16; Matt. 4:4; Rev. 19:13)

2. **My Words are Spirit and Life...**It is the Spirit who gives life; the Words that I have spoken to you are Spirit and they are Life. (see Jn.6:63)

3. **Remember His Sufferings...**We should remember His sufferings on the cross for us when we eat the bread during communion. We must not forget that His flesh was torn apart for our iniquities and He gave His life in our place.

6. Eternal Life In Jesus, The Good Shepherd

COMMANDMENT OF GOD	REWARDS FOR OBEDIENCE
Be My sheep and follow Me. (see Jn.10:26-27)	1. Jesus said, "My sheep listen to My voice; I know them, and they follow Me. 2. *I give them Eternal Life;* and they shall never perish; no one can snatch them out of My hand." (see Jn.10:28/NIV)

Jesus affirmed, **I am the Good Shepherd.** I lay down My life for the sheep. And His death on the cross proves His love and care for His sheep.(see Jn.10:14-15)

Characteristic of Christ's Sheep: 1.Those who are the true sheep of Christ **obey** His voice and **follow** Him. They are in constant fellowship with the Shepherd. The Shepherd gives Eternal Life to those who obey Him.

2. **Not of His Fold…**Those sheep which **stray** away from the Shepherd and refuse to listen to His voice, prove that they are not His sheep.

7. Eternal Life In Jesus, The Source of Living Water

COMMANDMENT OF GOD	REWARDS FOR OBEDIENCE
Drink of the water that I shall give you. (see Jn.4:14)	1. "Whoever drinks of the water that I shall give him will *never thirst.* 2. The water that I shall give him will become in him a fountain of water springing up into *Everlasting Life.*" (see Jn.4:14)

1. *Holy Spirit, The Living Water…*Jesus offers rivers of living water i.e., the Holy Spirit, to those who are thirsty. (see Jn.7:37-38)

2. **Continual Infilling of the Holy Spirit…**The drinking of the Holy Spirit is not a single act but rather a progressive, repeated drinking on a daily basis. Continual infilling of the Holy Spirit requires regular communion with the source of the Living water, Jesus Christ Himself.

3. Eternal Life…As the Word of God gives Eternal Life, the living water also springs up into Eternal Life. (Eph.3:16; 5:18; Jn.4:14)

8. Eternal Life In Jesus For Being Poor In Spirit

COMMANDMENT OF GOD	REWARDS FOR OBEDIENCE
Be poor in spirit. (i.e., be not spiritually self-sufficient) (see Matt.5:3)	For you are blessed and *yours is the Kingdom of Heaven.* (see Matt. 5:3)

1. This Commandment is taken from Jesus' Sermon on the Mount. To be poor in spirit is to depend on God for everything rather than on your own abilities.
2. **Woe to those who are wise in their own eyes**, and prudent in their own sight! (Is.5:21)
3. This is what the Lord, Your Redeemer says - "I am the Lord your God, who teaches you what is best for you, who directs you in the way you should go." So be not wise in your own eyes; but **Fear the Lord.** (see Is.48:17/NIV)
4. **Trust in the Lord** with all your heart; and lean not on your own understanding. In all your ways **Acknowledge Him** and He will direct your path. (see Prov.3:5-7)

9. Eternal Life In Christ -
By Exceeding The Righteousness Of The Pharisees

Jesus states that unless your righteousness exceeds the righteousness of the Scribes and Pharisees, you will *by no means enter the Kingdom of Heaven."* Obedience to His Upgraded Commandments will enable you to surpass the righteousness of the Pharisees. (see Matt. 5:20)

The upgraded commandments are listed in **Chapter 4 on "Christ's Righteousness"** in the following areas:

Anger & Reconciliation, Adultery, Divorce, Oaths & Retaliation, Neighbors & Enemies, Piety & Almsgiving, Prayer & Fasting, Eyes and Ears, Masters and Money, Anxiety and God's Kingdom, Judging and Hypocrisy, Forgiveness, Will of God, Test of false prophets, etc.

10. Eternal Life For Enduring Persecution For Christ

COMMANDMENT OF GOD	REWARDS FOR OBEDIENCE
1. Suffer persecution for righteousness' sake. (see Matt.5:10)	1. For you are blessed and *yours is the Kingdom of Heaven.* (see Matt.5:10) 2. If you should suffer for what is right, you are blessed. (1 Pet.3:14/NIV)
2. "Rejoice and be glad when people insult you, persecute you, and falsely say all kinds of evil against you because of Me."	For you are blessed and great is your reward in **Heaven.** (see Matt.5:11,12/NIV)

Who will separate us from the Love of Christ?

Shall trouble or hardship or persecution
or famine or nakedness
or danger or sword?

Thus saying, Apostle Paul encourages us to endure persecution for Christ's sake. Paul poured out his life as a drink offering for the sake of Christ but still kept the faith. Therefore, the crown of righteousness awaits him. (see Rom.8:35; 2 Cor.11:23-33; 2 Tim. 4:6-8)

Many are the afflictions of the righteous; but the Lord delivers him out of them all. (Ps.34:19). It is worth suffering for Christ!

11. Eternal Life For Sacrificing Your Life For Christ

COMMANDMENT OF GOD	REWARDS FOR OBEDIENCE
Sacrifice & Find Life : Lose your life for My sake. (i.e., sacrificing your life for Christ's sake.) (see Matt. 10:39)	1. For he who finds his life will lose it. 2. He who loses his life for My sake will *find it.* (Eternal Life) (see Matt. 10:39) 3. Be faithful, even to the point of death, and I will give you the *Crown of Life.* (see Rev. 2:10/NIV)
Apostle Paul who later on sacrificed his life for Christ said, "I am ready not only to be bound, but also to die in Jerusalem for the Name of the Lord Jesus." (see Acts 21:12-13/NIV)	

12. Eternal Life Through Jesus, The Narrow Gate

COMMANDMENT OF GOD FOR US TO OBEY	REWARD FOR OBEDIENCE
Enter through the narrow gate. (see Matt.7:13/NIV)	1. Because narrow is the gate and difficult is the way which *leads to Life* and there are few who find it. (see Matt.7:13-14) 2. **"I am the Gate;** whoever enters through Me will be *saved"* declares the Lord Jesus. (Jn.10:9/NIV)

1. When you deny yourself of worldly pleasures, your ambitions, your own ways and will, for the Lord's sake, you walk through the "narrow gate."

    It is a difficult path. It is very sad that only a few find it.

2. **Rich men, be warned...**

    i. Jesus said, "It is hard for the rich man to enter the Kingdom of Heaven." And the disciples were astonished at Jesus' words. But Jesus answereth again, and saith unto them, "Children, how hard is it for them that trust in riches to enter into the kingdom of God!

    ii. It is easier for a camel to go through the eye of a needle than for a rich man to enter the Kingdom of God." (see Matt. 19:23-24; Mk 10:23-25)

13. Eternal Life In Christ For Fulfilling God's Will

Pray that you might be filled with the knowledge of His Will in all wisdom and spiritual understanding; that you might walk worthy of the Lord and please Him in every way. (see Col. 1:9-10)

COMMANDMENT OF GOD FOR US TO OBEY	REWARD FOR OBEDIENCE/ CONSEQUENCE OF DISOBEDIENCE
Do the will of My Father in Heaven. (see Matt. 7:21)	1. So that you will enter the Kingdom of Heaven. (see Matt.7:21)
	2. You can **prophesy** accurately, **cast out demons, do many wonders** in Jesus' Name. And you can even say to Jesus, **'Lord, Lord.'**
	3. But after having done the above four things, if you have still not done the will of God for your life, you will *not enter into the Kingdom of Heaven,*
	4. For Jesus will say to you, **I never knew you; depart from Me,** you who practice lawlessness! (see Matt.7:22-23)

Find out the purpose for your life...

1. **Live a Sanctified Life...**By the will of God, we are sanctified through the sacrifice of the body of Christ once for all. (see Heb. 10:10)

2. **God wants all men to be saved** and come to the knowledge of the truth. (see 1 Tim.2:4)

3. **Do Not Be Carried Away By Miracles...**People, especially the ministers of God, can be carried away by the mighty miracles that happen through them, totally missing out on the will of God to reach out to the lost souls. (see 2 Peter 3:9)

14. Eternal Life For Child-Like Conversion In Christ

COMMANDMENT OF GOD	CONSEQUENCE OF DISOBEDIENCE
Be ye converted and become as little children. (see Matt. 18:3/KJV)	1. Or else, you will **not enter into the Kingdom of Heaven.** (Matt.18:3/KJV) 2. Jesus said, "Let the little children come to Me, for of such is the Kingdom of God." (Matt.19:14) 3. "Assuredly, I say to you, whoever does not receive the Kingdom of God as a little child will by no means enter it."(Lk. 18:17)

1. We receive Christ as our Savior when we have at least one of the following qualities inherent in a little child: innocence, humility, dependence, teachable and trustful nature.
2. For example, the Lord revealed Himself to Nathaniel as the Messiah. He was a man in whom there was no guile. (see Jn.1:49)
3. The Truth i.e., Jesus, will come your way; only humility will accept it, or else the Truth will pass you by.

15. Eternal Life in Christ - By Forcefully Possessing The Kingdom of Heaven

COMMANDMENT OF GOD	REWARD FOR OBEDIENCE
Be forceful in laying hold of the Kingdom of Heaven. (Matt. 11:12/NIV)	For the Kingdom of Heaven has been forcefully advancing, and forceful men lay hold of it. (see Matt. 11:12)

Apostle Paul who pursued the Kingdom of God against all odds, stated,

We are hard pressed on every side, but not crushed.
Perplexed, but not in despair; persecuted, but not abandoned.
Struck down, but not destroyed.
I have fought the good Fight,
I have finished the Race,
I have kept the Faith. (see 2 Cor.4:8-9; 2 Tim. 4:7)
We also, like Apostle Paul, should pursue the Kingdom of God as a valuable treasure and a goodly pearl.

16. Eternal Life For Forsaking Your All For Christ

COMMANDMENT OF GOD	REWARD FOR OBEDIENCE
Forsake all for Christ: Forsake houses or brethren or sisters or father or mother or wife or children, or lands for My Name's sake. (see Matt.19:29/KJV)	For you shall receive a hundredfold blessings - houses and lands, brothers and sisters, fathers and mothers, and children on this earth with persecutions; and in the age to come, ***Eternal Life.*** (see Mark 10:30)

*Apostle Paul who forsook his all for Christ, says...*To this very hour we go **hungry** and **thirsty,** we are in **rags,** we are brutally treated, we are **homeless,** we **work hard** with our own hands. When we are cursed, we bless; when we are persecuted we endure it; when we are slandered, we answer kindly. Up to this moment, we have become the scum of the earth, the refuse of the world. (see 1 Cor.4:11-13/NIV)

17. Eternal Life For Taking Your Cross & Following Christ

COMMANDMENT OF GOD	REWARD FOR OBEDIENCE
Deny yourself, take up your cross and follow Me. (see Matt. 10:38; Matt. 16:24)	1. "And *he who does not take his cross* and follow after Me is ***not worthy of Me.***" 2. For "he who finds his life will lose it." (see Matt. 10:38-39)

1. I have been crucified with Christ; it is no longer I who live, but Christ lives in me.(see Gal. 2:20)
2. Be imitators of me as I am of Christ, said Apostle Paul. (1 Cor.11:1)
3. God expects us to overcome the 3'P's - **Pleasure, Power and Pride**. You should deny yourself of the vain thoughts, filthy words and works of the flesh which are pleasing to you and not to God. When you crucify your sinful desires for the Lord's sake, it is like carrying your cross and following Him. (see Luke 14:26-27; Rom. 6:6-7; 1 Jn. 2:15-16)

18. Eternal Life In Christ Through The Acts Of Love

COMMANDMENT OF GOD	REWARD FOR OBEDIENCE
Parable of The Sheep & The Goats: Be like the sheep on Christ's right hand on the judgment day. (see Matt. 25:34)	1. For the King will say to them on His right hand, "Come, you blessed of My Father, ***inherit the Kingdom*** prepared for you from the foundation of the world." 2. Christ declares, Whatever you have done unto one of the least of My brethren, you have done it unto Me. (see Matt. 25:34, 40)

1. "The sheep" represent the righteous people. Jesus will reward the righteous (sheep) on His right hand with "Eternal Life" for their acts of love to His brethren. (see Matt. 25:31-46)
2. ***This is how we know what love is…*** Jesus Christ laid down His life for us. And we ought to lay down our lives for our brothers.
3. If anyone has material possessions and sees his brother in need but has no pity on him, how can the love of God be in him? ***Let us not love with words or tongue but with actions*** and in truth. (see 1 Jn.3:16-18; James 2:15-17)

19. Eternal Life In Christ -
To The Faithful Servant Who Multiplies His Talent

COMMANDMENT OF GOD	REWARD FOR OBEDIENCE
The Parable of the Talents: Be like the good and faithful servants who multiplied their talents. (see Matt. 25:16-17)	1. The Lord commended the faithful servants and said, ***"Well done,*** good and faithful servants; 2. You have been faithful over a few things; I will make you ***Ruler*** over many things; 3. ***Enter into the joy of your Lord*** i.e., Heaven. (Matt. 25:23)

1. **Great is our God's faithfulness** to all generations. (see Lam. 3:23; Ps. 119:90)
2. Our place in Heaven depends on **our faithfulness** and on the use of our talents for the Lord's service here on earth. He that is faithful in the least is also faithful in the much. (see Luke 16:10)

258

LIFE WITHOUT JESUS IS DEATH

What Leads To Eternal Damnation?

Sin, Sin and Sin! Sin separates us from the Lord Jesus Christ, The Eternal Life. (see 1 Jn.5:20)

1. Eternal Damnation To The Wicked & Lazy Servant (Who Does Not Multiply His Talent)

COMMANDMENT OF GOD FOR US TO OBEY	CONSEQUENCE OF DISOBEDIENCE
The Parable of the Talents: Do not be like the wicked and lazy servant who hid his one talent in the ground. (see Matt. 25:18) (If you don't use it, you will lose it.)	1. The Lord called him, "wicked and lazy servant." 2. The Lord said, Take the talent away from the wicked servant and give it to him who has ten talents; and *cast* the unprofitable servant *into the outer darkness,* where there will be weeping and gnashing of teeth. (see Matt. 25:18, 24-30)

Points to Ponder...

1. In the parable of the talents, Jesus points out that a believer's place in Heaven depends on the faithfulness of his life and service to God here on earth. (see Matt. 25:29)

2. A talent represents our abilities, time, resources and opportunities which God expects us to multiply so that His will can be fulfilled in our lives. In this parable, the servant who brought back his one talent to the Lord without multiplying it, was **cast into Hell fire** and Jesus called him wicked and lazy.

3. Scripture says that a wicked man walks with a perverse mouth; perversity *is* in his heart. He devises evil continually, he sows discord. **Therefore his calamity shall come suddenly**; suddenly he shall be broken without remedy. (see Prov.6:12-15

4. Laziness brings on deep sleep and an idle soul will suffer **hunger**. (Prov.19:15)

2. *Eternal Damnation For Rejecting Christ*

COMMANDMENT OF GOD	CONSEQUENCE OF DISOBEDIENCE
"Whoever will not receive you nor hear your words, when you depart from that house or city, shake off the dust from your feet. (see Matt. 10:14)	1. Assuredly, I say to you, it will be more tolerable for Sodom and Gomorrah in the **day of judgment** than for that city!" (see Matt. 10:15) 2. **Whoever does not believe stands condemned already** because he has not believed in the Name of God's one and only Son, Jesus. This is the Verdict. (see Jn.3:18-19/NIV) 3. **God's Wrath for Rejecting Jesus...** Whoever believes in the Son has Eternal Life but **whoever rejects the Son will not see life,** for God's wrath remains on him. (Jn.3:36/NIV)

1. Today, if you hear His Voice, **do not harden your hearts**. (Ps. 95:7-8)
2. He who is often rebuked, *and* hardens *his* neck, will **suddenly be destroyed**, and that without remedy. (see Prov.29:1)

3. Eternal Damnation For Refusing To Repent

COMMANDMENT OF GOD	CONSEQUENCE OF DISOBEDIENCE
1. Repent. (see Lk.13:3,5) 2. Remember therefore from where you have fallen; **repent** and do the first works. (see Rev.2:5)	1. Or else you will all **perish**. (see Lk. 13:3,5) 2. Or else I will come to you quickly and **remove your lampstand from its place** -unless you repent. (see Rev.2:5)
1. Jesus began His ministry with the message of repentance. He assured people of their inheritance in Heaven when they truly repent of their sins. He said, "The kingdom of God is at hand: repent ye and believe the gospel." (see Mark 1:15) 2. Christ will remove any congregation or church from its place and destiny in His Kingdom if it does not repent of its evil doings.	

4. Eternal Damnation For No Fear of God

COMMANDMENT OF GOD	CONSEQUENCE OF DISOBEDIENCE
1. Fear Him. 2. Do not fear those who kill the body but cannot kill the soul. (see Matt. 10:28) (Jesus declared, "**I and the Father are one.**" (Jn.10:30))	For He is able to destroy both ***soul and body in Hell.*** (see Matt. 10:28) (Jesus stated, "**I have the keys of hell and of death.**" (see Rev.1:18/ KJV)

5. Eternal Damnation For Blasphemy Of The Holy Spirit

COMMANDMENT OF GOD	CONSEQUENCE OF DISOBEDIENCE
Do not blaspheme the Holy Spirit. (see Matt. 12:31)	1. For all manner of sin and blasphemy shall be forgiven unto men; but the blasphemy against the Holy Spirit **shall not be forgiven unto men.** (see Matt. 12:31) 2. Whosoever speaks a word against Jesus Christ, it shall be forgiven him, but whosoever speaks against the Holy Ghost, it shall *not be forgiven* him neither in this world, **nor in the world to come.** (see Matt. 12:32/ KJV)

Revere the Holy Spirit of God...

1. Blasphemy against the Holy Spirit shows lack of reverential fear for the Holy Spirit.

2. For example, **David** had such reverence for the Spirit of God that he would not harm King Saul even when he had the chance to kill him; because Saul once had the anointing of the Holy Spirit. (see 1 Sam.9-11)

3. On the contrary, the **Pharisees** were so hardened in their hearts that they dared to blaspheme the Holy Spirit by saying, Jesus casts out devils by Beelzebub, the prince of devils; when Jesus had cast out devils by the Spirit of God. (see Matt.12:22-32)

6. *Eternal Damnation For Hindering Other Believers*

COMMANDMENT OF GOD	CONSEQUENCE OF DISOBEDIENCE
Do not cause one of the little ones who believe in Me, to sin. (see Matt. 18:6) (The little one represents a child or a child like believer.)	1. Or else, it would be better that a millstone were hung around your neck and you were drowned in the depth of the sea. (see Matt. 18:6) 2. ***Woe* to that man** by whom the offence comes to the little one. 3. It is better for you to lose one of your eyes or hands or feet and enter into Heaven; rather than having two eyes or two hands or two feet, and be *cast into the everlasting fire.* (see Matt. 18:6-9)

Points to Ponder...

1. Whoever claims to live in Christ must walk as He did. (1Jn. 2:6)

2. A believer must set an example to the other believers in speech, in life, in love, in faith and in purity. (see 1 Tim. 4:12;)

3. Especially preachers, being the shepherds should not be a hindrance to other believers; for the judgment must begin in the House of God. (see 1 Pet. 4:17)

7. Eternal Damnation -
For Living For Yourself & Not For Christ

COMMANDMENT OF GOD	CONSEQUENCE OF DISOBEDIENCE
Live not for yourself : Do not find your life, meaning, do not live your life for yourself. (see Matt. 10:39)And	1. For "he who finds his life (lives for himself) will *lose it* and he that loses his life for **My sake (Christ)** shall **find it.** (see Matt. 10:39) 2. For what good will it be for a man if he gains the whole world, yet **loses his own soul?** (see Matt. 16:26/NIV) 3. Apostle Paul says, "To me, **to live is Christ and to die is gain.**" 4. *For Jesus is the Life.* (see Phil. 1:21; Jn.14:6)

8. Eternal Damnation For Going
Through The Wide Gate

COMMANDMENT OF GOD	CONSEQUENCE OF DISOBEDIENCE
Do not go in by the wide gate. (see Matt.7:13)	For wide is the gate, and broad is the way that leads to *destruction.* And there are many who go in by the wide gate. (see Matt.7:13)

1. **A man's own folly ruins his life**, yet his heart rages against the Lord. (Prov.19:3/NIV)

2. There is a way that seems right to a man, but in the end it *leads to death.* (Prov.14:12/ NIV)

3. If you go in your own way and live as you like in the pleasures of this world, then you are walking through the wide gate damning your soul. So lead a righteous life before God by entering through the narrow gate.

9. Eternal Damnation For The Hypocritical Teachers of God's Word

No Intimacy With God...Jesus condemned with "Woes" the religious leaders of His time who had compromised the Word of God. They had replaced "The Word" with their own ideas, tradition and interpretation. (see Matt. 23:3-4)

Blinded to their Messiah...The teachers of God's Word were so blinded by their tradition and rituals that they did not see the Messiah who was in their midst. Many of them were responsible for the crucifixion of Jesus Christ, their Savior.

COMMANDMENT OF GOD	CONSEQUENCE OF DISOBEDIENCE
Do not shut up the Kingdom of Heaven against men. (see Matt. 23:13)	1. **Hypocrisy...Woe to you,** teachers of the law, you hypocrites! For **you neither go to Heaven** yourselves **nor will you let others** who are trying to go in. (see Matt. 23:13) 2. **Blind Guides**...Woe to you, blind guides! You travel over land and sea to win a single convert, to make him **twice as much a son of hell as you are.** 3. **Shrewdness**...You serpents! You brood of vipers! How can you escape the damnation of **Hell?** (see Matt. 23:13,15-16, 33)

1. Hypocrites are the ones who appear to be righteous outwardly but are unrighteous in their personal lives. Jesus called the religious leaders of His time hypocrites.
2. Let God's Word Be Your Guide...In these last days, you must be careful whom you follow. Whenever you hear message through any preacher, you should always check whether it is in line with the Word of God.

10. Eternal Damnation To The Evil Servant For Not Being Ready For Christ's Coming

COMMANDMENT OF GOD	CONSEQUENCE OF DISOBEDIENCE
The Parable of the Evil & Faithful Servant: 1. Do not be like the **evil servant who was not ready** for his Lord's coming. 2. Be ye ready; for the Son of man, Jesus, will come at an hour when you do not expect Him. (see Matt.24:44, 48)	1. The evil servant lives as he likes, saying in his heart, "my Lord delays His coming" eating and drinking and smiting his fellowmen. 2. And the Lord will come unexpectedly and cut the evil servant to pieces and assign him *a place with the hypocrites*; there will be **weeping and gnashing of teeth. (Hell)** (Matt.24:48-51)

Pause & Think...

1. **Filthy... Become More Filthy...**The time is at hand. He that is unjust, let him continue to be unjust; and he who is filthy, let him be filthy still;

2. **Holy...Continue to be Holy...**He that is righteous, let him continue to be righteous, and he that is holy, let him continue to be holy.

3. **Jesus' Reward for us...**Behold, I am coming soon! My reward is with Me and I will give every man according to what he has done. (see Rev. 22:10-12)

11. Eternal Damnation - For Lack Of Love To Christ's Brethren

COMMANDMENT OF GOD	CONSEQUENCES OF DISOBEDIENCE
Parable of The Sheep And The Goats : Do not be like the goats on the judgment day. (see Matt. 25:33-34; 41-46) (The goats represent the wicked people.)	1. The King will say to them on His left, Depart from Me, you who are **cursed,** into the ***Everlasting Fire*** prepared for the devil and his angels. 2. Christ declares, Whatever you have not done unto one of the least of My brethren, you have **not done it unto Me.** (see Matt. 25:41, 45-46)

1. Anyone who knows the good he ought to do and does not do it, sins against God. (see James 4:17)

2. The Lord will judge the wicked with everlasting punishment for the following reasons :

   - For not feeding those who are hungry.
   - For not giving water to those who are thirsty.
   - For not providing clothes to the needy.
   - For not helping a stranger.
   - For not visiting the sick.
   - For not visiting those in prison.(see Matt. 25:40-46)

12. Eternal Damnation – For Rejecting God's Invitation To Accept Christ

COMMANDMENTS OF GOD	CONSEQUENCES OF DISOBEDIENCE
Parable of the Marriage Feast: 1. Come to the wedding banquet of the King. 2. Do not ignore the king's invitation to his son's wedding banquet. 3. Go to the street corners, and invite to the wedding anyone you find. 4. Wear a wedding garment to the king's banquet. (see Matt. 22:4-11/NIV)	1. **Invitations to the Chosen...**The Kingdom of Heaven is like a certain king who arranged a marriage for his son and sent out invitations. 2. **Lame Excuses...**Those who were invited made light of it and went their own ways. Some of them even murdered the king's servants. 3. **Judgment...**When the King heard about it, he was furious. He sent out his armies and destroyed the murderers. 4. **Good and Bad Invited...**The King said that those who were invited to the wedding were not worthy and sent forth his servants to gather all the people they could find, both good and bad. 5. **Unworthy Cast into Hell...**The King was displeased with the man who was without the wedding garment and cast him into the *outer darkness,* the hell; where there is weeping and gnashing of teeth. (see Matt. 22:2-13)

1. **Father God invites us all** to attend His Son, Jesus' wedding just as the king did in the parable.
2. Today is the day of Salvation. **Give Christ a chance in life.** If you have any doubts about who Christ is, ask Him to reveal Himself to you and He will.
3. **Two categories of people will be thrown into Hell fire:**
   i. Those who reject God's call to acknowledge Christ as their Messiah.
   ii. After having accepted the invitation to attend the wedding, if anyone presents himself before God unworthily i.e., without the **Helmet of Salvation** and the **Garment of Righteousness,** (which we receive freely when we accept Jesus as our Savior) will be thrown into hellfire.

13. Eternal Damnation When You Persist in Sin - Sins of the Flesh

If we **deliberately keep on sinning** after we have received the knowledge of the truth, no sacrifice for sins is left, but only a fearful expectation of **judgment and of raging fire** that will consume the enemies of God. (see Heb.10:26-27/NIV)

COMMANDMENT OF GOD	CONSEQUENCES OF DISOBEDIENCE
Do not practice the works of the flesh. (see Gal. 5:19-21)	1. For those who indulge in the works of the flesh will *not inherit the Kingdom of God* but end up in the **Lake of Fire**. (see Gal. 5:19-21) 2. **Enemy of God...** Being carnally minded is enmity against God. (see Rom.8:6) 3. Friendship with the world is enmity against God. (see James 4:4)

1. **Hell If You Forget God...**The wicked will be **cast into Hell** and all the nations that forget God. (see Ps. 9:17)

    The fool says in his heart, "There is no God." (Ps.14:1/NIV)

2. *Consequences of Sin...*

    i.   **Slave to Sin...**Everyone who sins, is a slave to sin. (Jn.8:34/NIV)
    ii. **Your Soul Dies...**The soul that sins will *surely die*. (see Ezek.18:20)

3. *Redemption from Sin...*

    i.   **Jesus Died For Your Sins...**Remember, the death Jesus died, He died unto sin once.
    ii. If you are alive in Christ, sin will not have dominion over you.
    iii. Whom the Son sets free, is free indeed. (see Jn.8:36)
    iv. When you walk in the Spirit, you will not fulfil the lust of the flesh. (see Rom. 6:10-14; Gal.5:16)

Workers of Iniquity	**_Seven Things Are An Abomination to God_**
Scripture says that the adulterers, the fornicators, the idolaters, the homosexuals and abusers of themselves (those who commit masturbation), **cowardly,** the fearful, **all liars,** the **unbelieving,** the abominable, the thieves, the **greedy,** the **drunkards,** the **slanderers,** the **cheaters,** the murderers, the sorcerers; and those who indulge in uncleanness, witchcraft, **hatred,** discord, **jealousy,** wrath, **strife,** heresies, orgies, sedition, etc. These will *not inherit the Kingdom of God* but end up in the Lake of Fire. (see Gal. 5:19-21, 1Cor 6:9-10; Rev 21:8)	1. A proud look, 2. a lying tongue, 3. hands that shed innocent blood, 4. a heart that devises wicked schemes, 5. feet that are quick to rush into evil, 6. a false witness who speaks lies 7. and a man who stirs up discord among brothers. (see Prov.6:16-19) **Upon the wicked God will rain coals, fire and brimstone** and the burning wind; this shall be the portion of their cup. (Ps. 11:6)

14. Sin of Adultery

COMMANDMENT OF GOD	CONSEQUENCE OF DISOBEDIENCE
1. Do not look at a woman lustfully; for anyone who looks at a woman lustfully has already committed adultery with her in his heart. (see Matt.5:28/NIV) 2. Pluck out your eye and cast it from you if it causes you to sin. (see Matt.5:29) 3. Cut off your hand and throw it away if it causes you to sin. (see Matt.5:30/NIV)	1. He that commits adultery **destroys his own soul.** (see Prov.6:32) 2. The house of the adulteress is the *way to Hell*, going down to the chambers of death. (see Prov.7:27) **3.** It is better for you to lose one part of your body than for your whole body to go into **Hell.** (see Matt.5:30/NIV)

1. **Judgment of God for sexual sin**…E.g., Sodom and Gomorrah and the surrounding towns who gave themselves up to sexual immorality and perversion will suffer the punishment of Eternal Fire. (see jude7)

2. **Judgment of God on House of Eli**… E.g. God swore unto the House of Eli, the priest that the iniquity of Eli's house will not be purged with sacrifice nor offering forever; and his two sons will die in one day. (see 1Sam. 3:13; 2:34) For the sins of Eli's sons were very great in the Lord's sight because they lived sexually immoral lives and also abhorred the offering of the Lord. (see 1 Sam.2:13-17,22) So be warned!

| *Adultery Through Divorce:*

4. Do not divorce your wife for any reason except sexual immorality. (see Matt.5:32) | 1. For if you do so, you will **cause her** to commit adultery.

2. And **anyone who marries** her who is divorced commits adultery. (see Matt.5:32)

3. **Adulterers will not inherit the kingdom of Heaven.** (see Gal.5:19,21) |

This is the only exception for divorce permitted by the Lord Jesus. For God hates divorce. (see Mal. 2:16)

15. Sin of Idolatry - Lust for Money

COMMANDMENT OF GOD FOR US TO OBEY	CONSEQUENCE OF DISOBEDIENCE
1. Do not store up for yourselves treasures on earth. (see Matt. 6:19/NIV) 2. Do not serve two masters; God and money; for either you will hate the one (God) and love the other (money), or else you will be loyal to the one and despise the other. No one can serve two masters. (see Matt.6:24)	1. It is hard for a rich man to enter the Kingdom of Heaven. 2. And the disciples were astonished at his words. But Jesus answereth again, and saith unto them, Children, how hard is it for them that trust in riches to enter into the kingdom of God! 3. "It is easier for a camel to go through the eye of a needle than for a rich man to enter the Kingdom of God." (see Matt. 19:23-24; Mk 10:23-25)

Pause & Think!

1. God wants to have first place in your heart. It is not "having the money" but "making it an idol" that is wrong in the eyes of God. For example, Agur, in Proverbs 30, said that he did not want to have too much wealth because he was afraid that he would disown God and say, 'Who is the Lord?' (see Prov.30:8-9)

2. Watch out! Be on your guard against all kinds of greed; a man's life does not consist in the abundance of his possessions. E.g. Lot's wife, Ananias and Sapphira. (see Luke 12:15; Gen. 19:26; Acts 5:1-11)

Eternal Damnation When You Persist In Sin -

16. Sin of Unforgiveness

COMMANDMENT OF GOD FOR US TO OBEY	CONSEQUENCE OF DISOBEDIENCE
1. Forgive your debtors. (see Matt. 6:12) 2. Forgive men when they sin against you. (see Matt.6:14/ NIV) 3. Forgive your brother's sins not seven times, but up to seventy times seven i.e., 490 times. (see Matt.18:22)	**Forgiveness of God, Conditional…**Forgive men when they sin against you, only then your Heavenly Father will forgive you. If you do not forgive men their trespasses, *neither will your Father forgive* your trespasses. (see Matt.6:14-15)

1. **Get rid of all bitterness,** rage and anger and forgive each other, just as in Christ, God forgave you. (Eph. 4:31-32)

2. For example, Joseph's brothers who had sold him into captivity were later afraid of what he would do to them in revenge, since he was in power. But Joseph said to them, "Don't be afraid. Am I in the place of God? You intended to harm me, but God intended it for good to save the lives of many. Forgiving all their wrongdoing, Joseph spoke kindly to his brothers and reassured them by saying, "I will provide for you and your children."

3. Forgive and repay evil with good as Joseph did. (see Gen. 15:19-21)

Eternal Damnation When You Persist In Sin -

17. Sins of Anger & Murder

COMMANDMENT OF GOD FOR US TO OBEY	CONSEQUENCE OF DISOBEDIENCE
Physical Murder: 1. You shall not murder. (Matt.5:21) (This is the 6th of the Ten Commandments in the OT. (see Ex.20:13)	1. Whoever murders will be in **danger of the Judgment.** (see Matt. 5:21) 2. The slanderers, **the murderers** and those who indulge in hatred, discord, strife and wrath will *not inherit the Kingdom of God* but end up in the fiery lake of burning sulfur. (see Gal. 5:19-21; 1Cor. 6:9-10; Rev.21:8)
Heart Murder: 2. Do not be angry with your brother without a cause. (see Matt.5:22)	Whoever is angry without a cause will be in **danger of the Judgment;** (Since the judgment for murder and anger is the same, it is like breaking the 6th Commandment in the eyes of God.) (see Matt.5:22)
Tongue Murder: 3. Do not say to another "You fool!" (see Matt.5:22)	1. For you will be in danger of **Hell Fire.** 2. He who guards his lips guards his soul, but he who speaks rashly will come to **ruin.** (Prov.13:3)

1. Anger is equivalent to murder in God's eyes. E.G., Cain's anger turned into rage that led him to murder his brother, Abel. (see Gen. 4:3-8)

2. **Deal with anger in a Godly way…**In your anger, do not sin. Do not let the sun go down while you are still angry. (see Eph. 4:26)

3. Only by the help of the Holy Spirit you can overcome anger.

CHARACTERISTICS OF THE KINGDOMS

Inward Signs That Will Manifest Through You

Kingdom of God/Heaven	Kingdom of Satan/Hell
1. When you are in God's Kingdom, "**righteousness,** peace and joy in the Holy Spirit" are the unique qualities you will possess.	1. When you are in the kingdom of Satan, your life will be centred around the things of the **world** and **flesh.**
2. Power of the **Holy Spirit** to overcome the flesh, world and Satan is offered to us by God Almighty to live a victorious life.	2. You will be afflicted with disease and infirmity and live in **bondage.**
3. You will walk in the **truth** of God's Word.	3. You will operate in **deception** and falsehood.
4. You will live a life of **holiness.**	4. You will live in **sin** and indulge in wickedness.
5. Your **light** will shine forth to others.	5. You will love **darkness** rather than light.
6. You will have reverential **fear of God.**	6. You will **fear the Devil** more than God.
7. **Divine love** will flow out of you.	7. You will have more **love for the things of the world** than God.
8. **Spirit of obedience** will be found in you.	8. You will have the **spirit of rebellion** & disobedience.
9. You will have unwavering **faith** in God.	9. You will doubt God's love and power and live in **unbelief.**
10. You will be **humble** before God and man.	10. You will have a **proud** look and an egoistic attitude.

Think! In which direction is your life moving – Kingdom of God or kingdom of Satan?

2. Outward Signs That Will Manifest When You Are In The Kingdom...

Kingdom of God/Heaven	Kingdom of Satan/Hell
1. Salvation is the foundation of the Kingdom of God.	1. Damnation of your soul in Hell will be the end result of your life when you choose to follow the ways of Satan.
2. You will lead a fruitful life for Christ.	2. Your life will be unfruitful and self centred.
3. God will perform miracles through you to win souls and you will deliver people from demon possession.	3. Those who follow Satan will be demon possessed and perform counterfeit miracles to deceive people and lead them to Hell.
4. God will equip you with the gifts of the Holy Spirit for the benefit of others.	4. Sorcery, witchcraft, alcoholism, drug addiction and occultism are the signs of Satan's kingdom.
5. People will see the fruit of the Holy Spirit and the Christ-like nature in you. E.g. self-control, kindness, forgiveness, etc. (see Gal. 5:22-23)	5. You will manifest the acts of the flesh. E.g. Adultery, fornication etc. (see Gal. 5:19-21)

Now all has been heard; here is the conclusion of the matter;
Fear God and keep His Commandments,
for this is the whole duty of man.
For God will bring every deed into Judgment,
including every hidden thing,
whether it is good or evil.
(Eccl. 12:13-14)

LIST OF ARTICLES IN THE BOOK

Part II

Part III

LIST OF PARABLES IN THE BOOK

LIST OF MIRACLES IN THE BOOK

ABOUT THE AUTHOR

TESTIMONY OF DR. ESTHER V. SHEKHER

Greetings in His Holy Name from Christ Rules Ministries!

Salvation Experience...I come from a Hindu background and I accepted Christ as my Lord and Savior at the age of 18. During the course of my salvation experience, two facts became crystal clear to me - (*i*) *Jesus loved me so deeply that He would even die for me.* (*ii*) *He hated sin so much that He would bear the suffering* and shame *of the cross* **to deliver me from that awful sin.** I understood at that early age that I too must hate sin and I started longing for His righteousness.

Infilling of the Holy Spirit... Nobody else but Jesus Christ offers us the power of the Holy Spirit, His own Spirit, to overcome sin, satan and the world. After yearning for the Holy Spirit for a year, God filled me with His Spirit for about 3 hours. I also attended "Jesus Calls Evangelical Training Program."

Promise of God Fulfilled... Jesus Christ became my passion and I spent a lot of time talking to Him daily. He became my closest friend. While I was doing my medical training, one day, after crying out to the Lord for about six hours, longing to see Him, to hear His voice and to know His will for my life, the Lord promised me through the Scriptures *(Acts 22:14)* that I would see the Just One, hear Him speak and know His will. This promise came to pass seven years later, when I was in USA.

Calling of God... In America, I spent almost 3-4 hours daily praying in the Spirit and listening to His Word. On March 18, 1992, while I was pouring my heart to God in prayer, I heard His **audible voice** saying, *"I died on the cross for you, what have you done for Me?* Will you do my ministry until you have your last breath?" From then on, I heard Him almost every night, waking me up at 3 a.m. saying, **"Stand in the gap and cry out in the middle of the night with agony for the perishing souls."** I obeyed Him as He instructed me.

God molded my character over a period of five years by taking me through a great deal of trials. He trained me to die to self and to depend on Him instead of my own abilities. His awesome Presence, *His precious Holy Spirit, like a ball of fire cleansed the temple of my spirit everyday* and filled me, preparing me for His Ministry.

Publications... I have already published this God-inspired book *"All the Commandments of God"* from the Gospels of Matthew and John, in English and Tamil in Asia. Nothing is more important than obeying the Commandments of God and thereby receiving His blessings. This book is the first in the series. The second book "All the Commandments of God" from the Epistles of Galatians, Ephesians and Philippians and Colossians is under publication.

*Mission Trip...*God called me as a missionary. I obeyed His call and preached the Gospel in India and Overseas.

*Ministry...*By the grace of God, I set up "Christ Rules Ministries" in 2008 to enable me to preach the Gospel, to raise up Intercessors for the Kingdom of God and also to conduct Discipleship Training Courses based on my book "All the Commandments of God" to help Pastors and Believers to be rooted and grounded in the Word of God.

Presently, I am focusing my preaching on End Times through powerful Power-point Presentations to bring awareness about the Rapture and Second Coming of Jesus Christ. Since 2010 I have preached in about 35 Pastors' Conferences on this topic and various churches in several nations.

International Prayer Network... The Lord gave me a divine strategy to establish Prayer Cells through International Prayer Network (IPN) which I started in 2010 to intercede for the salvation of lost souls in every nation of the world. I have been successful in implementing this strategy in India, Sri Lanka, Malaysia, Singapore and US.

By God's grace, approximately 6555 Prayer Cells have been established so far in these nations; 1400 Prayer Cells in Malaysia alone on 5 mission trips; 800 in Srilanka; 155 in USA; 3950 in India; 250 in Andamans.

Since June 2012 I preached in many churches in Northern California, USA, sowed the seed of prayer in the hearts of people and started about 155 prayer cells. Praise be to our God!

TV Ministry... By the grace of God, I started the TV Ministry in 2011 to preach on End Times and the Commandments of God on Holy God TV which is being aired from France covering 198 nations of the world, to prepare the churches to meet our Bridegroom Jesus Christ in Rapture.

All the promises that the Lord has given me so far are coming to pass one by one. I humbly yield myself to the Master, to be used for His glory. My desire is to fulfil His will each and every day of my life. Blessed be His Holy Name!

MINISTRY MOTTO: PRAY, GIVE, GO OR SEND FOR THE KINGDOM OF GOD

CHRIST RULES OFFICES

To Contact the Author, Write /Call:

In USA

Dr. Esther V. Shekher

P O Box 994

Galt, CA 95632, USA

Dr. Esther +1 (626) 450 – 5973

Michelle +1 (480) 251 – 1979

Darla +1 (209) 401 – 1696

Vincent +1 (626) 430 - 6674

Email: christrulesnations@gmail.com/christrules@hotmail.co.uk

Website: www.christrulesnations.org

Facebook: Christ Rules Nations

If this book has blessed you, please do write your testimony and/or prayer requests.

In Singapore

Call Ms. Maya +65 98277554

In Malaysia

Contact: Pr. Nathaneal

E-07-12, PPR Muhibbah,

Jalan 15/155 of Jalan Puchong Taman,

Taman Muhibbah 58200, Kuala Lumpur, Malaysia.

Cell No. +60173204571

In India

H/3E, Sunshine Apartments

West Jones Road, West Saidapet,

Chennai 600 015, Tamil Nadu, India.

Call +91-9994709461/9791198673